Walking with Dignity

RUDOLPH WALKER

An Autobiography

With a foreword by Rev. Rose Hudson-Wilkin

This First Edition published: September 2024 by
Chronos Publishing

ISBN:
978-1-914529-58-0 Paperback Edition
978-1-914529-59-7 E-Version

This book is a memoir, reflecting the author's present recollections of experiences over time. Some names and characteristics have been changed, some events have been compressed, and some dialogue has been recreated. Memory can be a fickle thing, so the Author trusts that any minor errors in times, dates and details of particular events will be understood.

Contents

Dedication

I wish to dedicate this book to:

- My mother *Carmen Bishop*, whose inner strength and dignity has been the platform on which I built my life.

- My *aunts Miriam Taylor (Ada), Margery Bishop, Millicent Bishop* and *Merle Moore*, the four women whose guidance and love helped to mould me into who I am today.

- My children *Darren* and *Sheona Walker* - they fill me with tremendous pride and help to keep my feet firmly on the ground.

- *Lorna Walker*, a fantastic mother who has remained a true and trusted friend.

- My grandchildren *Josh, Loveday and Latimer,* the future is in good hands.

- *Neil Giuseppi*, for his true and loyal friendship over many, many years.

- *Yusuff Ali*, a dear friend, gone but not forgotten.

- My late cousin *Dr Patricia Bishop TC*, always inspiring me by example and continuous advice.

- *Carmen Munroe OBE* and the late *Earl Cameron CBE*, my mentors when I started. Their advice, guidance and encouragement helped me to navigate through the many challenges I faced as a young actor in the UK.

- To the actors who went before me and on whose shoulders, I stand – *Ira Aldridge, Clarence Muse, Hattie Mc Daniel, Paul Robeson, Josephine Baker, Richard Pryor, Ossie Davis, Sydney Poitier, Maya Angelou, Earl Cameron, Errol John and many, many more.*

Foreword

'The circumstances that surround a man's life are not important. How that man responds to those circumstances IS IMPORTANT. His response is the ultimate determining factor between success and failure.' Booker T. Washington, Black educator, author, and leader in the late 19th and early 20th centuries

Rudolph 'Malcolm' Walker in his long-awaited autobiography epitomises all that the above quote seeks to address. His childhood story resonates with hundreds and thousands of people who grew up at a similar time in the Caribbean – the strong matriarchal women that were not to be messed with; the absent fathers and the mothers who fathered their children; the supportive roles directly and indirectly played by the extended family and other adults in the community; the strict educational system that believed in using the cane with impunity.

Rudolph writes with an openness and honesty that invites those who read his story to have a ringside seat into the journey that he has travelled. He lays bare his soul as he takes us through the joys and pain of childhood: the creativity he exhibited with his friends as they made the toys that they played with, the fruit trees they climbed so were never hungry, and the exploits they got up to as children and young people growing up within their neighbourhood; but also the level of brutality suffered at the hands of trusted loved ones and in this case his mother in the beatings matched only by the level of her rage.

We stay ringside as he follows his dream to perform on the stage and screen. We again see him taking a lesson from the proverb – 'When you han eena alligator mout, tek time pull I out.' [When your hand is in an alligator's mouth, take your time and pull it out.] The lesson to be learnt is that if you make a quick withdrawal, the alligator will anticipate the move and snap down, taking your hands in the process. Although Rudolph did not always receive the respect due to him, he never reacted in a way that was detrimental to himself and his fellow actors. He kept focused on the end game of achieving his goal to become an accomplished actor.

Life for Rudolph the man and the acclaimed actor has not been a crystal stair. Adulthood has not spared him from painful moments, but he basks in the joy of being a father and a grandfather. His successes can probably be attributed to his dogged determination to keep moving forward and an amazing conscientious sense of being part of the change that he wants to see. He never tires of giving back into the community and this is reflected in the numerous school visits he does, the charities that he supports and the work that he does through his own Foundation working with young people.

Rudolph has hit many firsts in his career and accomplished much within his chosen field, but his ability to laugh and to make others laugh shows that he has remained grounded, a caring, gentle, gifted and unassuming man with a mission. In reading his autobiography, I have laughed and cried and found myself thankful for the privilege of living in his time.

The Rt Revd Rose Hudson-Wilkin
Bishop of Dover

La Trinity! La Trinity!
The place where many people crave to see,
Its Maracas Beach, its cocoa fields,
All of matchless scenery.

Come with me, come with me,
Come with me to the Land of Dreams,
Where the hummingbirds sing
Many a church bells ring
Where the beaches blend with their lovely bays.

by Rudolph Malcolm Walker, aged 14

Introduction

'Until the lions tell their own story, tales of hunting will always glorify the hunter' - African proverb

---

2020 was an extraordinary year for me. If anything could happen, it did happen that year. It felt like a culmination of everything that went before, a maelstrom of conflicting emotions, personal achievements, and serious challenges. Not just from Covid-19 and Black Lives Matter, but from the re-awakening and re-fashioning of the very foundations on which I have built my career.

I was being forced to be reflective, to take a stance on contemporary issues and in my 84th year, decide what my legacies are going to be. As a black man with a career spanning over six decades behind me, am I going to 'open the palace gates from the inside', tell my tale as a hunter, or watch as the hunted flash past my doors and TV screen?

Within the last fifteen years, I have witnessed first-hand the plight of so many youngsters. I have seen the hopelessness that has made many students with great potential – including young people from the African and Caribbean communities within the UK – turn away in despair, resorting to knife crimes, drug dealing, gang wars, and becoming involved in postcode violence. (Each area in the UK has a postcode, and for instance, if one group of youngsters live in 1NH, another in 7NH, and there is a conflict between one or more individuals, it can easily develop into violence.)

But equally, there are also stories of success: the fantastic achievements of the recipients of the Baroness Amos Bursary Awards to help those entering further education. Like Wilfred Obeng, whose passion for technology led to a first-class degree in Computer Science, gaining employment with some of the major tech companies, and a number of awards for entrepreneurship, or George Imafidon, 2022 Young Engineer of the Year, co-Founder of a youth-led organisation helping young people from under-represented backgrounds to develop their STEM skills to solve global challenges. The outstanding achievements of just a few of the many students from the Eastside Young Leaders Academy run by the late Ray Lewis and Anne Collard: David Ejim-McCubbin, who gained a Masters in Legal and Political Theory at University College London and is now Head of Policy & Advocacy at the Social Mobility Commission; and Yaade Joba, who completed his degree and Masters in Law at Nottingham University and recently won a prestigious scholarship – the 11KBW for black students pursuing a career at the Bar, this scholarship only being awarded to one person each year. Amara Agwo came from a low-income family in Essex and gained a bursary place at Sherborne Girls School, aged 11. She was an exceptional pupil achieving top grades for all her GCSEs and A Levels, received the Rank Leadership Scholarship and is now studying European, Social and Political Studies at UCL; she also works with a mentoring programme for black girls.

Rev. Rose Hudson-Wilkin – the first black woman to become a bishop in the Church of England – who previously had served as Chaplain to Her Majesty Queen Elizabeth II, and Chaplain to the Speaker of the House of Commons and is now the Bishop of Dover. Knighthoods for Lewis Hamilton and Clive Lloyd. The appointment of Ansel Wong as the Chair of the Black Cultural Archives and his own CBE in the Queen's 2020 Birthday Honours. The Golden Jubilees of Professor Andrew Ramroop OBE CM, as the first and only black Master Tailor on Savile Row; and John LaRose, fellow Trinidadian, founder of the first black bookshop in the UK: New Beacon Books.

In a matter of months, the Black British presence, through its activists, pioneers, and achievers, was becoming more understood. In the face of constant urgings from colleagues, friends, and family, I could no longer find excuses for not capturing my own story of my journey from humble Barataria in Trinidad to London in Britain: to capture my experiences and thoughts and to add them as my contribution to the recording and archiving of this presence. But the very thought of writing frightened me. I am an actor, not a writer. Was I competent enough to undertake such a task?

Then two separate incidents sealed my fate and made the decision for me.

First, there was an invitation that I could not refuse: to open the Notting Hill Pensioners' Day Centre in West London, and to rub shoulders again with a joint guest of honour, someone for whom I have the greatest admiration and respect: Sir Bill Morris, the then General Secretary of the Transport and General Workers' Union. Bill had risen through the ranks from a humble beginning in Jamaica to become one of the most powerful trade unionists in the UK. He wore his badge of office with tremendous dignity and is a shining example to our troubled youngsters. In attendance was a Jamaican-born photographer, Armet Francis, whom I met at the Keskidee Arts Centre in North London many years ago in the 1960s.

Unprompted, Armet asked whether I had considered putting into print my experiences over the years. He said that I owed it to future generations, and it would be an inspiration to many. I promised to give it some serious thought. But it was an encounter, several weeks later, in the Portobello Road market in London that really set me thinking seriously about putting pen to paper.

I was on my way to meet a young student film director, Miss Frances-Ann Solomon from Trinidad, who wanted advice on a short film she was doing for her school and wanted me to appear in it. I was a bit early, so to kill time I did some window-shopping. I was gazing at some African artefacts in a window when a voice over my shoulder said, 'Good morning, Mr Rudolph Walker.' I turned to gaze into the face of a senior citizen of African descent with the countenance of a sage, whose penetrating eyes bore into my own in a way I found faintly unsettling. I merely returned his greeting by nodding, as he did not extend his hand, an action that would have been the normal response.

Like some ancient mariner, he bellowed that I was 'a gifted actor'. He further emphasised that he had followed my career over the years and that I was being under-used. Then, as a parting shot, he fixed me with that same all-seeing eye and told me sternly and to the point, 'Young man, you must start writing. It is the only way you will get the quality parts you deserve and ought to be playing. You also need to leave something in writing for the future generation.' Having delivered his piece, he turned on his heel and headed off with a perfunctory 'Bye'.

Unnerved, I turned and walked in the opposite direction. I stopped, looked back, but he was nowhere to be seen. One minute he was there, the next minute he was gone. I felt the hairs rise on my skin. The encounter was a bit strange to say the least, and really set me thinking very seriously. The apparently barely literate, barefoot, black boy peering at the privileged few through the gaps in the high hedge of the tennis courts in Trinidad, the good-for-nothing, who endured serious beatings from his mother, was now a recognised achiever, no longer waiting in the wings.

Therefore, despite my lack of confidence in my ability to write, it is with deep humility that I have ventured into this new role. As I recall and paraphrase a popular and well-used quotation, it is my hope that all aspiring youngsters, especially those of colour, who read this honest narration of my life will realise that: 'the race is not always for the swift and the privileged, but for those who dare to struggle against all odds and aspire to reach the finish line'.

They should also recognise that it does not matter to me the number of Hollywood legends I have acted alongside, the privileged status of being amongst beloved soap stars. Gaining the respect of my colleagues was always far more important. And over and above that, there is always my love for my homeland.

I still yearn for the sights, the smells, and the sounds of Trinidad, to where I return every year I can. When I set foot on the plane, it is no longer as a boy returning to an impoverished home with its memories of flogging and humiliation, but as a man who has walked a walk few others have dared to take, who despite his lowly birth has pushed himself to the limits and succeeded beyond every expectation.

In Trinidad, when someone achieves more than was ever anticipated, people say that 'the boy done good for himself' and certainly this boy has travelled far and come an awfully long way since those early days.

I step onto my native land as a man who has taken on the establishment, risen above the racism he has encountered, tried to set trends, open doors for himself and others – and has lived to tell the tale.

PART ONE

Trinidad

MY MOTHER

In the whole world full of beauty
In the whole world full of love,
In the whole world full of friendship
My mother, she is above all.
What awful pains I brought her,
What tears I made her shed,
All because she loves me
And vowed to do God's will.

by Malcolm Walker, aged 14

CHAPTER 1

Trini To De Bone

'It takes a village to rear a child'
African proverb

My journey on earth began in the wee hours of the morning of 28 September 1939, at number 10, Tenth Street, Barataria, in the twin-island country of Trinidad and Tobago. Today, my birth certificate is the only proof I have of this beginning.

Christened Rudolph Malcolm Walker, I was called Malcolm when growing up, and I am still called Malcolm by my family and old school friends – no one ever called me Rudolph and it was a name I only began to use when I introduced myself to fellow passengers on board the ship that brought me to the UK. I did not even know that I was named Rudolph until I was well into my teens and needed my birth certificate for travelling purposes!

Trinidad is beautiful. It is the larger of the two islands in the Republic of Trinidad and Tobago, and the most southern group of islands in the Caribbean, though still small: only thirty-six miles in total from north to south. Barataria, the area where I was born, is in the north-west, about four miles from Port-of-Spain, the capital.

The geography of Barataria seemed to be well planned, with streets each about two miles long, all numbered running from north to south and avenues about a mile long, east to west also numbered, so for instance, I lived at number 10 Tenth Street, no problem for a visitor to find the house. It had a village atmosphere, where many people knew your business. The population today numbers about nine thousand; it would have been half that when I was going to school, with a large percentage of well-known families, so a stranger stopping someone on the street and asking for the Pierres or the Thompsons, or the Bishops or Gobins, would be directed to the appropriate house.

It might sound a cliché if I say I came from a poor family, but that was genuinely the case. We never actually considered ourselves poor though, and the term was certainly not part of our daily vocabulary. We were just pretty much the same as everyone else we knew in the area. There weren't many luxuries as we know them today. Our luxuries were from the natural island itself – the sunshine on my back, the sea breeze blowing in my face, the fine sand on the beaches. There were no mobile phones or computer games, or swish cars or fancy clothes. Simple pleasures – pleasures to which I love to return, and value highly, even though nowadays I can afford more material possessions. As the Calypsonian David Rudder eulogises in verse, I am 'Trini to de Bone'.

Islands in the sun
Islands in the fun

Welcome, Welcome one and all to the land of fete
Trini to de bone, Trini to de bone
When it come to bacchanal, Well they can't beat we yet
Trini to de bone, Trini to de bone . . .

It is a Trinidadian's belief that your connection to the country of birth cannot be broken if you fulfil two main conditions – your navel-string (umbilical cord) is buried there and you have eaten cascadura, a small local catfish with tough scaly skin. As far as I know, my placenta was disposed of in the backyard of 10 Tenth Street, Barataria, Trinidad, and I have eaten cascadura several times, so I will always feel a strong, proud connection to my birthplace.

The house I grew up in was very small but meticulously clean, with the floor well-polished, but this still did not stop the odd rat or two trying to share any food we left exposed at night, and some of these were big and smart son-of-a-gun thieves. We would often set a rat trap at night with cheese and bread – which we could ill afford – but the rascal rodents would often ignore the tempting picnic and go instead for the last piece of sweet bread that I thought I had tucked safely away. When a rat was caught in the trap, it was my job to remove it, so I would poke it with a big stick to make sure that it was dead before getting close, just in case it suddenly sprang up at me!

Our little world consisted of a kitchen, a sitting/dining room with a table and a rocking chair and a grandfather clock that chimed on the hour, plus one bedroom with a beautiful four-poster brass bed, which was my job to polish with Brasso, especially around Christmas time. I shared the bed with my mother, then when my sister Aliena was born, all three of us slept in the same bed. As I grew bigger, a little wooden bed was built and placed alongside the big bed for me, and later another bedroom and kitchen were added when my younger sister Veronica was born.

By today's standards, the house was a shack. We had no electricity or piped water until shortly before I left Trinidad in 1960. For light, we used kerosene lamps and candles. Every morning, from as far back as I can remember, before going to school it was my job to fetch water from the standpipe a block away. To do that, I would wake up very early, usually around five o'clock, a habit I still have after so many years, and head off, armed with buckets. I enjoyed those early morning trips, especially during the mango season as I would be up earlier than most of the other boys, so after I had filled our barrel with water, I would then visit the various gardens in the area before the other boys did, to pick up any mangoes that had fallen on the ground during the night. Today, most of the gardens are fenced in. How times have changed!

Like many at the time, we were a single-parent family. My mother, Carmen Bishop, never married and had three children without a husband: myself, my sister Francillia Robinson (often called Eileen or Aliena) who is four years younger than me, and Veronica (known as Dawn) four years after that. It was very common for women throughout the Caribbean to have children but not necessarily want to settle with anyone. I also had a younger brother, but he died when he was a few days old. I was about three years old then, and two or three days after the birth, the doctor came to the house and then the baby was simply gone – I did not know why or how he died, or even his name. Just that one day he was in the house and the next he was not, and no one said a word. He was never mentioned afterwards, and my mother was the sort of person that you did not ask about her business. I certainly never questioned her life choices or asked her why she never married my father.

She worked extremely hard to maintain us, mostly cooking and cleaning for some well-off families, and I admire her courage and strength in bringing up three of us – two girls and a boy – without a man in the house. What about my father? My mother might say to me on a Friday night that in the morning I had to take the bus to Tunapuna to get some money 'from Ralph'. She never referred to him as my father – and referring to a father by his given name was not uncommon in our society – although at some stage she must have told me he was my dad.

I never questioned this when I was growing up. I carried his surname, and the name Rudolph was chosen for me because his name was Ralph, or so I was told when I learned of the name in my teens. So, I accepted that he was my legitimate father, although I have always regretted not asking my mother directly if he was my real father or not. But when I was growing up a child would never dare question their parents on such matters. You accepted what you were told.

I would walk the five miles to his house, using the bus fare my mother had given me to buy maybe a rock cake and a mauby – a bitter-tasting drink made from the bark of a tree – or whatever other drink took my fancy that day. My father would give me a few dollars for my mother and sometimes, depending on his mood, he would give me an extra ten cents for some pocket money that I would carefully put away before making my journey back on foot to Barataria.

I have over the years felt a definite gap in my life of not being able to talk about a father-son relationship. Sometimes I felt pained when seeing a father playing cricket or football with his son, or flying a kite, or teaching the young lad to ride a bike. That should have been me with my father. I trust I have been able to break that cycle by making sure I was around for my own son and daughter, and to witness today my son's pleasure in himself being a father. I believe it is so important for fathers to step up and shoulder their responsibilities, regardless of the circumstances.

I wish I'd had a closer relationship with my mother too; I wasn't able to throw my arms around her, hug or kiss her and don't remember her ever cuddling me. She kept everything to herself, especially her emotions. Occasionally, when I had the opportunity to observe her enjoying herself with her close friends – and there were not many – she would explode with some real belly laughs, which often took me by surprise.

However, I was certainly not bereft of love. The minute I walked out of my doors onto the streets, I was bombarded by love. From a very early age, I gravitated towards my aunts and uncles, my godparents and neighbours, who welcomed me into their fold as part of their families. They say it takes a village to rear a child. Well, there were a lot of women around to help rear me, and four women to whom I became attached and from whom I drew a lot of guidance. These were the matriarchs who were major early influences in my life, teaching me so much that has been useful. And when I look back at the women I have chosen to share my own life with, I realise that the strong women of my childhood have each in their own way influenced the way I see women: I gravitate towards women who are strong and capable, able to make the best of whatever circumstances they find themselves in. I have never been attracted to meek, submissive ladies. As a working actor, however, any lady in my life had to be able to be self-sufficient as the nature of my career often meant I would be working away a lot.

First, however, I must mention Roselyn Bishop, my mother's mother. My grandmother. I was told by my other relatives that I was the apple of her eye and in her active days, while I was still a toddler, she apparently took me everywhere she went but I was too young to really remember her. Sadly, she became ill and had to spend a lot of time in bed before she died. I was no older than three or four at the time, and I remember being very scared as all our relatives stood on either side of the coffin and according to the local tradition the smallest child – me! – had to be handed over the coffin from person to person. It was one of the only times that I ever saw my mother really cry.

And so, my Aunt Ada – my mother's aunt – became a loving substitute for my grandmother. The matriarch of all matriarchs, the eldest and tiniest of the quartet of women but by far the most powerful. I learned so much from her as I grew up. A mother of three, a grandmother of seven, and with three great-grandchildren at the time of her death, Aunt Ada was small in stature, but she ruled her household with a strength that even at an early age I came to recognise and admire.

She taught me discipline and the need to take responsibility for my actions, whether good or bad. And she taught me manners too. In Aunt Ada's dining room, there were two tables: a long table for the adults and a much smaller one for the children – or so I thought for a while, but you had to graduate to sit with the adults; you had to know how to handle a knife and fork and how to politely converse with the older members of the family.

I clearly remember the moment I 'graduated'. It was a Sunday lunchtime and most of the family were sitting around the table helping themselves from the variety of dishes placed in the centre of the table. My cousins and I - the three of us - washed our hands and raced to our table remembering to slow down just before we got to our chairs.

Two plates of food were already placed for my two cousins, but nothing for me, and Aunty was already sitting with an empty chair next to her. 'Malcolm, come and sit here.' Promotion? Aunt Ada had set a place for me at the big table. I should have been looking at my cousins in triumph; instead, I was petrified, it was so sudden, no warning, no indication that this was going to happen. My food was already dished out, so that saved me the agony of having to reach over and help myself as the others did. My cousins were giggling quietly at my discomfort, and I kept looking back at them for support, until Aunty very quietly said to look in front and eat my food. I tried to concentrate on doing all the things I was taught, like take your time and chew properly, don't gobble down the food in an attempt to dash out and play with my cousins and their friends, when asked a question don't answer with a mouth full of food.

I was aware of Aunty quietly saying to me a few times, 'Speak up, Malcolm.' I'd never been told to speak up before, as I had a strong voice as a child. I was extremely slow, and everyone at my table had finished eating and had either left the table or were chatting, and my cousins had already left their table and gone outside to play by the time I finished eating. I asked to be excused and was just about to go when Aunty told me to sit back down. My immediate thought was: have I done something wrong? I quickly sat, then she asked me if I had finished eating. I said, 'Yes, Aunty.' She asked me again if I'd finished eating; there was more food left in the various bowls on the table, but the last thing I wanted was to sit and eat more food. My plate was empty, so of course I had finished eating, and had asked permission to leave. Why then had she asked me twice if I had finished? Then, before she asked a third time, I realised: I had not closed my knife and fork together on the empty plate. Manners. The right way to behave when eating in someone else's house or out in a restaurant as an adult. It was a lesson I never forgot.

Then there was Aunty Merle, a Barbadian – Barbados being to the north of Trinidad and Tobago – who was married to Uncle Albert, a Trinidadian. He wasn't a blood relative, but his mother was my mother's godmother. I loved to sit at the table in her house and watch Uncle Albert eat. Albert Moore was a towering man, well over six feet: an enormous man, but one who would sit and cut his food with the delicacy of a surgeon. He was a church minister on a Sunday and a Government Building Surveyor, a Building Contractor and Inspector during the week.

Aunty Merle, large, buxom and motherly but with no children of her own, taught me how to be understanding, to listen and to learn. And she was always open to giving me advice if I had any problems. Later, when I was grown and living in the UK, I would still call her to talk through any problems, and hers was always my second port of call whenever I visited Trinidad during my early return trips. She and Uncle Albert both died within hours of each other, he from a diabetes-related illness and she from cancer. And I still miss them.

Aunt Millie – a white Trinidadian married to my Uncle Roy – was also full of advice. 'Malcolm, stand straight, walk tall!' she would counsel, as if preparing me for hard times ahead or to atone for the harsh times at home. She truly loved me, treating me like a son, and she taught me that love was colour blind and to always hold my head up. There were undoubtedly a few raised eyebrows when as a child, we would go to the shops together and I would be holding onto her hand or skirt and calling her Aunty, because she was white. But her marriage to Uncle Roy – who worked on board a ship and was often away - was strong and loving and showed me at this early age that there should be no barriers towards whom one loved. She also knew how to have a huge amount of fun! Especially at Carnival, when she played mas every year. At a Trinidad carnival, you can go along and watch all the bands parade on the streets, mainly in the capital city Port-of-Spain, or you can join in – which is called 'playing mas'. This means paying a fee for the costume, joining a masquerade band, wearing a fabulous costume and make-up and dancing on the streets all day till you drop! If you think Notting Hill Carnival in London is spectacular, you should experience a Trinidad carnival. The Monday and Tuesday immediately before Ash Wednesday is when the main celebrations take place. Uncle Roy and Aunt Millie lived at the top of a steep hill with steps and rails that cars could not access, and I can clearly remember on several occasions, especially around carnival time, helping Aunt Millie, barely five feet tall, to climb up the hill when she had had one too many drinks. She did enjoy her rum!

Another of my favourite aunts was Aunt Marge, wife to one of my mother's brothers. He was good to me and would take me to the cinema to watch films, usually Westerns. Aunt Marge loved him very much, but he was the sort of man who would deserve being called a bit of a 'bad boy' or 'a player'. He chased after other women and, as was not uncommon in Trinidad at that time, would regularly beat his wife. It always upset me as a child. We lived in a male-dominated society and men felt they had to be in control; some women would boast that their husband or boyfriend beat them because he loved them. I have never agreed with that. I remember going over on a Sunday morning for breakfast and I noticed that Aunty had a puffed-up cheek and a swollen eye. I sat quietly and had my breakfast – fantastic fry-bakes - but afterwards, I felt confident enough to sit on my uncle's knees, telling him he shouldn't hit Aunty, that I loved her, and it wasn't a nice thing to do. It took courage from me, but sadly nothing I said – a child! – would stop him ill-treating Aunt Marge. As a man today, it would never cross my mind to treat a woman like that. I always respected women. Why might I want to hit a woman? Certainly not an example I'd want to set to my children. However, Aunt Marge taught me that despite hardship and pressure a person can still walk with dignity, and she always had a smile for me.

The four women were all different personalities, but each did give me something that withstood the test of time, although these experiences are, truthfully, Victorian à la Trinidad style: strictness, discipline, a good attitude to doing chores or schoolwork, along with respect for those in authority and my elders. Interestingly, today, in addition to parents, there are teachers, social workers, psychologists, therapists, counsellors, lawyers, probation officers and others, all highly paid officials, available to help young people facing problems, and yet so many still go astray.

I had my matriarchs.

And my mother, of course. As a child, I was quite afraid of her, because of what appeared to be any excuse to beat me, for the simplest of reasons. People living in my area when I was growing up would often say that I got licks for all the boys in the neighbourhood. Looking back at these frequent bouts of punishment, it was obvious that parents then believed that sparing the rod spoilt the child – though if I was raised like that these days in the UK, my mother would almost certainly have been dragged before the courts for child abuse. It was just the Trinidad custom when I grew up – I certainly wasn't the only boy who would get a hiding if I got into trouble! I got flogged for everything and anything. It could be for foolish things, like pitching marbles with my friends when I should be inside; or staying back and playing in the savannah after school; or talking to someone whom my mother thought was rough. I really got some serious blows, and it was the kind of licks that never seemed to stop. Now the house was very small, and I mean really small. If I stood on one side of a room and my sister was on the other and I pointed my finger at her with an outstretched arm, there was a danger of poking out her eye. There was definitely no place to run from any onslaught.

I had a big voice as a child, so sometimes I would scream out loud enough, hoping that one of the kind neighbours would hear me and come to my rescue. None ever did. My mother would shout at me demanding that I stop the loud crying, whilst the licks were still raining down on me. I would force myself to stop, hoping that she too would stop when I did. But no! She would suddenly shift the emphasis when I stopped crying and would say to me, 'Is hard yuh hard, yuh cah feel!' and that was topped by her favourite saying – 'Hard ears don't hear! Don't care, yuh go feel.' It was a Catch 22 situation. If I cried, I got licks; if I did not cry, I still got licks!

CHAPTER 2

The Best Gunslinger in Barataria

'Success is only meaningful and enjoyable if it feels like your own' Michelle Obama, lawyer, writer and former First Lady of the USA

Growing up, I was often busy doing simple chores for my aunts or other elders in the neighbourhood, for instance running errands to the shop, cleaning out the chicken coop, collecting eggs, sweeping, and cleaning the yard.

But there was always time to play. I considered most of the boys with whom I went to school and played with in my neighbourhood to be my best friends. Over the years, I have kept in touch with many of them – one or two have even visited me here in the UK. Some stayed in Barataria all their lives and I always touched base with them when I came back to Trinidad, and we have shared a lot of laughs over our adventures as children.

We had an abundance of toys that we made ourselves that were used in various games. The materials for making these items were often taken from within our homes or were waste or discarded materials, each person contributing so that no one person had to produce the lion's share of materials or equipment. The games themselves were traditional ones, and many were unique to Trinidad and even local areas.

From an early age, we were using our initiative, creativity, and daring to produce our own toys and create novel and local rules for their use. It often involved many intricate and complex skills, some acquired by trial and error and following traditions handed down from generation to generation, while others came from advances made with the introduction of new technologies and materials. We learned a lot! Carpentry and other skills, plus – importantly – heaps of using our imaginations. A homemade toy can feel so much better, so much more personal, than something you have just opened out of a box. And I feel sad for some of today's kids who get all their entertainment on screens or delivered to the door – imagination is a wonderful thing when you are a child.

We were experts at making kites to fly high across the nearby Aranguez or Barataria savannahs, or even in our backyards. I loved flying kites, the making of which involved a long process.

There were different types and shapes, but the most popular was the basic prism-shaped kite, called a Common Kite to distinguish it from the more elaborate versions like the Mad Bull, which was shaped without a single tail and made a lot of noise when flown. I've never forgotten my kite-making skills. As recently as a few years ago, I got all the materials together and made one for my grandson Latimer. We then went out and flew it together over the Wiltshire countryside.

We always began by creating a sturdy 'bow-and-arrow' frame from the stems of fronds taken from the branches of the coconut tree. This crossbow and arrow shape created the infrastructure on which we then affixed sheets of coloured tissue paper. To get a taut, wind-resistant surface, flour was mixed with water to glue the frame to the kite paper, especially at the corners.

Then we needed to make a tail for the kite. Scraps of discarded bed sheets were good, but the prized material that made the best tail was old typewriter ribbon about three-quarters of an inch wide. The final touch would be to add razor blades or very sharp pieces of glass from a broken bottle to the tail, using lagley, resin from the breadfruit tree. When the resin was hardened, we chewed it or rubbed it in the palms of our hands until it was soft enough to use. This added feature enabled you to have aerial combat with other kites, the goal being to cut or entangle the threads of other players and force their kite to 'ayeo'!

But it was the mastery of the kite in flight, playing your kite, that set you above the rest, giving you bragging rights for ducking and weaving it in intricate manoeuvres. Best of all was feigning 'ayeo' but recovering from the lowest levels near to the ground to soar, zigzagging, with tantalising movements of the tail to ascendancy in the air.

Without doubt, of all the toys and childhood games available, pitching marbles was my absolute favourite. I had a vast array of multi-coloured marbles, lovingly captured and kept in a bulging bag, then brought out to pitch, to fling and to knock opponents clear out of the ring. They were my prized possessions and Mother knew it. On occasions, when her slaps and smacks did not get the desired reaction, she would confiscate my bag of shiners to punish me in a way that was worse than any beatings: she would throw them down the latrine or cesspit – a six-foot hole dug in the earth and covered with a hand-made wooden toilet seat. Yet, regardless of where they were thrown, I would hold my breath, lean in, use a long hook to retrieve my prized marbles, disinfect the lot with a strong disinfectant and live to play another day. Along with the pollution in the canals, it is a marvel I did not succumb to any infections!

Of course, at times, we got involved in making mischief. I remember during crop time when the sugar cane from the fields was being harvested and taken down to the factory on open train carriages, I would go with my group of friends down to the train line and pull off pieces of cane in defiance of the shouting guards, who rode in the covered carriage or the engine room. Although we grew sugar cane in our garden, somehow the ones we pulled off the train were sweeter. Also, coming up to Christmas time, I remember times when trucks transporting apples overturned on the highway. Even though we had no telephone at the time, the news spread like wildfire, and we were all rapidly on the spot, scrambling to snatch as many apples as possible. Eating an apple was a luxury for us in those days. They were costly. We made sure to suck all the sugar cane and eat all the apples before going home, because some of us would be sure to get flogged for stealing. Funnily enough, although my mother somehow always knew if I'd been up to mischief, I was never punished for grabbing sugar cane or apples.

We played cricket all year round, as long as it wasn't pouring with rain. About four or five times a week on average – cricket was like the national sport then. The most popular area was on a dirt road about a hundred yards from where I lived, at the corner of Tenth Street and First Avenue, with most of the boys with whom I played living within a radius of about half a mile. It wasn't unusual when just travelling about three-quarters of a mile from school to home, you'd run into a group playing and join in and get carried away, getting home late to find a cross parent waiting.

We used bats made from the lower stems of the branches of the coconut tree; also, some of us with the necessary carpentry skills would make one from a piece of discarded timber, and for bowling we used a wind ball (lawn tennis ball) sold loosely for that purpose. Many times we had to improvise, so would substitute a very young breadfruit or a green orange as a ball. Our wickets for most games were an empty oil or kerosene tin. When one couldn't be found, we used a piece of timber propped up with a stick, and if neither of those were available, for an impromptu game, then two big stones were placed on the ground about four feet apart. The batsman would stand in an imaginary crease about a foot or two in front of the stones, in the middle of them.

This really developed our skills as batsmen. We became great timers of the ball, displayed excellent use of our reflexes, and developed precise foot movements. We tried to emulate our heroes: the three great West Indian batsmen known as the three W's – Weekes, Worrell, and Walcott. My hero was Sir Frank Worrell with his delicate touches. I tried to match his style and play with real technique. One thing that sticks in my mind is that I was never a natural hard hitter of the ball, but I could rack up the number of runs I made. I believe I still hold the record of the most runs made at our street corner of 96 runs not out!

More expensive treats than playing in the street had to be earned, as for most of my mates. I got money for shopping for a neighbour, cleaning my aunts' yards, or collecting the eggs from under a neighbour's house. The last task I would do with some trepidation because if the hens were around, they would attack and I often hit my head on the floor above, trying to escape a vicious hen.

With money in my pocket, the cinema was a major treat. My local cinema on the Eastern Main Road was the Ritz, a flea-ridden emporium, so everyone was guaranteed a scratching session when they came out. As boys, we went mainly to see Westerns, so fleas or no fleas, scratching or no scratching, we immediately dashed home afterwards and re-enacted the fight scenes. My first memory of a homemade toy is of wooden guns to replicate these Hollywood gunfights and the battles between cowboys and Indians that we saw at the cinema. We spent hours mastering the draw of our weapons from our holsters – usually just the waistband of our trousers. Who drew first was always a bone of contention, but I was fast!

War movies and other action films were also great favourites. We walked and talked like John Wayne or pretended to be the greatest swordsman in town when we saw Tyrone Power in *The Mark of Zorro* or played at being accurate archers after seeing Errol Flynn in *The Adventures of Robin Hood*. We were real actors too. We knew how to collapse when the enemy spotted us first and would shout at us, 'Bang, yuh dead.'

I realised later that the falls we executed then seemed to have been coming straight out of the Royal Academy of Dramatic Art in the UK, but with a touch of Trinidadian bravado thrown in. Everyone had their own style; one would die in slow motion, and another would just drop down like a stone. Yet another would hold onto a tree trunk using it as a prop, sliding down slowly like a snake until – too late – he would discover that the tree trunk was full of biting ants and he would start to scratch, so instantly he was no longer dead.

I was always looking for a way to outwit my friends by crawling through the bushes and other gardens and coming up from behind. The winner was the last man standing. No prizes, just the title for that moment, the best gunslinger in town. My favourite way of falling was to drop the gun, clutch my chest and collapse on the ground, with several painful groans thrown in.

There were no audiences to applaud when one fell, but it was still done for maximum effect, holding your prostrate position for long enough to get the applause. The joy was that we all came out alive and well apart from a bruised or cut knee if you were unlucky enough to fall on a sharp stone or broken bottle; we always lived to fight another day after a good laugh and jokes all around.

Sadly, today it is for real, no joking matter. The guns are real, the violence is real. This is not to say Trinidad was devoid of violence in those days, but it was in the main confined to bottles and stones, fists, wood, and occasionally a knife and cutlass, but fatalities were few and far between. The men of my generation who were involved in violence as youngsters walk around today with a few scars as mementos, not a headstone in a graveyard. Now it is all different.

One positive change for the better today is how, of course, many actors of colour now feature in movies. As a child, I never questioned or challenged the fact that all the heroes we were watching on the cinema screens were white, even Tarzan who landed in the jungle from America and communicated with the animals was white, while the black African people who had been born and lived amongst the animals for well over a century apparently couldn't. Our roles in most of those movies were as spear carriers. Sadly, I was to find that nothing much had changed when I began looking for theatre roles in the UK in my twenties. Spear carrier, it was!

Despite all our antics, we rarely had any injuries at all. We walked barefoot through cow dung and animal faeces and whether it was a cut foot or a squashed mango, the remedy was the same: wash it, put on some iodine, and move on.

There were no doctors or dentists on hand. I cleaned my teeth with the stem of the hibiscus plant (called datwan) and soda powder from the coal-pot, not the well-packaged and advertised toothpaste that we use today. My first encounter with a dentist was about three or four years after I arrived in the UK, and the first time I ever saw a doctor was at the age of twenty-four, after I had emigrated to England. Up until that time, my mother would find a plant to boil, which would cure any ailment. If Mother could not sort it out, then some old woman down the road would take care of me. Bush medicine – we call it herbal medicine today – was standard back then.

The only thing that Mother could not deal with was Obeah – the science of witchcraft that uses spiritual powers to help someone to do evil or good. Like most women in the neighbourhood, she was adept at sorting out children, men, and the authorities, but she feared what she could not see, touch or command – the spirit world.

I must have been about ten when I noticed my mother's commanding presence was shaken by a series of inexplicable night-time noises. She swore that a man who lived not far from us was an Obeah man and was out to get her. To protect us, she burned incense and sprinkled salt around the doors, and it all scared the living daylight out of me.

That all changed on a day after another terrifying night. There had been a heavy downpour of rain followed by some high winds. I was sitting and drawing when I heard the same sounds as during the night. I reasoned that ghosts do not operate during the day but only at night-time, so there had to be another explanation for the noise. I decided to investigate, and there it was – the branch of a coconut tree that was scraping against the galvanised iron roof!

Nevertheless, it still took me two or three weeks before I dared reveal to Mother what I had discovered. She did not believe me anyway and continued to blame the Obeah man. But I slept peacefully at night thereafter, even if Mother did not.

But there were other dangers, real dangers that could suddenly arise – nothing to do with Obeah, but from those whom I thought I could trust. I had been raised to have great respect for older people, but this respect had got me very close to being abused by the son of my mother's older friend when I was only about nine or ten years old. They were a family with a few brothers, big men at the time, and I visited their house several times with my mother. During the mango season, and in that yard, there was a tree laden with my favourite mango – mango vert. It was customary in those days that if a child passing a house on their way home from school saw any ripe mangoes on the ground, he would just call out, walk in and pick them up. On one occasion after school, I was on my own and one of the brothers invited me in for a few more mangoes which he had on the table.

I did not think it unusual, even when he sat me on his lap and asked me about my schoolwork. Although I felt uncomfortable, I still did not think it odd, but when he started rubbing his hand on my privates, I thought to myself, this is not right, he should not be doing that. When I was a baby, it had been fine and necessary for my mother to wash and touch any part of my body. But a grown man?

I jumped off his lap, frightened like hell, snatched up my school bag, which was outside the door, and kept running until I got home, minus my mangoes.

At that age, I had no idea what he would have done to me. I never went back, certainly not when he was around. I never mentioned it to my mother or my other school friends; if I had done so, his life would have been absolutely hell, because they'd have been going past his door calling him names.

Years later, this same man set up home with another man, a domestic situation that was a source of gossip in the community as same-sex relationships were considered abnormal and against God's will. By then, I was in my teens and working, and one day I saw him in the distance cycling towards his home and turned into his entrance, and on the spur of the moment, rather than continue walking past his house as I had done on a number of occasions, I decided to knock on his door. It was not unusual in Trinidad culture for people to unexpectedly call, we rarely locked our doors and so, my going to his home would not have been unheard of, it was more of a concern that I could have been spotted by friends which would have led to a lot of uncomfortable comments sent my way and speculation as to why I was there. As I approached the door I wondered, would he just ignore me, or open the door and chase me away? Or did he have a bad dog he would set on me - or would he apologise for what he had done or attempted to do when I was a child?

I knew I was brave and strong enough to stand up to him. He opened the door after a moment. Very polite greetings were exchanged, then his partner appeared behind him and invited me in, which I accepted, but I'd worked out in my mind that if they tried anything funny I was young and strong enough to fight them off and beat the hell out of there. Failing that, my screams would bring the neighbours running.

Fortunately, nothing like that happened; they were very polite, offered something to drink which I refused, asked me about my apprenticeship, but by this time I realised that no apology was forthcoming. It was clear that his partner knew nothing of what had gone on and so I said my goodbyes and left. I felt relief that I had faced my fears, perhaps the interaction would have been different had his partner not been there, but I was able to put the incident behind me and walk away.

CHAPTER 3

L is for a Little Lamb – My Stage Debut

'*To educate is to emancipate*' Dr Eric Williams, Prime Minister, Trinidad & Tobago 1962-1981

School, of course, features prominently in any young person's life and I was no exception.

The first school I attended was Miss Morton's Kindergarten. Miss Morton was referred to as 'Tanty Morton'. Miss Morton, a very strict Afro-Trinidadian lady, was my Aunt Marge's aunt, but that did not allow for any form of favouritism. Teachers then did not hesitate to discipline pupils in their care, but I was in awe of her and hardly ever got smacked. The memory I have of attending kindergarten is of reading stories, and I vaguely remember her always complimenting me on something: my handwriting, my tidy clothes.

Many years later, on a return visit with my three-year-old son Darren, I was emotionally moved to witness Miss Morton lifting him onto her lap, much as she would have done to me at the same age. She died in her 90s, having given up the kindergarten school just before she passed away.

At the end of the Christmas term, every year, she put on a show for the parents as she was very keen on the Performing Arts. I recalled one year she had us lined up on stage each with a letter of the alphabet to recite. There must have been fewer than twenty-six of us able to perform, so some were given two letters. I had: 'L is for a little lamb; his fleece was white as snow'. I was not satisfied with just the one letter – I wanted more – but Miss Morton would have none of it. This was my first acting experience on stage that I recall, and that image has stuck with me all these years.

On leaving Miss Morton's Kindergarten School, I went on to Barataria E.C. School: a secondary/elementary school, with pupils from seven to sixteen.

Here, I always thought I was just very average as a pupil. Not academically inclined, and the apparent lack of education would come to haunt me from time to time in later life. I did just enough to get by and to keep out of trouble. It is ironic that those same traits surfaced in both my children. Their school reports often read 'capable of doing a lot better'.

The only subjects I excelled in were mathematics, geography, and drama. Mathematics was called arithmetic in my school days, and I loved it because I enjoyed the challenge of outshining my classmates, being the first to deliver the correct answer. I loved geography, because I was interested in gaining knowledge about other parts of the world. And drama, where I felt I was the best in the class. I did just enough in other subjects to pass.

Mr Evans Rampersad, a portly East Indian gentleman, was the headmaster of the primary school. The day began with

Rampy, as we secretly called him, ringing the bell on the school steps, and regardless of where we were – in the school, in the grounds, across the road, or playing in the savannah – we would stop and pay attention immediately. The ringing of the second bell was an order to move as quickly as possible to the school ground and to line up according to classes. The class teacher would then inspect our clothes. Everything had to be tidy, shirts in our trousers, fingernails clean, or a rap was given on the knuckles with a ruler.

I always took pride in my appearance while wearing my school uniform, which comprised of a pair of khaki trousers and a blue shirt, and I made sure that they were always as impeccable as possible. I would clean and whiten my Bata plimsolls with Blanco shoe polish at least twice a week. If we were one of those whose parents could not afford plimsolls, our feet still had to be clean.

A third bell would then ring for us to go to our classrooms quietly. During all that time, Rampy would be standing on the steps casting his eyes over the area for latecomers. Punctuality was very important, and it was a foregone conclusion that if a latecomer was not armed with a valid excuse, preferably written by his or her mother or father, he or she would be caned. There were a number of times that I caught myself playing on the road several yards away from the school, heard the bell and covered the distance in record time.

In spite of his harsh discipline, I had tremendous respect for Mr Rampersad. I believe his overall disciplinary measures, as headmaster, did help to **mould** me into who and what I am today. No working actor can afford to be unprofessional, to turn up late or unprepared, or ignore necessary rules, and the self-discipline Rampy instilled in me has been of real value. On one of my trips back home, while living in England, I decided to visit Rampy at his home in Tunapuna. This was long after he had retired, so he was a little frail but still very alert. He remembered me but said with some sadness that I was the only past pupil from those earlier years who had returned to the island and visited him.

Drama was calling to me already. In my first term at Barataria E.C., when I was about seven years old, I saw the senior pupils perform a play. It was around Christmas time, and I seem to remember it being very colourful. When I saw it, I immediately felt that I wanted to be part of something similar – wanted to be up on stage with them. When we returned after the Christmas holiday break, I immediately asked to join the school's drama group. I was too young to think of this in any way as being a possible career, but I do know that I was simply excited by the idea of being in a proper play.

The drama group was usually only for the older students, but the teacher, Mr Dyer, accepted me and I became the youngest member. They met near the time of planning a production, but before any casting was done, sessions included learning and reciting poetry up on the stage. Some people could freeze when asked to stand up alone and recite, but I loved it!

My first role was in a Christmas musical play, *We Three Kings*. I was playing Melchior the king bearing frankincense, and it was the first time I got to dress up for a play. Mother made my costume for me, a long purple robe. At school, I made a cardboard crown, then covered it with gold paper. I felt really proud of what I had produced, and Mother also made me proud of her sewing skills by making the robe.

I can still remember walking onto the stage. I suppose I was no more than ten or eleven at the time and had to sing the verse 'Frankincense to offer have I'. It was very stylised. We had to move our hands up, in time with the other two kings, and slow down our delivery. The audience comprised parents, friends, and other supporters of the school. I understood that Mother was proud of me – in the audience then and for future productions, supporting me – but I could never remember her saying, 'That was good!' or, 'That was excellent, Malcolm!' She simply wasn't a woman who expressed herself in that way, she would just give a broad smile, so I knew deep down that she was pleased when I did well.

My next school play was entitled *Papa Bois*, and I performed the lead role as Papa Bois himself - the star, even though I was one of the youngest member! Papa Bois is a Caribbean folklore character, 'The Father of the Forest', feared by all children because he chastises those who are naughty or disrespectful to him. I was offered the role over many of the more senior pupils and I thought that I might have been chosen because Papa Bois had a big booming voice and I had the strongest voice and presence in the school when I stepped on the stage, according to one of the drama teachers, Miss Franklyn.

We made a sack outfit out of a crocus bag – a porous brown material in which sugar and flour were shipped. The crocus bags were not discarded but were taken and washed to be used for clothing, floor mats or any other item as the need arose. The outfit was covered with mud to make me look like a person who lived a rough life in the woods.

Mr Dyer, the teacher who directed the play, also asked me to take over the rehearsals whenever he was unable to attend. This was an invaluable though rather scary experience, helping me to understand how to control a group and how to get the best out of everyone, getting the whole cast to really pull together. Following on from this, it didn't only happen in the drama group. I'd often be picked out to take over one of the classes of younger children if a teacher was absent – helping them learn early arithmetic, for instance. And when I came to school leaving age, although I didn't think I was one of the brightest pupil, the school suggested I stay on as a pupil-teacher, going on to college to qualify properly. Teaching, of course, doesn't need the most academic person; there are other skills required. I sometimes wonder how my life might have turned out had I taken up that offer. I think I would have eventually opened my own school, with graduates leaving well rounded and fully equipped to lead, a view held by my friend a retired Head Teacher of Tulse Hill School Mr Ken Noble now living in Tobago who has written the blueprint for a school that is second to none.

I always worked hard to be a good actor. Whenever I was given a poem to recite or a play to do, my commitment increased by 150 per cent. It also inspired me to try and write for myself. At about the age of eleven, I went through a period when I wrote several poems. Many of them I would start during the day and armed with a pencil and copybook continue to scribble in the dark after my mother turned off the kerosene lamp. I was reading other people's verse on stage but wanted to read my own too.

CHAPTER 4

Laughing Shoes

'Intelligence plus character = that is the goal of true education'
Dr Martin Luther King Jr., Baptist minister and leader in the civil rights movement of the 1960s

---

After our fight, Gobin and I became good friends. And he became complicit the first time I ever played truant – or 'made l'ecole biche', as we called it. He was a master at it!

The reason for this was down to my shoes. As a result of our financial situation at home, I was only able to get one new pair of shoes at the start of each term. Now boys will be boys, and I was no exception. I played many games, at lunchtime, tea break, and of course on the way home after school. Inevitably, on one occasion, my plimsolls were split at the front. Now, had it been split in the back, it would have been all right, but not in the front, because when it came to the attention of my school friends that would only result in fatigue – verbal teasing – down the line.

In a typical jocular tone, they would ask, 'But, Malcolm, how ***come*** your shoes laughing so?'

Worst of all, the girls would be looking down and giggling when they should be looking at me in my eyes and saying that they liked me. For girls were beginning to become quite important to me these days. So one evening, when my shoes were torn, I begged my mother to buy me a pair the following morning before I went to school, and of course the answer was in the negative.

I tossed and turned in bed all night thinking of my laughing shoes and how I would face going to school the next day. I got up the following morning and pleaded again with Mother to buy me a new pair.

She did not relent; in fact, to add insult to injury, I got a good licking before I left for school for being so rude as to ask again.

Now I had never played truant before, but I decided to do so that day and I got a willing partner in Gobin. We went down to an area called The Coconut, so named because of the acres of coconut trees and just the odd house on its fringe, dotted with other vegetation in between. It was situated well away from everyone. There were narrow tracks which were difficult to negotiate during the rainy season, but in the dry season, it was a haven. We ate mangoes, broke open dried coconuts and ate the nuts, pitched marbles, and played cricket.

We had a good time, but through it all, I kept having what in today's terms can only be described as a cold sweat, especially as home time got closer. I knew my mother would not be there – she was four miles away in Port-of-Spain for the entire day, so I ought to have been safe, and I was sure that no one had seen me. We did not have a telephone, and it was not customary for a teacher to drop by and see a parent if a child was absent for a day or two.

It was a Thursday and I only had to do it again for one more day, Friday. A trip into Port-of-Spain on the Saturday, to any of my favourite aunts, might certainly have solved my problem – new shoes would be on my feet by Monday, I felt sure. I got home in good time and tried to do all the normal things that would please my mother, such as filling the buckets with water in case she needed any and sweeping the yard.

In retrospect, I just didn't know what time my mother would get home. I was in the backyard, stooping down and pitching marbles with a couple of friends when she arrived. About two minutes passed without a word from inside. I was just about to give the thumbs up to my friends when I heard, 'Malcolm, come here!' in a tone of voice I only associate with a licking.

In my pocket, I had a handful of kitchen salt wrapped in a piece of brown paper. There was a theory amongst us children that if a person was about to get licks, and he threw some salt over his right shoulder and spun around three times before going inside, he would escape the licks. I had decided that I might as well protect myself, just in case.

It did not work, because as soon as I stepped inside Mother exploded: 'Why you didn't go to school today, and where you went?' I did not even have time to tell a lie, because she demanded, 'Where's the belt?'

It was not in its usual place because when I got home, I had hidden it inside our grandfather clock. That turned out to be a big mistake because it elevated her anger to another level. After dropping the first two lashes across my back, and she was a powerful woman, she demanded I take off my pants.

It was not a joking matter in those days when a mother told a boy child to take off his pants. Some mothers seemed to hit harder than fathers. In my case, there was no father around, so she had double strength. I decided to make a quick dash to under the four-poster bed and to creep to the far corner, but as I dived under the bed I knocked over the posey (chamber pot) filled with wee. It must have been the first thing Mother had done when she got home. You see, we did not have an inside toilet and the cesspit was way down in the backyard, so Mother must have used the pot when she got in. I was bathed in it, but that was the least of my troubles. I thought I was safe in the far corner since I am talking about a five-foot-wide brass bed.

I swear my mother was a limbo dancer or a contortionist in her younger days, because she bent down and let fly some lashes with that belt. Every time she fired a lash the very tip would catch me, and that was worse than the full belt, and at the same time she was shouting at me to come out. When I realised she was getting angrier and angrier, I decided to make a run for it from under the bed, through the back door and into the backyard. I manipulated my body in an effort to negotiate fewer blows on my bare bottom as I leaped over the four steps.

Unfortunately for me, as I was flying in mid-air, who should I glimpse to my right, standing by the wire fence looking on, but the girl from next door – my current girlfriend! I did not know what was worse – staying inside and absorbing my licking, or the humiliation of a girlfriend watching my little private part dangling in front of me as I ran around the garden pursued by my mother with a belt in her hand.

In those days, there was modesty and a degree of innocence. Quick-thinking as I was, in desperation, I dived into the outside toilet, the latrine. Mind you, there was no lock on it, so it would not have stopped the licks, but it would have confined us to a small area and out of the sight of my girlfriend's eyes.

Going into the toilet was my saviour, because after flinging open the door and shouting for me to come out, Mother stopped. As frightened and embarrassed as I was, I wedged myself behind the seat because there was the danger that if either of us got too physical in there, we could go through the floorboards and end up in three to four feet of pure shit.

Lord! Why didn't I think of this before? I thought.

I remained in there and cried for ages and only ventured out when I heard a call from my mother demanding that I come inside for my dinner, and I could see that my girlfriend had gone. I knew then that the worst was over.

Or was it?

Highly embarrassed, I still had to go to school the following day with my laughing shoes. Now, no child relishes being frog-marched to school escorted by a parent with a face set like thunder. By the time I arrived in the playground with my mother, it seemed like the entire school knew what was happening.

I anticipated she would take me straight to my then teacher, Mr Robin, a very soft-spoken man who I admired. With this quiet demeanour, he was a disciplinarian whose style of punishment was to lean you over the desk and with his tamarind whip administer four lashes, no more, in quick succession. This was done in front of the class and in full view of most of the senior school, as it was a large, sprawling, open-plan building.

Being familiar with Mr Robin's method of flogging, I had decided that morning to put on two pairs of khaki pants. My reason was that they would cushion the blows on my bottom, which was still very sore from the night before.

However, when Mr Robin planted the first lash, and a particular sound reverberated around the class, there was an initial quizzical hush. The rest of the class did not know if they were to laugh or to applaud, because no one had used their initiative or thought of padding like that before. Unfortunately, it did not fool Mr Robin. He made me take off the top pants. Surprisingly, all I then got was an additional lash in the palm of my hand. Was I being rewarded for my ingenuity? Was my public humiliation sufficient? I never knew.

I was certainly relieved, as a student was branded a wimp if he cried in front of the girls, and when we broke for the first recess, one of the female teachers took me to the teachers' room, found some strong glue and helped me to stick together the front of my plimsolls. I cried my heart out there and then. Nevertheless, that was the first, and last, time I played truant.

It was also one of the last times I got a licking from my mother. This was due to a piece of acting by me! One evening, I was again on the receiving end of my mother's fury, naked from the waist down, and with quick thinking, I decided to act as if I were dead. I closed my eyes and made one dramatic fall backwards, and remained still, but I made sure that I turned slightly on my side to protect my private parts – I was not stupid: I did not want that damaged!

After four lashes, I held my breath, playing dead. I then heard, 'Malcolm! Malcolm! Malcolm!' The belt was quickly replaced by a hand turning me over. I had never touched a dead person before, but I imagined that the body would be cold and frigid, so I stiffened my body, and I must have been cold anyway because I was scared to death that the whole thing might backfire, and the licks would continue with more ferocity.

Mother, I sensed, was just beginning to panic, but I did not know what to do from there. As if by magic, I heard a bicycle bell in the front garden. It was my mother's partner who lived round the corner from us. She dashed to the door and dragged him inside. It gave me a few seconds to take some deep breaths. Then he gently said, 'Malcolm' several times. By that time, I really knew how to hold my breath. Next, he asked her for the smelling salts. Well, I had to do something. Just before she brought the smelling salts, I started groaning faintly, and saying in a very faint voice, 'Don't hit me, please.' By the time he had the smelling salts, I was breathing. The relief that came over my mother was something to behold.

A few nights later, I decided to take the bull by the horns and confront her. It was a very brave thing to do, even though she had panicked a few days before. I waited until my mother's partner was around; he was much older than her, almost like a grandfather, and had a calming influence on her.

'Excuse me, Mother,' I said, 'I don't know what happened a few days ago, but why do you have to beat me so? I'm not bad.'

She replied, 'You are too damn harden!'

I repeated, 'But I'm not bad. Desmond and his friends are bad boys, not me; I'm not like them. When I do something wrong, why not talk to me and I'll listen, instead of you beating me so?'

Her partner then chipped in with, 'I think you are beating the boy far too much!'

Mother, with all her strength, had no answers, but just said, 'We'll see about that, now go and play.'

I am happy to say that it was the last licking I got from my mother, though it certainly wasn't the only time I did something I knew she'd disapprove of.

Her world view dominated my upbringing in Trinidad. In many respects, she was herself moulded by the colonial determinants that shaped everyone – skin colour, ethnicity, social status, poverty and British values. Cultural norms, religious dogma and language were all Anglo-Saxon. British to the bone. To her, anything native to the region or which related to our heritage was treated with suspicion. So, it is not surprising that Mother insisted that I should avoid any association with the steel band players. And I'd been dancing in the street to just such bands.

The steel band is the only original instrument created in the 20th century and its birthplace is Trinidad. This cut no ice with Mother. She believed in the popular belief at the time that players in these bands were rough: gamblers, vagabonds and the unemployed. Very few women if any played in a steel band.

Today Trinidad and Tobago is justifiably proud to be the home of the steel band: instruments that replicate the full orchestra, performing any type of music as soloist, ensemble or full orchestra. The music has come a long way from the bands that Mother knew. Today, our musicians and artisans have elevated this local art form onto a global stage. One of these innovators is Dr Patricia Allison Bishop TC, one of the first women to arrange musical compositions for the steel band. I am proud to be related to 'Pat' Bishop, who, with others, has been instrumental in taking the pan to a very high level of respectability. She has conducted the steel orchestra at places such as Carnegie Hall in New York and the Albert Hall in London.

I loved to dance to the music, but I never learned to play myself.

Skin colour – another colonial heritage - was something which we all noticed, and I was one of the darkest in my class, so teased by pupils as a result. Nugget was the name they called me. We all knew that the lighter-skinned youngsters did clearly have privilege – they would be the ones more likely to be offered jobs in banks and similar, a colonial legacy which still persists in many ways, even today in the UK – why else would so many in the Black community use 'skin-lightening' products? Then a teacher – Mr Farrell, very tall and imposing, with a dark complexion – had simply said to me one day: 'Don't let that affect you. Just smile and be proud of your dark skin. Just say to them, "It's a strong and beautiful colour." From that point onwards, I know I felt very differently about it. I was black and I was proud of it.

But I still joined in the jokey comments at school – no one was ever ridiculed for skin colour, though as for myself sometimes given a nickname, but in the Trinidadian way, we all threw jokes at each other all the time and any feature that was prominent about someone was a good starting point. If a person could not take jokes – or fatigue, as we call it – then his or her life could be a living hell.

Teasing and joking can easily morph into flirting, as it did as we got older. As most teenage boys of my generation, I was beginning to chase after the girls; if a boy did not, then everyone thought something was definitely wrong with him.

One of my favourite games had always been hide-and-seek. One person was picked to do the finding. With eyes closed, that person would count to fifty, whilst the rest of us dashed off and hid. That person would then set about to find us. That exercise could take a long, long time, depending on the ingenuity of the ones who were hiding or when our parents called us in to bed. The first person to be discovered became the seeker for the next round, and so it continued. It was a game I loved. And as we grew older, that game developed into something with a different motive – to spend time with the girl of our choice!

I remember Valarie, a schoolteacher's daughter, whom I liked a lot. She was a year younger than I was. Playing the game, we would disappear separately but knew where and when to come together and remain together for the longest while. Compared to what even younger children are doing in public today, our little frolics in the dark in those days look tame, like child's play, and indeed they were. I believe that for a whole year, we held the record for never being found in the hide-and-seek games that we played.

I found it incredible I was that brave to strike up a relationship with her anyway, because her father – Mr Thompson - was a much-feared man, a schoolteacher. I knew if we were ever discovered, I would first get a flogging from him, and then I would be marched off to my mother. Worst of all, I would be banned from visiting their home, and that would have been a total disaster for me, because they were a beautiful family and their mother was the kindest person in the neighbourhood. It was therefore a very sad period for me when I realised that she started losing weight and had to be confined to bed. It was the first time that I had ever heard of cancer and seen its effect. Typical of the society in which we lived, her illness was blamed on her husband, whom it was rumoured was having an affair with another woman, who surely had worked some black magic that had caused her illness and, ultimately, death. Our relationship, such as it was, was only short-lived anyway, and Valarie herself emigrated to Canada when she was older, a couple of years after I'd left. We have stayed in touch though and in one of our conversations recently she recalled that I would get her brothers, sister, and friends together in their gallery and tell them stories all made up by me.

I will also always remember one particular girl, Cyrilla, who attended my school. Most of the pupils lived within walking distance of the school as they grew up in the area, so there was a strong togetherness and camaraderie among us. We all knew each other and the parents. But Cyrilla was different. She had not been to our Kindergarten but came in much later. She also lived quite a long way from school and had to take a taxi for part of the way.

From day one, I was smitten. Cyrilla was beautiful. She walked with a grace that would make Naomi Campbell, the supermodel, look like an amateur. She was not very dark but just had a smooth honey-colour skin with no blemish that I could see.

Even better, she seemed to appreciate my interest. Why then would she, on most mornings, choose to walk on my street to go to school? It gave me the opportunity to carry her books, to hold her hand from time to time, and to kiss her on the cheek.

Cyrilla always appeared to be a little more mature than the other girls in our class, and I decided to take her home to meet my mother because I felt it was the right and proper thing to do. It was risky because if for some reason my mother took an instant dislike to her, just one word and a look would send my girlfriend scampering and I assumed that would have been the end of our burgeoning relationship. There was also the added danger that some of the neighbours along the route to school would have spotted me, nearly every day, walking alongside this very attractive girl. They would most likely tease my mother, so I decided to do as the old saying goes: 'take in front before in front takes you'.

However, to my relief, Mother was extremely pleasant to her and even offered her something to drink, which left me totally bewildered. This was it! The girl of my dreams had my mother's approval. Things were too good to be true. But a few days later, as soon as I arrived from school, having just parted company with Cyrilla around the corner, Mother asked me if the woman who passed the house twice a week with a basket on her head, selling fish, was Cyrilla's mother. I said that she was, and Mother exploded angrily, 'Well, what you doing with her daughter, could you not find a better class of friend? I do not want her back in this house again.'

Now I might have been a quiet boy, but I had a determined streak in me. Mother was not about to stop me from seeing my jewel in the crown. The relationship continued for some time, getting very much closer, until I arranged to meet her one Sunday morning. I met Cyrilla at a prearranged spot and we went for a walk through the market. While she shopped, I carried her bags. The plan was that we would take a taxi to her home, where I was going for the first time.

We were standing at the corner, waiting for a taxi when a car pulled up. The guy behind the wheel called Cyrilla over in a rather familiar tone of voice. She hesitated only long enough to say to me, 'I'll see you in school tomorrow, bye.'

He kissed her on her lips when she got into the car. He was much older, of course, so I was not about to run after the car. I had spent weeks kissing her on her cheeks, respecting her, thinking that I was doing the decent thing, taking it slowly. I felt that we had been committed to each other. But after witnessing that scene, I was shattered! So back home I went with my tail between my legs, feeling totally humiliated.

I left for school on Monday morning, hoping against hope that Cyrilla wasn't waiting around the corner to walk to school with me because that would be pouring salt on the wound. As luck would have it, she was not there, neither was she at school that day. However, on the Tuesday, she quietly slithered into school just before the bell rang, and with a very gentle nod of the head she acknowledged me. We continued to be very polite to each other until she left the school a year before me, but where she went, I did not know.

My mother often quoted the famous saying that beauty is only skin deep, but from then on I also adopted as my own saying: never put all your eggs in one basket. I do believe that, to some extent, this experience with Cyrilla shattered my trust in girls or women, making it tricky later in life for me to open up, let anyone get really close, always instead making sure that there was a part of me that was holding back. I did not want to be hurt again.

CHAPTER 5

My Final, Final Cut-Tail

'The future belongs to those who prepare for it today'
Malcolm X, American 1960s human rights activist
and Muslim minister

At the age of fourteen, I took my acting a stage further, and formed my own drama group. I had decided to do this so we could put on different shows and go elsewhere to perform, places where we'd be paid too. I got about ten to fifteen people involved, many from my school drama group. Not many of my personal friends were that interested in the theatre, but a few loved poetry and so were happy to be a part of it too. I could pick bits from plays that I wanted to perform, but mostly we would develop little skits from ideas we had ourselves, short pieces lasting about ten or fifteen minutes, then recitations of poetry. The group had as its members a teacher and some already in full-time employment as apprentices. Rehearsals were held either at The San Juan Government school or at the home of one of the members. I faced two challenging situations during that period. One was because of a very attractive classmate, Jocelyn, who I desperately fancied. Her mother, however, was very strict and would not allow her much freedom. She was keen on drama, so persuading her to join the group was no problem, but persuading her strict mother was a non-starter. However, Jocelyn suggested I write a letter to her mother, spelling out the group's activities, which I did, and she agreed to allow her daughter to attend.

Unfortunately, this was the start of my problems, for I soon discovered she was not interested in me at all but in another member of the company, who happened to be a pupil-teacher at my school! He became a problem for me, generally. During the day, I had to listen to him and respect what he said but, in the evenings, when I was in charge, the roles were reversed and he found it extremely difficult to deal with this and, instead, sought to undermine my authority. If I suggested one way to direct a scene, he would belittle it. I would select a piece of poetry; he would come up with something completely different. It was my first experience of seeing how one actor's ego can be so disruptive for a production, and I was too young to know how to handle it, so I left the group, but felt I had learned another valuable lesson. By then I had also found another outlet for acting. I had joined the leading amateur dramatic group in Trinidad, 'The Company of Players', which had amongst its members all the leading Trinidadian actors of the day. The group had been going on for years, but what drew me in was the casting of a play to be staged in the Botanic Gardens in Port-of-Spain, an open-air Easter production – *The Way of the Cross*, or a similar title. I went along for an audition and got a small part. I was on stage with some of the leading actors of the day, like Freddie Kissoon, who played Judas, and Horace James, who was like a mentor to me during his period in the UK. It was a fantastic experience not only working with those actors, but performing in the open air, in one of the most beautiful gardens in Trinidad, adjacent to the base of the then Governor General of Trinidad and Tobago.

"I was about fifteen, almost ready to leave school. Drama teachers from the UK sponsored by the British Council came over to do courses on the techniques of acting with the Company and I went to those as a member of the Company."

I was also to encounter a seriously influential mentor: Derek Walcott, a young and very prolific playwright and poet, who cast me in a play he was directing, *Our Town* by Thornton Wilder, about life and death in an American small town. Derek then launched, in 1958, The Trinidad Theatre Workshop and invited me to be one of the founding members, I was the youngest member of the group that included leading and well-known actors of the day: Errol Jones, Stanley Marshall, Eunice Alleyne, amongst others, and the opportunity to learn from them.

I loved listening to the great singers: Nat King Cole, Johnny Mathis, Paul Robeson, and groups like The Platters. At times I fancied myself as a singer. There was always a birthday party or a wedding to attend and at most of them someone would always get up and sing a song; many held their own and were enjoyable to listen to, but others just had to stop and hastily admit defeat. I never had the confidence at the time to take the plunge.

However, living not far from me was a churchgoing family. The children there did not attend my school, but it was a route I would sometimes take to go to my school, so I got to know them. They attended a Pentecostal Church. Two brothers and a very attractive sister, who I fancied. They were a musical family; the father played the piano, the two boys the guitar and all were fantastic singers. With their sister, they had created a family Gospel group. I loved the challenge of Gospel singing. So, after hanging around with the family over a period, and occasionally joining in when they were having a practice session, they suggested I join them, so I did. I must admit the sister was my ulterior motive, but my interest in her faded as she was very, very prim, proper and far too religious, and lacked any adventurous streak. So, after a few concerts I decided to leave.

For my next venture in singing, I played it safe with an all-male group. A member of my drama group was Gene Pierre, who had a fantastic tenor voice. As a result, he often did a solo spot at our shows. We were both invited to join a duo called The Tulips, making it an a cappella quartet with our inclusion, with myself singing the bass. We tried to be Trinidad's equivalent to the American group, The Platters, and we did several shows culminating in a popular talent contest on the radio hosted by a well-known personality, the late Holly Betaudier. During the final rehearsal, Holly observed that one of us was at times flat. I knew it was me, so on the night of the live show, before an audience, I was so scared of going off key that I decided to mime most of the song. We came second.

Two weeks later, I entered the contest again, reciting one of my own poems, '*I Was Born A Hero*', and I came second again. This time I was beaten by Felix Roach, a young pianist who went on to become one of Trinidad's most celebrated entertainers, known as 'Sugar Fingers'. I was fortunate enough to hear him play in 2019 when he played at a private house party held for me and some of my friends. It was the first time we had met since our appearance on the Holly Betaudier radio talent show as teenagers. Entertaining us that afternoon were two other outstanding Trinidad artists: opera singer Miss Anne Fridal, holidaying in Trinidad at the time, and Emmanuel Joseph, a young and in-demand pianist and arranger, already the winner of several National Awards.

I left school at sixteen, without the sort of qualifications that would take me on to college and then university, and in any case, my mother could not have afforded the school fees. I had to find a job, as I couldn't sit around all day not doing anything, so obtaining some sort of employment was definitely expected of me. It was right that I should have to contribute to the household expenses. My sister's father had retired from the civil service as an employee at the Government Printing Office, and he suggested I apply for an apprenticeship. It was a sought-after job with a secure future. A few weeks before leaving school I therefore wrote a letter to the Government Printer, Mr Dunstan Clarke. Several days went by before I received a reply asking me to come down for an interview. Once or twice a year there is an intake of apprentices to be trained as machine operators or compositors.

For several days before the interview my mother went about gathering various plants, I believe with the help and advice of some of her older friends. It was a common belief amongst certain sections of society that taking a bush-bath would give you an advantage over others. I don't know how much I believe in that – after all, what if the parents of the other applicants do the same? Is it the one with the stronger mixture of bushes who'll succeed? But we Trinidadians are superstitious, so I wasn't going to risk not doing as my mother wished. Funnily enough, actors often have their own superstitions too – lucky rituals or mascots before a first night, for instance. Anyway, the morning of the interview, Mother filled two buckets of water and crushed all the collected bush into it and with a calabash then poured the water over me, at the same time rubbing the bush all over my skin. Some of the leaves were sharp! I wasn't allowed to use soap and had to dry myself with the towel leaving what I thought was a strange smell on my body.

Yardley cologne was very popular amongst youngsters, so I made sure I dabbed some on my shirt to hide any bush smell before leaving home. Looking sharp in my brown pants, white shirt and tie, I arrived at the Government Printing Office on Tragarete Road, Port-of-Spain, and was ushered into a waiting room, where there were about a dozen youngsters like me waiting to be interviewed by Mr Dunstan Clarke the boss. We were given a sheet of paper to fill in our names and an Arithmetic test which for me was very simple. We were then called in one by one into Mr Clake's Office. The ones who came out said very little so I had no idea what to expect. Then it was my turn. Mr Clarke, a tall slightly greying gentleman was sitting behind his desk, I said good morning, sir which he responded, he took my paper. He looked at it while I remained standing, although there was a chair in front of his desk, I wasn't going to sit in it unless he offered. I was so nervous I'm not sure if he was smiling or serious, when he finally suggested I take a seat. He then asked me a few questions about my school, why I wanted to work there, he described the two options that were open to me if they employed me, and that was all. We were all then taken around the Printery to see how it operated, saying hello to some of the workers. It appeared to be a very relaxed atmosphere. Our tour over, we were told to leave and wait until we get a letter stating if we were successful in securing an apprenticeship.

On my way home I decided to pay Aunty Merle a visit, just to fill her in on my interview and to ask if there was anything she needed from the shop. Soon after Uncle Albert turned up, and I had to explain why I looked so smart. What he said next took me by surprise. He offered me a job as a timekeeper to earn some money until hopefully I got offered the apprenticeship. He was a Clerk of Works and in charge of the day-to-day running of a new fire station that was being built on Wrightson Road, Port-of-Spain. My job was to get there early and tick off the names of all the workers, the same at the end of day. There was the odd occasion when a man would arrive a few minutes late and I wouldn't penalise him for it. Most of the labourers came from a place called Laventille Hill, a very picturesque area but with a bad reputation for violence. After about six weeks I received a letter from the Government Printing Office offering me a place as an apprentice compositor.

My mother and her partner were delighted. A good job with a secure future.

We got paid monthly: a little brown envelope with cash. Obviously, I had to give my mother a sum every month, but I still had quite a lot of cash left. Or so I thought. Travel costs took a fair bit, and lunchtimes were usually food bought at a local woman's house – Miss Dolly. Rice and peas and stews or soups. It meant I didn't need to eat much at dinner. What with these costs, and taking my girlfriend, Jean, out, I'd sometimes run out before the end of the month and not have enough money to get to work. Charlie, or Charlo as he was mostly called, was a moneylender who came in very handy. I certainly wouldn't admit to my mother that I'd spent it all. High interest! So, I soon learned to budget better. Throughout the three and a half years of apprenticeship, I did just enough to hold down the job, because my heart was set on leaving the island, as soon as it was financially viable for me to pursue a career in the theatre, either in the United States of America or in England. In the meantime, I attended City and Guilds evening classes as part of my apprenticeship - you could be dismissed if you failed the exams or had poor attendance. I was never late for work, but I struggled with the classes, because I often chose to attend rehearsals for a play instead.

A part of the growing-up process for me was also getting involved in various new relationships. One with another employee at the Government Printing Office.

Jeanette Prescod was much older than I was, a single parent and a very warm-hearted person. Within a year, we were courting. I had been scared to get too involved with this lady at first, especially as she had a young child and was so much more experienced. I thought that maybe she might have been expecting me to support her child on my apprentice pay, but no! She did not ask for or take a penny from me. In fact, she was determined to bring up her son with or without the father's help or help from any man for that matter. Just like my mother. The father of her child – her ex-partner, whom I met – did not pose a threat to our relationship, neither I believed did a guy named Ray, whom Jeanette had ditched several months before I met her, but who kept trying to befriend her again. Our relationship developed slowly and amicably, and I really liked her. But life does not always run smoothly, and Jeanette's ex-boyfriend, Ray, suddenly reappeared.

It was a beautiful moonlit night. Now I am a very romantic and demonstrative person and I love holding hands. Doing so on a moonlit night in the Caribbean, with someone you love, is heavenly. That, and the sound of rain falling onto a galvanised roof when you are indoors with your sweetheart. Anyway, Jeanette and I were walking home hand in hand, eyes only for each other, when we heard hurried footsteps from behind like someone trying to catch up with us. We both looked back at the same time, and coming towards us was a short, stocky guy with a very determined look. All I heard Jeanette say was, 'Ray, no!' in a tone that spelled danger. And she gave me a push. It was clear that she was in no danger, but I was.

That was my cue. I was out of the blocks like a flash. I took the first corner and I heard Jeanette shout again, 'Ray, no, don't! Ray, don't!' I didn't look round, but from the pounding of feet behind me, Ray was getting closer - he was quick! Now I was much younger than he was, so there was no way he should catch up with me, but I kept thinking, 'This man is going to kill me, I am not going to see England!' Suddenly I heard something sing through the air and felt a sharp pain on my back. It was a cat-o'-nine tails, a multi-tailed whip used for severe physical punishment. Well, a spark lit. Looking back on that incident, I cannot help likening it to the sight of Usain Bolt in the Beijing Olympic Games, running side by side of his competitors for the first twenty metres and then, as if by magic, leaving them eating dust. When the blow landed, I leaped twenty yards in less than a second, and at that point, I am sure that I became the fastest man on earth and would have out-run any Olympic sprinter, even Usain himself. I wonder if he would admit that licks from his mother or the threat of a cat-o'-nine tails had propelled him to run so fast.

I arrived at Jeanette's home, about two miles away, in no time at all, let myself in – I knew where she hid the key for the house - and locked myself in the bedroom. Jeanette arrived home about half an hour after, on her own, very upset and very apologetic. She said it would never happen again. I do not know what she did or what she said to Ray but that was the last time we saw him. However, my mind was still on leaving Trinidad, going to England or America.

At nineteen years of age, going on twenty, I knew I had to do something. I had already spent a few years acting with the leading amateur drama company in the island, The Company of Players, run my own drama company and become one of the founding members of Derek Walcott's Trinidad Theatre

Workshop. For me, working as a compositor at the Government Printing Office was never a lifetime option. I began to explore options available to pursue my career. I couldn't see myself being a printer all my life, with theatre just as a hobby. I knew that I wanted to develop my career in the theatre, and looking around at what was happening in Trinidad and Tobago and reading about people like Errol John and Edric Connor doing things in other countries, it seemed clear. To make it, I would have to leave. No question.

I wrote to several drama schools in England and the United States of America, about the various courses they conducted. I noticed they all had fees to pay though - I could not have afforded it. Hollywood was even more out of reach. There I knew that actors such as Sidney Poitier and Paul Robeson had become big successes, though good roles for black actors still seemed few in number. I wasn't really aware of racism at the time, but the theatre was my love and I felt there would be more roles for me in that area. It was a very restless period for me. The boys around me, members of my own company, weren't serious about theatre so there was no one around me who would really encourage me, or help me find out more, so when I did get the opportunity to talk to anyone who had experience, I grabbed it. And at this time Edric Connor, a much-celebrated actor in England, visited Trinidad and I was able to arrange a meeting with him. His advice was less than encouraging. He suggested I remain in Trinidad, work the amateur scene and get myself well-known, like the late Horace James had done. He even offered to introduce me to Horace, but what he did not realise was that I was already a good friend of Horace, who was also a member of the same Company of Players. I left the meeting feeling a little deflated.

Several weeks later, another celebrated Trinidad actor, Errol John, landed on our shores. Errol John lived in England but was fast becoming known in Hollywood with several American films to his credit. He had even appeared – even if uncredited – in The African Queen, a movie starring Humphrey Bogart and Katherine Hepburn! And had a small part in The Nun's Story, which starred Audrey Hepburn. I learned later that he had become frustrated at the lack of good roles available to him – often being offered a stereotypical bit part as soldier/African policeman etc, something I became familiar with myself later – and so had begun to write his own plays. His play *Moon on a Rainbow Shawl* was staged at the Royal Court in London and won a Play of the Year Award. The Trinidad newspapers faithfully reported any triumph for him – if someone from Trinidad did well in another country, then they would always be featured in the islands' papers. He would be a great person to ask for advice. Fortunately for me, at the time I was performing in a play, The Story of the Robe, at the Belmont Catholic Youth Organisation (BCYO), so I took the initiative, got his address and invited him to one of the performances. To my surprise, he turned up. He kindly agreed to see me the next day, and once again I expressed my keenness to further my career and asked his advice. His response was, 'Just pack your bag and go to England. It offers the best training, far better than the United States, and when you get there, if there is any help I can offer, I will be more than happy to do so.'

I left his home that day floating on air. He had seen me play two different characters the night before so I was sure that if he had considered me a hopeless actor, he would have discouraged me. That was just the first hurdle. Now I had to sell the idea to my mother. She had seen the play; in fact, she had seen everything in which I was involved, so I thought her support would be automatic. I was in for a surprise. She was not angry; she just said firmly, 'You have a good job in Government working as a printer. You are a civil servant and can work yourself up over the years and become Head of a Department. What do you want to go to England for?' That was final, as far as she was concerned. And it was unthinkable, for me, to go without my mother's blessing. I might have been nineteen/twenty by now, but I still could not step out of line. It would also have taken me a long time to save the money to go, so I also needed her support.

Several months went by with frustration building up within me, and then out of the blue, Mother came home one afternoon and said, 'Look, if you really want to go to England then you should, you have my blessing.' I was shocked. Why the sudden change of mind? Knowing my mother, I thought that I had better not ask her anything at that time. But I discovered a few years later that she had been on the bus coming home that evening and overheard a conversation between two women, one expressing her regret for not allowing her son to go to the United States when he wanted to, and how he had turned out to be a vagabond and blamed his mother daily for his missed opportunities. Of course, Mother did not want that to happen.

We spent about two months putting a leaving package together, $175.00 US. My mother borrowed some money from a local. In addition, Uncle Mitch, an old uncle of my mother, arranged with his godson, who was living in London at the time, to meet me on my arrival and also to find me a bedsit, a single-room accommodation. The apprentices at work organised a farewell dinner at a Chinese restaurant in downtown Port-of-Spain. It was also going to be my first trip abroad, so the time when the decision was made to emigrate to the UK and the departure date was finalised was one of mixed feelings: apprehension, not knowing what to expect. Three weeks on a ship to a place I had only read about. To stay with people who were strangers. Doubts, too. Would I truly make it? It was a brave thing to do, but at the time I was just filled with excitement at what was ahead. And then, on the memorable night of 20 August 1960, I stepped out of my uncle's car at the docks in Port-of-Spain and saw what was to me in those days a gigantic ship with the name Oranje Nassau painted along its side, a Dutch flagship, which for the first time was picking up passengers bound for England. I shook my uncle's hand as was the custom in those days, hugged my mother, who as usual displayed the minimum of emotion, hugged my Aunt Marge, my sister Aliena (Eileen). My younger sister Veronica (Dawn) was the most tearful of the lot. My girlfriend Jeanette I hugged and kissed last, with the promise that I'd send for her to join me when I settled. Sadly, I never saw her again because she died later of cancer. With my very large but manageable suitcase or grip as we called it then and a smaller one packed with homemade sweetbread and cake, ginger beer, sorrel drink, tamarind balls and anything my mother aunt and friends felt I was not going to get in the UK. I made my way up the ramp, turning back every so often to wave to family and friends.

The first thing to hit me when the ship pulled out of the harbour, and the family and friends melted into one – becoming part of the landscape of the beautiful island of Trinidad – was the realisation that I was heading to a new life which could be for better or worse.

'This is it!' There was no turning back for Rudolph Malcolm Walker.

PART TWO

England – And My First Footprints

THE SEA

Whoever gazed upon the sea
Upon the broad deep sea,
Where the wild waves play
Upon the watery plain
Where many fleets swept oe'r in vain.
Come with me, come with me
Come with me, out to see
Its rolling foams, its bubbling groans,
Its bubbling, boundless profound groans.

by Malcolm Walker, aged 13

CHAPTER 6

Barataria Arrives in Britain

'Life is like a book. Some chapters are sad, some are happy, and some are exciting. But if you never turn the page, you will never know what the next chapter holds' Anonymous

---

I joined the group of other new passengers from Trinidad & Tobago, together with some who flew or sailed from Barbados, to make the journey to England. We were then addressed by a ship's officer assigned to that deck. His first statement that I recall was, 'You are confined to this deck, you are not allowed above here.' I looked up to see only white faces looking down.

The officer then escorted us first to the dining room where we were to gather in an hour for dinner, then shown to our cabins. They were small, with two or three bunk beds to each cabin. There were four or six passengers in each cabin. My cabin had three bunk beds **six** of us. It looked like a prison cell, although I had never been in one, but I saw them in the movies, or maybe a slave ship minus the chains. Some of the beds were already occupied. The top bunks were preferred by most of the passengers, I chose one of the two bottom bunks remaining, the one nearest the door, reasoning that if we needed to escape in an emergency, I'd be the first out. Three or more weeks cooped up in there was a daunting prospect.

On board the Oranje Nassau was a diverse group from various islands, fifty-three of us – all young black men – heading to carve out a new life in the United Kingdom. I soon found common interests with several other passengers. The late Trevor Rhone from Jamaica also wanted to be an actor like me and was planning to enrol at the Rose Bruford Drama Academy.

Trevor went on to become a celebrated writer for TV and stage. He wrote such plays as Two Can Play and Old Story Time, both of which I appeared. He was travelling with another Jamaican, Frank Cousins.

Frank was in the Jamaican army, and hoped he would be able to get a better post or rank in the British Army by emigrating to the UK. Most of the journey he wore his uniform, unable to divorce himself from army life even for that short period, so at times he'd talk to us as if we were in his platoon. No bitterness or resentment was felt by any of us, and sometimes we joked about it. Unfortunately, his dream didn't materialise as his every application to join the British Army was rejected. Back in Jamaica he dabbled in the performing arts, so he turned to a life in the theatre as an actor and we ran into each other many times at casting calls or auditions.

The third of the Jamaican trio was Lloyd Gray, who was going to the UK to study engineering, we referred to him as 'The Pastor' as he was always ready and willing to offer a prayer before a meal or find a quote from the bible at any of our group chats.

The four of us struck up a rapport. For all of us, it was the start of a journey of great expectation, of adventure and excitement.

The first day out to sea revealed that the passengers on the ship were divided. This was a merchant ship adapted to take some passengers, I believe, for the first time from the Caribbean, but all the black male passengers were on the lower deck with the white passengers above, out of bounds to us. There was just one exception - a black male passenger travelling above, but he made no attempt to communicate with us, so for the first time in my life I found myself being aware of racism. I'd had no real experience of it in Trinidad, sure, we all knew that those with lighter skin tended to have more opportunities than those of us who were darker, and there were some clubs, especially in Port-of-Spain, which were exclusive to the Europeans, but the two worlds seldom collided, it was just a way of life that existed from birth and most of us just got on with it. I never really thought about it and wasn't involved in any of the politics when Dr Eric Williams led his party, the PNM (People's National Movement), to majority rule in 1956, while independence didn't come until 1962, two years after I had left. With Dr Williams, however, the islands did have a black Prime Minister – prior to this there had always been a white British Governor. Even the captain of the national cricket team Jeffrey Stollmeyer was a white Trinidadian who owned the Stollmeyer estate in Santa Cruz, an area I visited frequently as my godfather Mr Babb lived on his estate, surrounded by acres of orange, grapefruit and cocoa trees.

Now racism, or what some of us believed was racism, was in my face. The journey was to last for about twenty-one days, and we realised that the fifty or so black passengers below might never see the rest of the passengers on the ship. As young men, we wanted to experience everything we could, have a real adventure on board. We were also soon aware that on a couple of evenings we'd hear big band music coming from the upper deck; it was a record player, and the white passengers, all decked out in dark suits and tie, were dancing on the deck. Some of us who loved dancing would do our version of the waltz and cha-cha-cha, sometimes mimicking the white passengers' stiff upright stances, and we ended up in fits of laughter.

It was during one of those sessions that one guy from our group from Trinidad brought out his guitar and started playing and singing. Some of us joined in, either singing the popular calypsos, or negro spirituals, or imitating the black American singers – Nat King Cole, Louis Armstrong, Paul Robeson, Johnny Mathis. What started off as just a singsong mushroomed into evenings of great entertainment for us, poetry reading, storytelling, comedy sketches.

Calypso is hugely popular in Trinidad. It's a musical genre that is derivative of the Dahomey work song used by Africans enslaved and working on sugar plantations. Calypso was developed in Trinidad in the 17th century and then spread to the other West Indian islands. When the French brought Carnival to Trinidad, calypso competitions became a great feature, alongside the drumming and the masquerade processions.

It uses call and response stanzas and was widely used to make social comments and to poke fun at public figures, whether that person was the President, Prime Minister, teacher, road-sweeper or whoever he or she may be. No one escaped the verbal lashings of the Calypsonian! Fun was to be had and made from anything and anyone. In a way, there were similarities to reggae – which often used lyrics to make serious social statements – but this serious side was flavoured by masses of humour too. The more laughs the better!

We noticed one evening that two of the couples from the upper deck came down and stood watching what we were doing and seemed to be enjoying it, together with the crew member who was assigned to look after us. The following night when we performed – different songs, poems etc. – there were about six couples who chose to leave their ballroom dancing and come down to watch us perform.

The following day the purser asked if we'd agree to perform on the upper deck for those passengers. And so, Trevor, Frank, Lloyd and I decided to devise a ninety-minute programme with a mixture of sketches, poems, folk songs, calypsos and storytelling – to entertain all passengers on board the ship. I recited two of the poems I had written as a teenager, 'I was Born a Hero', and 'A Beggar am I', and both appeared to go down well, while amongst the other passengers were guys who could sing, so in total there were about a dozen of us taking part.

It was just one performance almost ten days into the voyage. But the show proved quite a hit with passengers and crew alike, and for the rest of the journey, during the day many of us – especially the performers from the lower deck – were allowed to mix with the passengers above.

The night before we docked, there was a huge dinner for the entire ship – a big British dinner. What a change of heart our gesture to entertain had evoked!

Lloyd in recent times recalled that his memory of me was standing on the deck and acting out bits of Shakespeare or reciting a poem to an imaginary audience out in the sea. Some of them must have thought, *Why is this mad Trinidadian going to England?*

I had never heard of sea sickness before a couple of days into the journey when guys were dashing over to the side of the ship and emptying their stomach. I thought at the time that the food was the cause. Some of the Jamaican passengers lodged a complaint about the quality and type of food that was dished out before I got on board, and an attempt was made to improve, but it still fell short of flavour and taste.

There were some terrifying days when the sea would suddenly turn rough and angry, and it felt like the ship was going to capsize. Some of us would make sure we were near a lifeboat, just in case, and as I couldn't swim I was going to make sure I was I'd be among the first to jump into any lifeboat.

There were also many days and nights when the sea was gentle. I enjoyed just standing on deck gazing at the stars and the moon, imagining what my life would be like in England. Walking on stage and delivering a speech with the audience applauding? Or going to a cinema and seeing myself appearing on a big screen? Returning to Trinidad to visit friends and family and being celebrated as Errol John and Edric Connor were? There were also moments of sadness when I shed a tear for the many friends with whom I spent the first twenty years of my life and that I might not see again for a long time, or never.

My first sighting of the English coastline was that of a grey still mass, which seemed lacking in life and movement. I had plenty of time to observe it as we docked on the south coast, but I remember the ship staying offshore for a couple of hours before we came into port. All I could see was greyness! And although I wasn't cold – I had dressed for arrival in my grey suit, handmade especially for the journey, as were my shoes – it was damp and dull, and this was August, the height of the British summer. What would the winter be like? I wondered.

There were several passengers amongst us who were not interested in drama or the performing arts whatsoever and felt their time was best spent gambling. The card games started with matchsticks, then progressed to money. Two or three of the players had lost all their money, without a cent in their pockets a few hours before we were due to land and were in tears. They pleaded to have some of their money back. Lloyd stepped in and worked out a deal that was acceptable to all.

The journey to London by train was uneventful, though initially I was shocked by the sight of chimneys puffing smoke.

'Are those houses on fire?' I questioned.

'Nah, man, just chimneys burning coal to keep the houses warm,' one of the boys with a little more knowledge told me.

I was also apprehensive. It had been arranged that my Uncle Mitch's godson Errol would be at Paddington Station to meet me, but the ship had been delayed. Would he still be there? Would he recognise me? I had never met him before. Most of the others I was travelling with were meeting up with relatives they already knew well, and I think I may have been the only one in our group to be heading totally into the unknown. It was scary, but the will to overcome any obstacles was very strong and paramount in my mind, nothing could go wrong.

Drawing closer to London, I saw something else that surprised me. England, I was led to believe, was one of the top industrialised nations in the world and if the streets were not exactly paved with gold, it was still a very rich country. So, it was something of a shock and even seemed hilarious to me and others when we saw people driving around in three-wheeled cars. Apparently, the price of petrol after the war had soared, so lots of three-wheelers were produced at this time as they were more economical. Bubble cars, little vans and others – now classed as classic vehicles and worth lots of money, but I had never seen anything like that, not even in the movies. In Trinidad, we were used to seeing only cars with four wheels.

After what appeared to be a very long journey the train pulled into Paddington Station, London. The station was massive, far bigger than the one in Port-of-Spain, Trinidad, with exits everywhere. I had the home address of Errol in case of emergency, but I had no idea of how I would get there if we missed each other. By a process of elimination and the descriptions we had of each other, however, I was able to contact Errol. Phew!

I parted company with Frank, Trevor, Lloyd and the others. It didn't occur to us to swap addresses – and in any case, I didn't even know where I would be staying. The sheer scale of London had not totally sunk in yet.

Errol on the bus said he was taking me to a friend's family home in Dalston, within walking distance of Ridley Road market; they had offered to put me up for the first two days and that he and his wife Jean were returning to Trinidad, and I was to take over their 'bedsit', one room in a shared house. My Uncle Mitch had mentioned that they were planning to return to Trinidad permanently, but I wasn't expecting it to be so soon.

On the way there, I began to feel a bit disappointed, because I had expected the surroundings and the streets to be exceptionally smart and clean. Instead, I found that many of the houses looked cold and grey some had an untidy, musty appearance, and were joined together, what Errol described as terraced houses. Most of the people looked dull and humourless too – not many smiles – and their clothes, in comparison with back home, seemed to lack colour or flair. Generally, the atmosphere was dreary. This certainly was not the vibrant and pulsating city I had imagined it to be.

I couldn't help but think of Lord Kitchener's famous calypso, 'London is The place For Me', when he arrived here on the HMT Windrush, in contrast to a Charles Kingsley poem, 'The Buccaneer', of which I could only remember one line: 'England is a cruel place for such poor folks as I.' Would London prove to be a 'lovely city' or a 'cruel place' for me?

After depositing my one large grip of belongings in the room, Errol took me to meet his wife Jean who had cooked us a meal, and to see the bedsit in Northchurch Road, Islington.

The room was right at the top in the attic. Very small, with space only for a single bed, a table and two chairs, a small wardrobe, with hooks on the wall to hang any extra clothes – and a paraffin heater strategically placed under the window to warm up the room in the winter. The sash window, which required a bit of muscle to open, looked out over the back yard. It occurred to me then and there that the space I was about to call home for the foreseeable future was even smaller than the home I had left in Trinidad. When you came out of the room, there was a step up into a little kitchenette where I could cook; this was shared with a Jamaican couple who occupied the front room, which was much larger, with enough space for a double bed and a sitting room with armchairs, table and wardrobe.

The next flight of stairs below had two sets of families living there with another kitchenette to share between them. Below, on the ground floor, was a family from Dominica who had the whole floor, whilst in the basement was an Irish guy.

I didn't see all of this of course on that first day. After viewing the room where I'd be living and being treated to my first Trinidadian meal since leaving home, Errol and two of his friends Carl - referred to as Carlo the barber, who lived a few houses away on the same street with his Irish wife - and Ben, a painter decorator, decided to take me out for the evening. They were all older than me, had lived in the UK for several years, and as Errol was returning to Trinidad in a couple of days, he felt that his friends Carlo and Ben would be able to teach me the ropes and look after my well-being.

They whisked me on a No 38 bus from the top of Northchurch Road to Central London. We sat on the upper deck so I could view the scenery on the way. It was already night-time so there was nothing spectacular to see on the way apart from a well-known dance theatre called Sadler's Wells, and huge buildings all jammed up against each other.

We got out at a stop that Carlo said was Leicester Square, and the first thing that struck me was that the whole area was all lit up, flashing colourful lights, people gathered in little groups all over the place, some standing outside what we call in Trinidad rum-shops but referred to in the UK as pubs, going in and out of well-lit buildings.

They took me for a walk along Shaftesbury Avenue, and although my new friends were not theatregoers, they pointed out several theatres on the street, like the Queens Theatre, The Lyric, The Apollo, and The Globe – which changed in 1997 to The Gielgud in honour of the great British actor Sir John Gielgud. Lots of well-dressed people were queuing up to see the plays, some of the women wearing long dresses, the men in suits. The names and pictures of the leading actors were displayed in bright lights outside the theatres. Would my name appear there one day?

A street away we entered an area referred to as Chinatown, obviously because of the number of Chinese restaurants in the area. It had been a long day, but I felt no hint of tiredness; it was very exciting, my adrenaline was pumping, and I was loving the new experience.

The atmosphere was far different from anything we had in Trinidad. Without warning we entered an area where women were going by wearing what appeared to be the minimum amount of clothing, some standing and smoking in underlit doorways, smiling at us as we slowly strolled pass, beckoning us to come over. We had entered Soho, labelled a red-light district.

Carlo, the ringleader of the little group, the elder statesman, went over and had a chat for a few minutes with one of the ladies - maybe someone he knew? She looked my way and smiled, and of course I returned the smile. Carlo then told me he felt sure that as I had endured twenty-one days at sea, I'd want to relieve myself in the company of what looked like a sexy-looking woman, and she would be happy to give me a good time. It was clear that although he and his friends all had girlfriends and wives, they had clearly tried what was on offer themselves.

'We'll hang around outside till you come out,' Carlo said. He even offered to pay for me, as a welcome treat! I politely declined. After my refusal, they felt I had seen enough of the West End for one day and suggested we head back home. The teasing and jokes on the way back because I refused to have sex was endless, and I had a hell of a job defending myself - luckily, I had a good sense of humour so could see the funny side of the banter.

Two days later Errol and Jean left for Trinidad, and I moved into their bedsit, and this was when my life in London really began.

I woke that first morning with butterflies in my stomach, the realisation that I was now truly on my own. There was no

Errol and Jean to call on; Trinidad was four thousand miles away, and I didn't have money for a return passage, so it was sink or swim for me.

Having a shower is one of the best forms of relaxation for me, and I needed one desperately to pull me out of anxiety, but to my shock, I was told by a tenant that the house had no shower facilities – there was no bathroom, and I would have to visit the public baths if I wanted more than just a wash down. I was used to having a shower twice a day in what was regarded as a third-world country, yet here I was in the Mother Country with third-world facilities, civilisation in reverse. She said that what was the norm was that you got a large plastic bowl or bucket, part-filled it with tap water, boiled the whistling kettle and poured in the hot water until it got to the temperature you wanted. You needed a wash rag and soap, she told me, and offered to lend me the items but I had noticed that Jean had left behind a bucket and a couple of towels. I just had to spread some newspaper over a small piece of the lino floor, strip naked and wipe myself down. That was my initiation to a bedsit daily bath.

For these first days of life in London, that was what I became accustomed to doing in order to clean myself, making sure I first turned on the paraffin heater to warm up the room. Having a full body wash was a luxury to be gained at the public baths, usually only once a week. I was beginning to realise that life for a large percentage of Londoners was not all that rosy. I discovered that many houses only had outside toilets – something that was fine in a warm climate, but I felt sure would be a severe discomfort during the cold winter months. Luckily, the house I was in did have an inside toilet – though it was three flights of stairs down in the basement, and was for everyone in the house to use, so you had to make sure you were not desperate. Many times, from my room in the attic, I could hear someone banging and shouting for someone to hurry up, or a tenant calling out that Paddy was in the toilet again.

After my week with the bowl and washcloth, I decided to try the public baths. Mr Ben and his wife Masie - both from Jamaica - occupied the room next to me, and he offered to take me there on his motorcycle on the Saturday morning.

I had never been a pillion rider on a motorcycle, and I was petrified, even though I had seen the ease with which his wife sat behind him when he took her to work every morning and brought her home in the evening. No amount of encouraging words from Mr Ben relaxed me, I held onto him for my dear life, always feeling that I was going to fall off at any time.

'Doh hold me so tight, nah man!' he shouted at me several times on the way. Pride, dignity, machismo, call it what you like, stopped me from telling him to stop, I'd walk the rest of the way. It was only five minutes on the bike, the longest five minutes of my life. I arrived soaked in sweat.

There was quite a queue already assembled, mainly white. At this point, I was looking forward to standing under a much needed, refreshing shower. I had to first buy a ticket, sit on a bench and wait my turn in the queue. A door opened in front of me and out stepped a burly white guy with a carrier bag and what looked like a towel on top, and I assumed his dirty clothes and toiletries below.

Through the door, I just could not believe what I was seeing. The cubicle had a big white bath, and I assumed that all the cubicles along the corridor was similar, being used by every Tom, Dick and Harry, meaning that anyone and everyone used the same baths.

As soon as one person had finished, an attendant would go in, swish it out and fill it up again for the next user. I asked Mr Ben if there were any showers, and he laughed, 'No, mate, it's all baths.' Showers, in fact, were not common in the UK at this time, partly because of the kind of heating systems used for water. At best, I discovered, a dual rubber hose with a shower head might be fitted onto the bath taps and then hooked up high enough to have a shower over the bath.

Then it was my turn. I noticed other users were putting their arm in the water to check the temperature and had cold or hot water added accordingly, so I did the same. The shock was instant – the water felt like an iced bucket. I thought that the attendant wanted to embalm me. In a strong cockney accent, he asked with a little smile, that I wasn't sure how genuine it was,

'Is it too cold for you, mate?'

'Yes, it is freezing, I just come from Trinidad where it's hot for so, I can't bathe in ice water!' He looked at me for a while without saying a word, and I started to think he wasn't going to do anything about it. Should I call Mr Ben, or not bother and go back to my digs and continue with my bucket?

After what seemed like an eternity he started adding hot water until it felt suitable for me. I closed the door, stripped and got ready to step in this thing.

I stood there for a while thinking of the number of people who had lain in that same bath before me. It made me feel really uncomfortable and perhaps it was my imagination, but I could have sworn that there was a line of muck from the previous occupant, and a few strands of hair floating on top of the water. To my relief, I learned that on future visits, if I gave a tip to the attendants, they would not only give the bath a special clean for you but also a refill, and the temperature would be OK first time. However, on that day, as a total novice, no sooner did I get in than the water turned from what I felt was warm to cold, and that was immediately followed by a knock on the door from the attendant, who informed me that my time was up.

That first encounter at a British public bath was a rude awakening for me, and to this day, I will only lie in a bath if I am having a soak with salts for aches and pains, but I will stand under a shower for a very long time and even for relaxation, if necessary.

When I came out of the cubicle, fear immediately overtook me at the thought of returning home the same way, riding pillion on the motorcycle. As Mr Ben was still in his bath, to exercise damage limitation and restore a little bit of dignity, I called out to him that I was going to go round to Ridley Road market – about a ten-minute walk away – to do some shopping, so I'd see him back home.

I couldn't tell Mr Ben that I was scared stiff to go back with him – he probably knew that anyway, and the whole house and friends in the area would sure to make even more jokes about the trip, as jokes were all part of the camaraderie and friendships that were to play an important part in helping to settle me into the society in those early days.

The jokes on my motorcycle experience came at me from his wife, saying, 'Why you had to squeeze up my husband so?' to the boys asking me if I had leanings 'the other way'. That was the last time I've ever ridden on the back of a motorcycle.

I had arrived with a few pounds in my pocket. The previous occupants of the bedsit, Errol and Jean, had left behind a few essential utensils and ingredients that'd last me a few days, but clearly, I needed to get a job quite soon. Luckily Errol had also been a printer, so he had given me great advice on which sorts of firms to approach for work.

I left Trinidad before I completed my City and Guilds final exams as an apprentice, taking home basic pay, and one step away from being a qualified compositor, but I felt I had acquired enough experience as a compositor to do any job, if given the opportunity. Life would have been much harder without these skills. If you gain a qualification as a youngster, there will always be opportunities for employment, and I feel sad when I meet young people who are just focused on earning some money in the short term but don't see the advantages of getting a good education or gaining some decent skills to build on. However, although I knew I had the skills necessary, that didn't stop me from being extremely nervous and apprehensive when I left my digs that Monday morning in search of employment.

The first and only firm I visited was Billington Press, a little printery on the Kingsland Road, Islington, not far from my bedsit. I had noticed their advertising board as I walked past on my way home a couple of times.

I got to this black door, with the sign on it saying 'Billington Press'. No bell, but the door was slightly open. There is an old saying, 'In for a penny, in for a pound', so, I took a deep breath, straightened myself up and walked into this very narrow corridor with stairs that led up to the next floor, as well as down to the basement where I could hear printing machines going. On my left was another sign, again saying 'Billington Press'. I knocked and a voice said, 'Come in', which I did. The office was the size of my bedsit with files neatly stacked on shelves, and in the corner was a desk with a slightly greying Englishman sitting behind it.

I said good morning, of course, which was part of my upbringing.

His voice was gentle. 'Can I help you?'

So, in my best Trinidadian ambassadorial display, I told him my brief history, the truth, the level of my qualifications etc. The only thing I left out was how I wanted to be an actor.

Mr Billington got up, and I realised then he must be well over six feet tall. He went to the door and called for Gerry to come up. Shortly after, Gerry entered wearing a white overall. He was introduced as the foreman and was instructed to take me downstairs and take me through a quick test – just setting a page, which was exactly how I'd worked in Trinidad. There was one other worker, Peter, a short white guy; he too was a compositor, because he was setting up a job. I guessed it was a very small firm of just two people, with Gerry the foreman operating the printing machine. A Heidelberg.

I didn't need any advice or instructions from anyone as everything was there, so I just got on with setting the test page, occasionally answering any questions about myself, making sure that my answers were as humorous as possible. Halfway through setting up my job, Gerry left and went upstairs, but only for a short period. Did I say something out of place, or are they racist? I wondered, smiling, but worrying deep down that they might not want a black man working in such close proximity. I knew I couldn't be accused of being too slow, because at the Government Printery in Trinidad we occasionally had a little typesetting competition between us, the apprentices, and most of the time I had been the fastest.

When I finished setting up the page, Gerry ran it off on the machine and I took it up to Mr Billington.

I don't think he scanned much of the page; he just said, 'If you don't have the offer of another job, can you start tomorrow morning at eight?'

It was the start of a wonderful relationship, with never a hint of racism from Gerry, Peter or Mr Billington. Mr Billington's son had the job of going out and canvassing for print work, but we hardly ever saw him. That was the sum total of the workforce! They all had a terrific sense of humour. Was there some unseen hand, a guiding light that was gently leading me on, clearing the path? Because I couldn't have asked for a better start to working in the UK. It was also well-paid, enough to cover my rent, eat and clothe myself and sometimes send a few pounds back to my mother. I immediately wrote to her to let her know my good news, as I knew it would take a weight off her mind, knowing I had a skilled job.

The houses in the area I now lived in were predominantly owned by white people; the one I occupied was owned by a Jamaican which was unusual. There was only one other house on my street that I knew of that was occupied by African and Caribbean people, and I understood it had the same landlord as mine. You travelled a few streets away towards Dalston and you found a greater percentage of African or Caribbean house ownership and occupancy - people liked to gravitate towards others of a similar background.

Dalston and Ridley Road market was the nerve centre of the Caribbean community. A visit on a Saturday morning especially in the summer was like back home in Trinidad, the only difference being it was a melting pot of Caribbean people. Jamaicans were the most prominent, but we had Vincentians, Barbadians, St Lucians, Dominicans, Grenadians, and many, many, more. It was an area where you would bump into someone you last saw in Trinidad, knew they emigrated to the UK, and there they are shopping like you, for home grown products.

My favourite place to hang out was Mikey's Barber Shop on Ridley Road, especially on a Saturday, I visited the shop not only to have a haircut but to lime (old talk), and this can take several hours. The discussions, or arguments (never overheated) covered a very wide range of topics from cricket to local and West Indian politics, to women, and always with plenty of laughter, as there was a great feeling of community spirit amongst us West Indians.

In the early 60's when walking in areas not frequented by Africans or Caribbeans, if you saw another black person, the immediate action was to wave or say hello, regardless of if they were from the West Indies, Africa or wherever, as long as they are black. Perhaps this happened because there were so few of us around, that the wave of acknowledgement was like an excited greeting.

Those with whom I shared the house in Northchurch Road had nothing whatsoever to do with show business, so any conversation about my ambition fell on deaf ears; they were post office workers, housewives, nurses, secretaries, mechanics. An average day for most of them was to leave early in the morning for work, back home, switch on the black and white TV, then dinner. On weekends, a game of dominos or cards in the sitting-cum-dining room, with background music playing, calypsos or reggae, and a heavy consumption of alcohol, though no one got drunk as I recall.

There was a group of about seven of us in the neighbourhood who loved dancing and going out to parties, so some Saturday nights especially in the summer, all sharply dressed, we'd go to a blues party in the basement of somebody's house, generally within a mile or two of where we lived. We all surreptitiously had to slip a donation to the owner of the house, as it wasn't a licensed premises. The owners went to great lengths to make sure they knew nearly all the people who turned up, as it wasn't uncommon for the police to have one of their officers in the party pretending to be a friend and later tipping off their colleagues who would turn up and demand that everything be shut down because they had evidence of alcohol being sold. Sometimes they would just pull up and asked that the music be turned down. It wasn't unusual to see several white girls turning up and enjoying themselves without a hint of racism, quite the opposite to some of the hostility we experienced on the streets.

The only thing I didn't like about blues parties was the cigarette smoke in such a confined space, so when I found myself surrounded by those who smoked, I'd have to go outside. Luckily none within my group of friends smoked, but I had the impression in London that most people smoked, and it was difficult to escape it in the pubs, the barber shops, public transport, theatre foyers, everywhere.

Most of the guys I hung around with had girlfriends, and going to parties I was always the odd one out. Within a few weeks of arriving in the UK, I had naively been led to believe that all you had to do was sweet-talk an English girl and she was yours – this information followed tales that were circulating amongst some of us aboard the ship bringing us to the UK. I had to put that philosophy to the test. It was during my first few weeks in London when I attempted to engage in a conversation with a very attractive white girl who was walking alongside me in Dalston. I said, 'Hello, how are you?' No response. 'I am new over here. You mind if I walk and talk with you?' which I thought was a normal friendly greeting. I had hoped that such a gentlemanly approach would lead to a little friendly conversation, exchange of addresses etc. Instead I got such a stern look and verbal rebuke, accompanied by a threat to call the police, that I beat a hasty retreat, and that was my first and last attempt at trying to chat up a lady like that. The very thought of the police arresting me for talking to a white lady, putting me in prison and then sending me back to Trinidad, humiliated and disgraced, wasn't an outcome I wanted.

We have an old saying in Trinidad that some of the boys used – 'Any port for a storm', meaning if you were desperate, any girl would do! I had been in the UK for several weeks and I hadn't succumbed to that level of desperation yet.

Did I have the wrong approach? I asked myself. A lot of the guys I knew appeared to be less polite when dealing with women. They were the ones I noticed even when I was growing up in Trinidad, the ones who the young ladies gravitated towards. Was I going to change my ways to impress the ladies? The answer was a resounding no.

The Astoria in Tottenham Court Road was a venue I was told where there was always dancing on a Saturday night, and for a small entrance fee you could dance until midnight or one in the morning; also a big band supplied the music. I thought that sounded like my kind of music, maybe like the dances I frequented in Trinidad with big orchestras like Joey Lewis and Sel Duncan blasting out popular tunes. It was in the West End of London, so I guessed the dress code had to be jacket and tie.

I turned up, paid the entrance fee, and entered the ballroom, and then with a quick glance around the room I realised I was the only black person there apart from some of the musicians on stage. I was aware of the odd glance in my direction, though without any hint of hostility. A waltz was playing, and couples were circling the dance floor in a kind of orderly fashion, going in the same direction, all doing the same kind of steps, hardly talking to each other. Am I at the wrong place? I thought. Was this some kind of dance school?

There were several girls leaning up against the wall, just gazing into the room, some in little groups chatting. Women far outnumbered the men, so I knew I wasn't going to have difficulty finding a partner. I kept scouting the room to see if any of the young ladies were looking my way; if I caught any just as much as looking at me, that would be the one I'd ask to dance, but no one did.

The band stopped, some couples stayed on the dance floor, others split and went their separate ways. I got myself a soft drink from the bar, and once again took up a position leaning against the wall. The band leader announced the next dance, a foxtrot, and I saw the guys going over to the ladies, putting out their hands and asking them to dance and they would readily oblige, but still no one looked in my direction. When the music started and I saw the way couples were dancing, almost skipping around the room in a robotic fashion, I was glad I wasn't out there. The band played about three foxtrot tunes, followed by quicksteps, and the same pattern. I decided to wait until they announced the waltz again; that was one of my favourite dances in Trinidad.

It must have been nearly two hours before the waltz was announced. I went to a young lady standing on her own and asked politely, 'Please may I have this dance?' She just looked at me and shook her head to say no.

I must have approached about six women around the room either standing alone or in small groups, and all turned me down either with a blunt no or with a shake of the head. I was beginning to get wet with perspiration, and I dared not look back to see if any of the ladies who had refused were looking at me and laughing.

The orchestra changed to another waltz, and I was coming towards the end of circling the room. I approached a group of three ladies who were having a chat and weren't looking my way; they were wearing what appeared to be more mature outfits and were more senior than the other ladies I had approached. By then I had decided that if this approach failed, I'd just slip out of the venue and head home, humiliated but with an old saying from back in Trinidad: 'He who fights and runs away, lives to fight another day'. So once again, I offered to dance. They all looked at me, and I wasn't sure if it was with surprise, warmth, or 'Who is this one? I've never seen him before.' Politely I asked for the dance without singling out anyone, and they smiled and looked at each other for a second - it felt like minutes - before the one nearest to me who appeared to be the more senior of the trio said, sure, she'd love to. By then I was so nervous that I had to dry my hands on my trousers quickly before I held hers.

I decided to follow the other dancers circling the floor. After a few minutes I relaxed and enjoyed the challenge, occasionally putting in a few Trinidad moves which made her smile as she appeared to be a good dancer and was led quite easily. She was happy to remain on the dance floor and complete the set of waltzes before I took her back to her friends, thanked her, and decided I'd had enough of the Astoria for one night, and would leave on a high whilst the going was good.

I returned to the Astoria many times after but always with the group of friends with whom I frequented the basement parties; although I didn't have a girlfriend, at least I could rely on one of the girls from the group to have sympathy and give me a dance or two. As a group we never followed the crowd that danced round the room; we did our dancing in one corner, adapting the rumba, foxtrot, jive, waltz or samba to suit us. Other times they'd encourage one of their friends who was at a loose end to join us, and also there were the odd occasion when someone in the dance hall would willingly agree to dance with me. I searched the dancehall on each of my visits for the group of ladies I had met on my first visit, but with no luck.

Then I met a nurse from Trinidad, Beulah. I received a letter from Errol and Jean saying they had settled back in Trinidad and had opened their own printing works in Port-of-Spain, and wanted to know how I was getting on, and if I had settled into my new environment. In the letter, they gave me the name and telephone number of a friend of theirs from Trinidad who was a nurse at St George's Hospital in Tooting. I called and arranged to visit her at the hospital when she was off duty, we went for a meal at a local restaurant, talked about Trinidad, found out she had known Errol and Jean for some time and had visited them on a few occasions at the bedsit I was now occupying. I continued visiting her when she came off duty for several weeks, during that time I found out she loved dancing, so I asked if she'd like to come with us to the Astoria, and she agreed.

She also agreed to stay the night - my first relationship nearly nine months after leaving Trinidad!

I decided to treat her to some home cooking on that Saturday of the Astoria visit. Got up early, went to the public baths, then a trip to Ridley Road market to buy some meat, rice etc to do a Trinidad style cook-up, one of my favourites and a safe dish.

I knew nothing about spirits so in my naivety I made sure I got a bottle of Stone's ginger wine; I drank it occasionally, so I thought everyone else did the same.

The table was beautifully laid out with tablecloth, napkins etc. I thought, very impressive: well, that was the verdict of my neighbours who popped in to see how I was getting on.

Beulah didn't strike me as someone who cared much for strong drinks and didn't smoke, but when I look back I wonder what her thoughts were when I offered her the Stone's ginger wine. She couldn't have minded too much because it was the drink I offered most of times she visited me, apart from the carrot or Guinness punch I sometimes made. It was a comfortable relationship, but it never really sparkled - there was always something I instinctively felt was holding her back, then after several months she suddenly broke off and said she was going to America. She admitted when pressed that she was committed to someone who was living in the USA, a long-distance relationship that did work out, I believe.

For myself, I had written to my girlfriend in Trinidad, Jeanette, but distance had finished the relationship, and sadly she died of cancer not long after.

Racism was something I had to deal with during those days, but I realised that I needed to make sure it didn't make me a bitter person or go around with a chip on my shoulder (a phrase that was used constantly when you challenged the way you were treated as a black person), or cloud my judgement or make me give up on my dreams. It made me determined to pursue my ambitions more intensely and with courage. And I was resolved to maintain the dignity that I had inherited from my mother.

But it was not easy to keep a smile on my face when confronted with such attitudes. One early regular experience – probably around 1961 - stands out in my memory. It involved getting on the number 73 bus, the bus that was said to travel the length and breadth of class and race in London from the affluent West End with its glittering lights and high-priced theatres, through to the less wealthy areas of North London. Just getting on that bus on a Saturday morning to go into the heart of London was an eye-opening trip. A black man could not be subjected to worse treatment, as every white conductor tried very hard to avoid eye contact. The disdain they displayed, at just the thought of perhaps actually touching a black man's hand to collect a fare, was a sight to behold.

My trick was to pause long enough to catch the conductor's eye, then watch the look of disgust on their face as I deliberately try to make contact with the palm of their hand as I paid them. The next bit of fun I had was with some passengers. By the time the bus reached The Angel in Islington, it would be full, but – surprise! surprise! – the only seat available would be the one next to me. The fact is that most of the white people preferred not to risk touching a black person and chose to stand rather than ease their tired feet. Rather than being bitter, I decided instead to enjoy these episodes very much, after all, on a crowded bus it meant more room for me. I felt like a king, and the smile on my face must have been clear to those who dared look at me.

There was a high percentage of black workers operating on the London Transport Service, but attitudes can take a long time to change. Years later, in fact, I recorded a few episodes in a very popular comedy series, On the Buses, including the very first episode, 'The Early Shift'. The series ran from 1969 to 1973 and followed the exploits of the driver and conductor on a particular bus, as they attempted to outwit their bus inspector. I was told that there was every chance that the role would be a running character, then quite suddenly the offer was dropped with no explanation given at the time. Several months later I was told, off the record, by Stuart Allen the director that the writers and executives of the company felt that having a running black character would not be good for the ratings.

Of course today, it's a very different story and it's no longer unusual to see a bus filled with so many different races. We may still have a way to go, but I have loved seeing how the UK changed and has embraced new cultures.

My first Christmas in England was a shock, just as my first visit to the public baths had been. About ten of us who were living in the house decided to visit the local church on Christmas morning. Mothers, fathers, children; we all strolled down Northchurch Road on that cold, wintry morning in our best clothes. We, the men, were well-decked out in our suits and winter coats with the ladies in their beautiful dresses; the children accompanying us were well behaved. We must have cut a very impressive picture, because the white people were taking a second look at us as we passed by. When we entered St Peter's Church, there was the usual buzz, until the congregation slowly realised that there was a large group of black people in their midst, after which they gradually fell quiet. The vicar himself even stopped greeting people just as we were approaching him, but it was so tactfully done that none of the others with me noticed his subtle departure. Back in Trinidad, with no influence or pressures from my mother or peers, I had worshipped in the Roman Catholic Church, the Baptist Church, the Pentecostal Church, the Church of England where I was baptised, the Church of God and with the Jehovah Witnesses. I had always felt from a little boy that I should be free at any given time to attend any place of worship that I liked, and be accepted with open arms by everyone, especially the priest or pastor. And back home it was unthinkable to be treated with disdain by any of the religious leaders, especially in the church building.

It was, therefore, a complete shock for me when I saw the silent hostility displayed by the priest and some members of the congregation. The members of our group were ushered to seats by an attendant, and my friends thought that his smile and the seats in which we were placed showed that we were welcomed. When the vicar delivered his sermon, he avoided any mention of us, but spoke of several other visitors from the North of England, and to add insult to injury, his sermon ironically was about love and the festive season. He also subtly avoided us on our way out.

It was my last visit to that church or any other in England, except on special occasions. I have always felt that God has no favourites and does not discriminate among His children. The incident that day only reinforced my early childhood teachings and beliefs that 'I should love my neighbour as I love myself' and 'do unto others as I would have others do unto me'.

When we got home, the love of performing was so well ingrained in my bones that I seized the opportunity to demonstrate and share true love the way I thought the church should have done, by singing Christmas carols on the stairs with the four or more kids between the ages six to fifteen who were living on the premises or visiting for the day.

We started with carols, with me pretending to be Paul Robeson – though clearly not with his wonderful bass-baritone voice. I was not sure if the dads who shouted, 'Shut up!' meant it; or the mothers who laughed were laughing at or with us; or the ones who applauded did so because they enjoyed it and wanted more. The kids were joining in and singing with me. They loved it!

It was whilst living at Northchurch Road that for the first time, I did what I thought at the time was a very significant walk-on part, in what was referred to as a crowd scene. It was a Saturday Night Play for television, set in Africa and starring Errol John, who had been such an encouragement when I met him in Trinidad. I said hello, but we had such different status on the set that I couldn't really approach him, and most of what I was involved in was also on location.

I was strategically placed in most of the crowd scenes and obviously I felt the director liked what I was doing because he kept giving me extra things to do; for instance, moving a dead body from one position to another and other similar activities. There were quite a few other black actors, but he kept picking me out to perform various actions. Of course I was excited, although it was a non-speaking part. This was the first thing I had ever done on TV.

When the play was due for transmission, I told every man-jack and child in the house and a few neighbours also, that I was going to be on television that Saturday night. I spent the whole week, nearly every day, reminding them. The excitement was building; even a family a few doors away stopped me on the street to say that they were coming over on the Saturday evening to watch with the rest of us.

The house where I was living in Northchurch Road, Islington had a mixture of Jamaicans, Vincentians, an Irishman we called Paddy – our own form of stereotyping! – who lived in the basement, Grenadians and myself, the only Trinidadian. We all gathered in the sitting room-cum-bedroom of Mr Ben; normally, if we were not out dancing, we would be playing dominoes, draughts, or bingo - certainly not watching a Saturday night play on television.

It was a real family atmosphere that night, everybody gathered in front of the box to watch me. Using my culinary skills, I made what Trins call a Guinness Punch, made with Guinness, two well-beaten eggs, nutmeg and ground cinnamon, evaporated milk and condensed milk. I also made a non-alcoholic carrot punch, using grated carrots, nutmeg and ground cinnamon, cow's milk, and condensed milk. Both were blended for the perfect taste and served with ice. Other drinks we often made included our own mauby, the bark being available in the market so we could boil it up ourselves.

Sea-moss was also a popular drink with meals; this was a clear white seaweed that we would wash and boil, then add condensed milk, a flavoured essence (like people add to cakes) and nutmeg to flavour it. Others brought in beers; some cooked food and with everybody sitting around, it was time to view my first television appearance in England.

Fifteen minutes of an hour's viewing went by, and then twenty-five. I was beginning to sweat.

'Rudy, you sure you in this thing, boy?'

'You sure is tonight?'

Half an hour went by and still I had not yet made an appearance, and suddenly in the background, through the crowd, I caught a glimpse of myself carrying a body. In a blink of an eyelid I was gone. Only two or three people saw me, and we didn't have the technology to rewind. I had to endure another twenty minutes waiting for another appearance and hoping better still for a close-up of my face, but it never came. Nobody had told me that as a walk-on, most of it ended up on the cutting room floor, meaning that the editors just discarded those aspects. That was only revealed to me in my later conversations with other actors, so that night I was the butt of the jokes for the whole household and for days after that.

Some of them even suggested I give up acting and stick to my day job! I wonder if this is why since then I seldom tell my friends and family when I am appearing on TV - they discover it themselves, sometimes being told by a friend.

CHAPTER 7

First Footprints on The Stage

'Everyone can rise above their circumstances and achieve success if they are dedicated to and passionate about what they do' Nelson Mandela, anti-apartheid activist and first Black president of South Africa

I had come to England to be an actor, and I was determined to give it my all, be a success, doing whatever it took. Full-time drama school would have been an obvious route to take, but I simply could not afford that, nor pack in a day job that paid my rent.

First, I enrolled at an evening class in St John's Wood to do ballroom dancing. Primarily, I went simply because I loved dancing, but I also knew it would be useful in my social life and help me become less isolated in the UK, help me to participate more fully, if I learned the right dances, and the correct way of dancing, in the UK.

I enjoyed it very much indeed, but one of the things I couldn't get used to was that it was so restrictive; I had to hold my body straight like a broomstick, I couldn't move my waist as I was used to, I had to hold the lady some distance away from me. I felt as though the rules were 'This is the man's space; this is the lady's space.' I was always getting corrected by the teacher. In Trinidad we exercised more freedom and rhythm, and if both dancers felt good about each other, you got closer and closer, if not you danced at arm's length. It felt more natural and spontaneous to me.

There were students there of all ages, shapes, sizes, and backgrounds, and I believe I introduced one or two to the Trinidadian way of dancing. One Jewish girl seemed especially to be on the same wavelength, and we always seemed to gravitate towards each other when the tutor said to take a partner, and when she wasn't looking at us, we'd do our own thing: a cha-cha-cha with a difference! We'd go for coffee afterwards and giggle and laugh about it. I fancied her a lot but got the feeling that she was from a very strict family and wasn't really allowed out much, as I invited her to come to the Astoria Club with me, as part of a group, but she always had an excuse, so I stopped asking. In retrospect, I think she knew that she would have needed parental approval for her to go out with anyone and did not think her parents would think me – black, non-Jewish – an acceptable companion.

I also enrolled for a three-year evening drama course at the City Literary Institute in Holborn. Tutors who taught during the day at places like the Royal Academy of Dramatic Art (RADA), Rose Bruford, and the London Academy of Music and Drama (LAMDA) held classes there in the evenings, making themselves some extra money, so I did not feel that I was short-changing myself. The key difference really was that there was no certificate at the end, as with the drama schools, and whereas someone saying at an audition 'I went to RADA' would make a director's eyes light up as they knew the person had professional training, the City Lit did not have the same clout.

We were a mixed bunch from all over the world: African, Jewish, Australian – all sorts of backgrounds. I signed up for everything to do with acting that the Institute had to offer. They held classes in speech, mime, fencing, dancing: everything one could study at a full-time drama school. We'd be given speeches to prepare e.g. from Shakespeare. Or a scene from a script which we would then read in the class, the teacher directing and the rest of the class then commenting on our performance. Movement taught us how to walk with a straight back, while there were also mime classes, things like putting across motion such as running while staying on the spot, and fencing, one of my favourite subjects.

I purchased my own foil and had a special leather cover made so I could just put it over my shoulder and walk along with it. Foils for fencing, of course, aren't dangerous weapons: they have a button on the end, not a sharp point, but I suspect I would be apprehensive carrying one around today in case someone got the wrong idea.

Each day after work, I would jump on a No. 38 bus from Islington and head for Holborn. If record books were available, I am sure that I would have been one of the students whose record would show that I hardly ever missed a class.

I remember one winter, for two consecutive nights, the fog was so thick that the conductor had to step off and direct the bus by walking in front of it. When I finally got to my classes, they had been cancelled, and it was quicker to take the tube to the Angel and walk the rest of the way home to Islington rather than try and catch another bus. The first time I saw London smog I was horrified: ghastly air. With so many chimneys burning coal, the air would get trapped and the whole of London would be blanketed in a nasty, unhealthy, smelly fog – what Londoners called a 'real peasouper'. It could be so dense that pedestrians would have to put a hand on a fence or hedge to keep in a straight line along the pavement, and children would hold hands in a line when going to school. How I missed the clean Caribbean air – the scent of the sea, the fresh breezes.

The period I spent at the City Lit was an extremely happy and productive one, and the camaraderie among the students from around the world was fantastic. Quite a few moved on to drama schools, or into the theatre on graduation, and a few became household names. One such was the late Mona Hammond, the Jamaican-British actress who became very well known for playing the role of a no-nonsense grandmother, Blossom Jackson, on EastEnders, before I joined the show. What a small world it was! Like me, Mona loved the mime, movement, and improvisation classes, run by Miss Margery Sigley and Mr Eric Wynn-Owen, who did drama.

In the summertime, the Institute ran some extensive weekend courses, from Friday evening to Sunday afternoon, at various country houses, one of which was a place called The Shornells in Surrey. Apart from the actual building with its unusual landing stairs, high ceilings and polished, wooden floors, the atmosphere was further enhanced by a breath-taking view of lush vegetation and beautifully landscaped gardens.

Before coming to the UK, I had thought that there would be far more big houses like this one, and after mostly seeing London terraces, this was a wonderful house to stay in. But although it had once been a family home, I could never envisage anyone living anywhere like this; the rooms were huge – we slept two or three to a room whilst staying there, and I still had more space than I had in my bedsit!

Sometimes, however, every upside in life can be followed by a downside and this occurred when we got back to London and one of the male tutors invited me back to his place for tea. He was in his early fifties and there was whispering among fellow students about his behaviour. Homosexuality was kept very much under the carpet in those days – it wasn't legal in the UK until 1967, and only then between two consenting adults over the age of twenty-one, and gay men it was alleged could face prison if they were arrested. When the tutor stopped me on the way out after class, brushed his hand on my behind then put an arm on my shoulder and suggested again I come with him for a meal, I told him in no uncertain terms that not only was he was barking up the wrong tree, but that I had respected him as a teacher and now that respect was out of the window, I surprised myself by my strong reaction – for after all, I believe one hundred per cent in the rights for everyone to live the way they choose – but I realised on my way home that the encounter I had as a child in Trinidad and kept silent about it, was somehow buried in my inner self, and once again the approach had come from someone who was in authority.

Luckily, attitudes were changing and in not much more than another five years, homosexuality stopped being a criminal offence, though it still took a long time before the LGBTQ community were accepted by some sections of society. I saw the tutor only once after that incident. I continued to attend classes, but it was noticeable that the tutor was absent from his classes and eventually replaced.

A few weeks after that encounter the principal of the institute, Mr Peter Trewelyan, a very kind and soft-spoken man, invited me to his office. Immediately I thought I was in deep trouble after the encounter with the tutor. I knew I did not share my experience with any of the other students, so there was no added gossip about him that I might be responsible for. Mr Trewelyan's greeting was warm and friendly – he sat me down and said that while talking to some of my tutors, they all felt that for the next term, I should be promoted straight to the third-year student classes.

'Why?'

'Because, Rudolph, you are good enough to be out there working as a professional actor.'

This came as a total surprise – I had thought he was going to tell me off for something, though I couldn't think what for – but this was quite something.

About the second week in August 1961, whilst still attending the drama classes at the City Lit, one of my tutors, Mr Eric Wynn-Owen, came in one night and said that a Mr Charles Marowitz, who was directing an American play entitled The Cave Dwellers by William Saroyan, was looking for a black actor. He had recommended me and suggested that I should talk to the director the next day. He also gave me Charles's phone number to call him that night and fix a time for the audition, as he was expecting my call.

Charles Marowitz was a well-known and respected Canadian director who went on later to establish and become the Artistic Director of the In-Stage Theatre Company, which had its home at Tottenham Court Road, London, so this was a massive opportunity to dip my toes into the profession I had travelled four thousand miles to pursue. So of course, I was extremely nervous of going for what was my first audition in the professional theatre in the UK.

I tried to convince Mr Wynn-Owen how futile I thought that might be, because of my lack of experience, and bearing in mind that Charles had already seen several established actors for the role. How could I possibly compete? Among actors in the play were experienced actors, including one who was to go on and appear in EastEnders: Leonard Fenton, alias Dr Legg.

However, Eric would have none of my objections, so I went up to the principal's office and nervously made the call. The next day, I took an extended lunch break from Billington Press and went over to see Mr Marowitz. The audition took place in the bar at St Pancras Town Hall, and was a gruelling one; it seemed to last hours, but in reality, took only about ten to fifteen minutes.

Charles was a tall man with piercing eyes that he rarely seemed to take off me. I was trying to concentrate as I read the part of Jamie, the assistant to the Wrecking Crew boss, read by Charles, who was all the time looking at me. It was a very small part, and I would only appear in the last scene of the play together with the Wrecking Crew boss. Charles asked me to do several interpretations of the character, so that by the time I finished I knew the lines. I was conscious of trying to both read the part and engage with him at the same time whilst he kept stroking his little goatee beard. What was he thinking? Eric had said he 'was auditioning', so he'd clearly seen other, more experienced, actors already. I was absolutely fresh, green. Yes, I had appeared on the amateur stage, but this was professional – a different ball game.

At the end of the audition, Charles said he would like me to play the part. Yes, I had been offered my first speaking part in the professional theatre in England! The play was set in America, in the ruins of a theatre about to be demolished, peopled with homeless no-name characters. I was to play Jamie, a member of a wrecking crew. It was noted in the script that the character should be black. An issue I was to encounter in my early career would be that unless it was specifically stated that the character should be black, I would not be considered for an audition.

At this point, I had to admit to Charles that I had a day job, but he was quite happy to work around me. Because I appear at the very end of the play and only in the one scene, getting away from work to rehearse in an extra-hour lunch break wasn't a problem. However, for the dress rehearsal and opening performance day, when the press would be present, that was a totally different challenge. I would obviously be required during the day. Although the printing firm was excellent about my taking the odd day off, I was reluctant to put in a request for the two full days I needed prior to the public opening night, as I knew the heavy workload they had at the time. I therefore decided to engage in a bit of deception.

My call for the dress rehearsal was for 10.30 a.m. on stage at St Pancras Town Hall, where the performances were taking place. The town hall was approximately a half an hour's bus ride from my workplace so, as I had not informed them of my plans, I went to work at 7.30 that morning, as usual. The actual printing works and typesetting were in the basement; one had to come up to the ground floor and negotiate a narrow flight of stairs to go up to the office.

I set up the print job and about 8.45 a.m., I took up the document for Mr Billington to proof-read. He read it and made the necessary corrections. Going back down to the print room, I made a very dramatic fall, tumbling down the stairs! It was a bit risky, seeing that opening night was just a day away, but having practised stage falls at drama classes, I felt it was a risk worth taking. And it was a great piece of acting!

My 'accident' brought everybody out, including Mr Billington. He got very worried and wanted to call an ambulance, or take me over to the hospital, which was across the road, but I insisted, saying, 'No, No!' Then he offered to pay for a cab to take me home and that I accepted, demonstrating a slight limp to show my injury. Of course, as soon as the cab dropped me off at my home, I legged it to the bus stop, and jumped a bus to St Pancras Town Hall, the limp completely gone – and with plenty of time before the dress rehearsal.

The next day, Thursday 2nd March 1961, we had to be in during the day to iron out any wrinkles that had been apparent during the dress rehearsal, and then – that evening – I made my debut on stage! The moment I prepared to walk on stage as a professional actor and as a black man, before an audience that was totally white, a moment of realisation hit me like a bolt out of the blue. Then and there, the first phase of my journey truly had begun and performing before such an audience might be my typical experience for a long time to come.

Was this what I truly wanted?

It was a moment when I asked myself two very serious questions; I had to be true to myself with the answers.

'Do I have not only the talent, but the strength, courage and resilience to climb that mountain?' And 'Do I really have what it takes to succeed in this business?'

I recalled how I had been advised by the late Edric Connor, back in Trinidad, to become known there rather than go overseas as roles for black actors were few and far between. I knew I would have to fight for any form of recognition, knew it would be challenging, but the moment I walked onto that stage, I realised that I had my answers. As I moved into character, into the role, I felt like I was where I belonged. I had no doubts.

This was endorsed when in the bar after the show, Mr Marowitz asked me what I intended to do with my career. I said I wanted to continue with evening classes, and work during the day for another year or so. His immediate response was that I should turn professional right away. After all, I realised, I had known that quite a few of the British black actors had gone for the part, although small, wanting the opportunity to work with Mr Marowitz, and I had got it. His support at this critical moment was such an amazing statement, and I am eternally grateful for the timely piece of advice he gave me.

I went back to work the next day following the press night, praying that none of my co-workers or Mr Billington read the papers and saw my picture in it – I chose to remain silent about my stage appearances at the Town Hall. It was a small part, and I was the only black actor, but the critics focused less on the actors and more on Charles Marowitz, as he was a controversial director who the press liked to feature quite a lot.

The following week the play transferred to the Pembroke Theatre in Croydon, opening on 13 March. It did not present a problem, as I legitimately finished work in time to get to the theatre.

The Pembroke was a theatre-in-the-round, where the audience surrounds the stage. This was a totally new and challenging experience for me, but one that was most enjoyable. It was the first time that I had performed before an audience that was sitting so close and all around me, that was an exercise we did only a handful of times at evening classes. I learned the importance of being truthful to the character I played, to immerse myself in the character, so even if parts of the audience were facing my back, they could get a sense of the character through my body actions, my voice, and my emotions.

After the play closed, I returned to Billington Press. I did eventually confess to Mr Billington about the fall, and he just laughed, but no longer did I have to fall down a flight of stairs to get the time off, I just had to ask, and Mr Billington kindly allowed me to go.

About this time, I got myself an agent. As stated earlier, I had met Edric Connor – the well-known singer, actor, and director – when he made one of his celebrated visits to Trinidad, so it was not surprising that in London I gravitated towards his wife, Pearl Connor, and her Agency that catered exclusively for African and Caribbean performers. Trinidad-born Pearl with a Portuguese/African father and a white mother, had legal training and was not only the first agent in London to cater for non-white actors, helping to bring more awareness of African and Caribbean culture to the UK, but she was also very vocal in defending and fighting for greater representation for us in the industry. She was a kind of Mother Superior, a loving guardian, a godmother to many of us, like Corrine Skinner-Carter who later joined the cast of EastEnders, Nina Baden-Semper who played my wife Barbie in *Love Thy Neighbour* and many more who Pearl helped to kickstart their career. The actors on her books did not go for big roles – Pearl was well known for providing walk-on parts, though not very many speaking parts. It was a great starting point, and I would not have been considered by any of the bigger agents at this stage of my careers. Those – all white – did take on one or two black actors each, but only those who were already established, working in the theatre or on television already, so, when a good, speaking role came up, producers and directors tended to go to those agents and select from this small group, then turned to agents like The Pearl Connor Agency or Oriental Casting for walk-on or supporting nonspeaking roles.

I continued to play walk-on parts on TV and in films, but I made sure I didn't reveal to my neighbours what I was doing for fear of being humiliated again!

I also continued to work at Billington Press, hoping that somehow, someone like a casting director would have seen my performance in The Cave Dwellers and would contact my agent to offer me a part in something, but days, then weeks, then months went by with the calls from Pearl only being for walk-on and supporting actor's parts.

During that period of inactivity, I was told that the BBC Radio World Service had a regular slot doing African and Caribbean plays. I did a demo tape and sent it to one of the radio producers, and within a couple of weeks I was cast in one of the plays. It was so well received that I then became one of the handful of actors who were cast regularly playing a variety of characters, and all recordings took place over the weekend, so it didn't affect my day job.

I continually looked for any opportunity to learn my craft, so when I heard that the Stanhope Institute in St Johns Wood, London, had a thriving amateur theatre company I joined, and no sooner than I did, they decided to stage Shakespeare's Othello and invited me to play the lead role. What better way to practise my skills, make mistakes and learn by them, hoping that one day I'd be asked to play the role in the professional theatre.

A chance meeting and conversation with a director in the BBC canteen at Bush House led to me fronting several documentaries for the Central Office of Information (COI). The two most memorable ones I filmed were being strapped up and climbing down the cliffs of Dover whilst interviewing a British Army Officer, and the other was being taken up in a window cleaner's cradle to one of the very tall buildings near Liverpool Street Station and interviewing a worker. What was remarkable and memorable about those two experiences is that I don't like heights, so I avoided looking down as much as possible.

From April 1961 to 1964 was a barren period in terms of getting speaking roles either on television or the theatre, and although occasionally a black actor would appear on the TV screen and in a stage play, the majority were struggling, and one by one some were giving up show business altogether, embarking on a different career, while others were returning to either Africa or the Caribbean, but I was determined to stick it out for as long as it takes.

One morning whilst working at Billington Press the foreman called us together, all four of us - by then they had added another worker in the machine department as an apprentice, a young man of Jamaican parents. He announced that the Trade Union had approached him with an offer for us to join the union, and that Mr Billington had no objection, so we all agreed.

The whole firm became unionised, and this meant that as a compositor within the union I could go to most printing firms, and as long as there was a job available, they would employ me, and that would have been ideal, if I had intended to continue in the printing trade – for it was an extremely well-paid occupation at the time – but it gave me a false sense of security. If I gave up a job to do an acting part, I could immediately go back to a printery, any printery, or newspapers, and almost certainly get another job. It would be security, but I could find myself doing more print work and less acting as a result. For a time, it worked well.

As I continued to search for work in the industry, I realised that somehow, I had to do something different to draw the attention of the directors and producers out there, as all the usual channels were not working. I did not want to spend my entire acting life as 'African President' or 'Nigerian chief' on the radio. I then came up with the idea of doing a mailshot and wrote to every director and producer at every TV station in England. I did the same with every artistic director of every theatre in the country.

I got the approval of Mr Billington and the foreman to produce a very impressive profile, free of charge, listing everything I had done as an amateur, including my training at The City Literature Institute.

From the first batch of about two hundred applications, I received not one single response. After about three weeks, I sent out another batch to the same directors, producers and artistic directors. This time, I was pleasantly surprised that I was rewarded with two notable responses, one of which resulted in my first speaking part on TV.

I received a letter from BBC Television to meet Mr Christopher Morahan, who was casting for a TV play called *Fable*, which was written by a very prolific writer, John Hopkins. The play was set in an alternate Britain, where there was reverse apartheid – much as Malorie Blackman later explored in her young adult novels, Noughts & Crosses. It was an exciting concept, and I was reading for the part of the policeman in the play. I had never met or seen Christopher Morahan before, and as I was ushered into his office by his secretary, this big gentleman, six feet plus, came out from behind his desk, towering over me, he extended his hand with a firm grip and with just a hint of a friendly smile and an imaginary label pinned around his neck which read 'Mr BBC'.

The audition was surprisingly very short, he didn't ask me to read but questioned me about my background, and at the end of it, told me that he wanted me to play the part of the policeman and handed me a copy of the script. I could not wait to get out of the room, as by then I was sweating profusely, and I was scared that if I had stayed any longer, he might change his mind. When I came out of the room sitting there to go in were two other actors including Trevor Rhone, who was a fellow passenger on board the Oranje Nassau when it sailed from the Caribbean in 1960. I hadn't yet read the script, so I had no idea what part he was being auditioned for, but I knew it certainly wasn't the policeman because I'd just got that.

Appearing in *Fable* was supposed to be a baptism of fire for me, because in those days it was said that Christopher had a reputation of being a very tough director – someone who did not suffer fools gladly. I felt that I had crossed the first hurdle when he cast me, a budding television actor, in what was a small but significant role, and one which I knew would not end up on the cutting room floor. The rehearsals – over three weeks – were nerve-racking, and throughout Christopher was very helpful, encouraging and supportive, but firm, I could not have had a better and more beneficial baptism into TV.

For a young actor like me, walking into a TV studio for the first rehearsal was very daunting. Walk-on crowd scenes had nearly always been out on location, but here I was faced with a battery of cameras and machinery all around, plus lots of crew congregating where the actual set was. I couldn't even immediately see where I'd be acting! And the pieces of equipment – cameras, boom mikes and so on – were enormous and heavy; if I didn't trip over a cable, I was worried I'd hit my head on a boom mike, as I believe has happened to at least one actor of my acquaintance, although obviously the floor manager is very aware of the actors' interests and the risks are minimised.

But I was the least experienced actor on *Fable*; the rest of the cast had all done work in TV studios before, so the setting felt normal to them, as it does to me nowadays. I was eager to learn from the more experienced actors.

During the rehearsal periods I would sit around at a distance and watch those experienced actors like Thomas Baptist, Eileen Atkins, Ronald Lacey go through their paces, how they react when Christopher gave them notes, the gradual growth of their character during that period, and the confidence they displayed on set in front of cameras on that first recording at the BBC TV studio in White City, London.

I was particularly enthralled with Miss Atkins' performance that when she was recording one of her strong scenes, I positioned myself close to one of the cameras, making sure I didn't get in the way of its movements, just to watch this brilliant actress at work, her controlled delivery, minimum but powerful movements and gestures. Immediately after recording that scene, she came directly to me and said loud enough so people close heard, 'Get the hell out of my eyeline, you are distracting me'. I apologised and moved away, feeling hurt, but not deflated, in fact it helped me to fuel the scenes I had later on with her.

I have learnt over the years, that a quiet word with the floor manager is the best way to approach problems like that.

People often ask how you can stay in character if filming scenes out of order, but in those days TV filming was more like being in the theatre in that we moved from one set to another, playing the scenes in order, just like in a stage play – but with an audience, which felt very weird to begin with. The most important focus now was the camera – there'd be three or four on the actors at any one time – but to myself as the actor, playing to millions of people is the last thing I think of. I have to make the character mine, as I want, following the guidance of the director. On stage, in the theatre, everything must be bigger – more obvious gestures, a voice that can project. In the TV studio, it has to be more truthful; more nuance is needed as there could be close-up shots. These were all things I needed to learn on the job. And *Fable* was where I began that learning experience.

Except for Ronald Lacey and Eileen Atkins it was an all-black cast, which meant that coffee breaks and lunch breaks were spent telling jokes and stories. We especially enjoyed those from the Caribbean, the native home of most of the cast. Amongst the cast was Carmen Munroe, an actress whose work I admired. She later said that for the actors it had been quite unsettling, behaving like a racist, 'because suddenly you were being asked to perform the sorts of acts that were performed against you in real life'. It seemed to be a bit unnerving to others too, with audience research afterwards finding that quite a few whites found the role reversal difficult to handle. And even the screening itself was put back a week to avoid it clashing with a London by-election where immigration was a key issue.

After the recording of the final scene most of the cast including myself went up to the BBC club to have complimentary drinks and snacks. The director, Mr Morahan, took the opportunity to compliment me on my performance. He might have said that to all of the other actors – it didn't matter; at the time it felt personal coming from him and the reputation that preceded him.

The late Leo Carera, who was also a schoolteacher, and Bari Johnson offered to give me a lift back to my digs as they both lived not far from me. I invited them up for a cup of tea, as by then I had sort of embraced part of this English custom – neither of them, as I had observed, drank much alcohol, so I felt comfortable in inviting them up for a cuppa. They were both very complimentary about my performance and my approach to the profession and predicted a bright future for me. Mr Carera also went on to say that, looking at the black actors around at the time, I brought something different and refreshing. I thought that was praise indeed coming from an actor so well established and respected in the industry.

I allowed myself a couple of weeks, hoping that I'd get a call from my agent to audition for another job but nothing happened, so I then decided, instead of returning to Billington Press I'd try getting a night job at one of the national newspapers, and holding a union card there was no problem, and it also freed me up during the day to go for auditions.

My attempt at working nights only lasted about three weeks, as I found it extremely difficult to adjust. I would arrive back home about six in the morning and go straight to bed as you are supposed to, but by nine o'clock I was wide awake and found it extremely difficult to go back to sleep.

I returned to Billington Press and once again they were fantastic, giving me odd jobs when I needed work, but I knew that if I left the union, this would no longer be an option. In the end, I took the brave, yet hard, decision to stop paying my union dues and take on the theatre full-time so that the security of a job to fall back on would no longer be available to me.

A leap of faith to be sure, but I was serious about pursuing a career as an actor, and this was a commitment I felt I needed to make.

However, I still had to pay the rent. There were agencies that placed regular advertisements for 'resting actors' in the theatrical weekly newspaper, The Stage. I considered the term used to be a deceptive, ridiculous yet humorous phrase, which simply meant that we were 'out of work'. The nature of the jobs advertised would often be for cleaning or gardening – virtually all for clients who were white and middle-class. I was never refused entrance to any of the houses I visited, but the look on some of their faces when they saw that I was a black man was sometimes horrendous. It was only because I was sent from an agency that specialised in finding part-time employment for actors that I was allowed entrance. However, I knew that had I just knocked on those doors and asked for a job, I would have been unceremoniously turned away.

A few of the clients, rather than leave me to get on with the cleaning, would literally follow me everywhere I went in the house, even into their toilet. At times I found the experience rather humiliating, and at other times highly amusing.

There was also a popular reputation in this era of the black man being particularly well-endowed and a great lover. Was that why some clients would follow me so closely into the bedroom? Once, I nearly put a client to the test. I was cleaning out her toilet and shower when I needed to pee, so I closed the door whilst she remained on alert outside that door. I wondered what might have happened if I had not closed the door and had just started to use the toilet without an announcement. It meant I spent the rest of the morning laughing to myself.

That way of life continued for most of the year until I had a call from Theatre Royal, Stratford London to audition for *The Road*, a stage play by a young Nigerian author Wole Soyinka in August 1964 directed by David Thompson, nine months after my last job.

The play was set in Nigeria and for this production, Equity, the actors union, permitted a few Nigerian actors to fly over and be part of the company. It helped several of us from the Caribbean, like Horace James, Bari Johnson and I gain valuable knowledge of Nigerian culture. Wole Soyinka paid us several visits during our rehearsal period and reassured us we were doing well.

The play was staged as part of the Commonwealth Festival and one night before we went on stage for the performance, we were told that Princess Margaret was in the audience.

During the first half, most of the actors kept looking to see where she was sitting, so the interval was spent speculating as to where; and would we have to line up on stage after the curtain call to meet her and shake her hand? We came off after the curtain call as usual, and waited in the wings for a while, but no one said anything so we all went to our various dressing rooms. The following day, the press released a photo of her attending the performance. The jokes that went around the cast as to the reason why she didn't come on stage to meet us after the show are unprintable.

Within two months of appearing at Theatre Royal Stratford I auditioned and was offered the part of Mark in a new play called *Fear of the Panther*, written by Jean McConnell and staged at the beautiful Richmond Theatre. It would be the first opportunity for me to work on stage with a well-established wonderful actress, Miss Carmen Munroe from Guyana, whose work I admired.

The play was directed by Robert Peake and on the press night, Barry Reckord a renowned Jamaican playwright and his brother, Lloyd Reckord, an experienced actor in England, who was also a director invited Carmen, Bari and I to the pub after the show, which I discovered was something of a theatre custom.

What happened next took me by surprise. Lloyd immediately launched a sustained attack on every aspect of my performance, from the way I walked or talked, calling it a bad example of a West Indian man. His brother, as well as Carmen, came to my defence, but he only stopped when he had his full say. It was a shocking learning experience for me – surely any responsible senior actor should have been less brutal to a young actor just starting out in the business. I did not cower, or burst into tears or even feel deflated, or challenge him. I just listened and tried to take it all in. Whatever was his agenda, what he did, really set me thinking about the way I should deal with criticism in the future, so he had in fact done me a service rather than a disservice. It also made me decide not to mix with other cast members after shows; instead, I would go home immediately after a performance and not join in any after-show gatherings. This suited me perfectly, since I didn't drink or smoke, and at the time British pubs were filled with cigarette smoke fumes.

Over the years, I have been criticised by the press, directors and colleagues. Some criticisms were very harsh, but I had to deal with them realistically and in a very practical way. After all, it is my belief that one man's meat is another man's poison. With this in mind, I never dismissed criticism of any kind about my work, but I always sought to determine if it was genuine, constructive and helpful to me. Obviously, I can't read the minds of any critics, but I do know that sometimes the critics may well dislike a particular interpretation of a role – especially in a very traditional play – although that interpretation might be exactly what the director and I wanted to achieve. Brilliant plays are open to all sorts of different direction – but the essential themes of love, jealousy, hatred etc – are universal, open to all human beings, regardless of their background.

Taking a play and putting it into a different setting e.g. setting Shakespeare into a World War II or Sixties setting, gives a new perspective. It works. But it also gives the critics something to focus on. Not always to the detriment of the play though – controversy can attract audiences!

A criticism by another actor of my performance can hurt, though, so Lloyd Reckord's comments felt wounding. Sometime after the run of the play, however, I received a letter from Robert Peak, the Artistic Director of Richmond Theatre in which he said: 'For someone who came in green, we are really very impressed, not only by the sheer vitality and innovation you demonstrate but what you brought to the part.'

This was praise indeed, and very encouraging to a young actor. What if I had decided, after Lloyd's comments, that I should give up acting? Never have had further opportunities to develop my skills. I wonder sometimes how many actors have been put off by early criticism. I always try to be encouraging to new, young actors I find myself working with. There are always positives to find about everyone's performance.

After *Fear of the Panther* came to the end of its run, there was no Billington Press to call on as I was no longer a member of the union and searching for a non-union printing firm would be a nightmare, so I had to look for temporary employment to eat and pay the rent.

In the 1960s and 70s, the media often described all immigrants – especially West Indians – as spongers, living off social security; that was an unfair criticism, given the small percentage who went to the local employment exchanges. But in those days, most actors without a family lived from day to day. It was never a question of having to save for a rainy day, as there was nothing to save. And this did mean claiming benefits at times. This included me; now and then I had to visit the Labour Exchange and 'sign on'. There was no Universal Credit then, nor online applications since computing was still at an early stage, so anyone unemployed had to go to their local Labour Exchange every week, queue up and sign to say they had done no work since their last visit. In return, a Giro cheque you could cash at the post office would be sent in the post or collected, it wasn't much, but it covered the basics and on top of the unemployment benefit, the social security department added sufficient to cover my rent.

CHAPTER 8

Further Footprints on Stage and Screen

'***No Blacks, No Irish, No Dogs***'
Sign in window in 1960s London

The house in Northchurch Road was owned by a Jamaican, and the time came when he announced that he was selling up to return to Jamaica, so unfortunately, we all had to move out. The house, I believe, was sold for just £4,000. Today, one must pay nearly six times as much just to tastefully fit out a new kitchen!

I began searching for new accommodation. I looked through the Evening Standard, the local papers, sweetshop windows, estate agents and other places of advertisements.

I experienced the same rejection that many from the Black community did trying to secure rented accommodation. Prejudice and racism famously reflected in the sign in the windows – NO BLACKS, NO IRISH, NO DOGS. It always intrigued me that we were top of this prohibited list, even more feared than dogs!

I never approached any landlord exhibiting such signs but many who didn't were equally unwilling to rent to black people. Their refusal was just more subtle – the room was just rented out and is no longer available, I am ever so sorry. The frequency with which this happened made me curious and, on a few occasions, I got one of my fellow English actors to call an hour or so later, and of course the room was always still available.

The message I was receiving was loud, clear, and everywhere. We were being told on the one hand that we should go home to our native countries; whilst on the other hand, the UK was begging us to come and run the railways, the buses, and the hospitals. They knew that if we left, those industries would collapse due to the shortage of labour, as there was always a demand for cheap or imported labour in England. The wealth of the island was also built on exploitation, be it from the blacks from Africa, the struggling West Indians, the Asians, or the poor from other European countries.

But politics aside, I was facing a serious dilemma. If no rented accommodation was available to me because of my colour, where was I going to get a place to rest my head? Surely not everyone was so discriminatory. How did others who arrived here before me cope? They weren't living on the streets, what was I going to do?

Wole Soyinka, the Nobel Prize-winning Nigerian playwright, wrote a fantastic poem, 'Telephone Conversation', describing exactly what I was experiencing. A poem I recited on many occasions.

But like many times in my life, fate, luck, a guardian angel, the Almighty, or someone else intervened. Finding myself at

Willesden Green Underground Station, I noticed a sweetshop displaying cards advertising Room to Let. The first one I called, a female answered, it was still available, she said, there was no hostility in the voice on the other end, although there never was. I said quite strongly but politely, almost as in the poem, 'In order not to waste your time or mine, I am black.'

'I do not have a problem with that! Do you?' the female voice replied. The response took me by surprise, I told her where I was and if it was possible to visit right then, she said by all means, again sounding very polite and friendly.

The house, a semi-detached, was located on Melrose Avenue, Willesden Green, just a few minutes' walk from the underground station. I rang the doorbell, still a little apprehensive. I could hear someone coming down the stairs, the door opened, and this lady extended her hand, introduced herself as Marion, and invited me to come in. She showed me the room I was to occupy, which was the front room on the ground floor, not hidden away in a back room upstairs, but should they have visitors, and they were in the back somewhere I'd be the one to open the door and let them in. The kitchen she said I would share and also the bathroom and toilet. The house was clean and tidy but for several toys scattered on the floor. They had two children: Tony, who was fast asleep in his crib, and Sabina (Bina) who was at kindergarten.

I was offered a cup of tea and was immediately made to feel relaxed and at home. She said when I asked, that the room was available; and it was the first time they were having a tenant. I told her that out of courtesy I had to give at least a week's notice to my current landlord, even though the house was for sale, and it would be just over a week before I was able to move in, and to secure it I offered to go to the bank and withdraw what little I had and pay the first week's rent. Marion would have none of it. 'Just give us a ring when you are coming, the room is yours,' she said. Were these once again unseen forces in play? It was as if I were guided there, or as the saying goes, 'What's for you. You'll get it'.

I kept in touch and ten days later I turned up with my two suitcases. The door was opened by Jack, Marion's husband, who warmly greeted me and showed me to my room followed by their young son Tony, who insisted on hanging around whilst I unpacked. Any attempt to remove him ended with screaming, so I encouraged Jack to leave him, then I began singing a Negro spiritual, which seemed to amuse him.

Marion and Jack Cassin-Scott were Jewish, and Marion's parents lived across the road. Jack designed and made miniature military figures on horses, from armies around the world – they were well sought after. He baked them in his little kitchen oven. Prior to that he was a theatre set designer. Lodging with the Cassin-Scotts became one of the happiest periods of my life in England. They were a young family at the time and had two children – a daughter, Sabina whom I adored and son, Anthony. I became part of that family, as the babysitter and the disciplinarian, because at that point I was the only person to whom Tony would listen!

After four years of living there, I moved out only because I got married. The room in which I lived, and until they died and sold the property, was always referred to as Rudy's room: I was their last and only tenant.

Moving to Willesden Green meant that I had to change the Job Centre/Benefit Office I used in Victoria that catered for actors and were sympathetic, to one in Harlesden North London who were less so.

I hated claiming any benefits full stop, finding it embarrassing, but needs had to be met if there were no roles on offer, nor any available work through the agency for cleaning or gardening. Even so, I had a problem convincing the department that I was an actor and not a compositor, nor a printer – though they could not find me a print job unless I re-joined the union. Acting was now my full-time job, but they would have none of it. As far as they were concerned, I had to do whatever they suggested, or they would stop my benefits.

After several visits, I was finally interviewed by a kind woman in the Harrow Road Office in Harlesden.

'Don't worry, Mr Walker,' she said. 'I will change your job description and register you as an actor.'

I left feeling elated, as if I reached a major milestone in my life. Even the unemployment offices now recognise me as an actor!

As an actor, black or white, female or male, gay or straight, you are forever engaging in competitive pursuits of roles and jobs, but not on a level playing field. For black actors there are additional hurdles to overcome, from agents, directors, producers, cast members and audiences. And in such an intense battleground, it means also battling with your fellow black thespians to secure one of the limited roles available.

During my career, I have found it easy to get along with all actors, but navigating my way through both theatre and TV, I have had to manage varied experiences and individuals, each with their own challenges, each shaping me as a person and as an actor, each preparing me for the next step on my journey.

At the risk of repeating myself ad nauseam, opportunities for black actors were few and far between; there was also definite prejudice, sometimes even from people who were trying to be helpful but who fostered stereotypes that were completely wrong.

I am not sure which of those was the most difficult to cope with, but the reality was that black actors were being marginalised, rather than being accepted as part of the mainstream acting profession. We were rarely chosen purely based on our skills or capacity to do the job.

In those days, the bulk of my work was playing an African or a black character of indistinct heritage. Such roles came and went, influenced by contemporary events that resulted in plays being written, documentaries on the Caribbean or fictional accounts of political turmoil in Africa. If on the rare occasion, a black actor was offered the part of a doctor or lawyer, it was deliberately scripted and always stipulated and emphasised that there was a dramatic reason why that character had to be black. We did not get auditions for 'doctor' or 'lawyer' unless the race had previously been stated.

And there was often no artistic leeway to interpret a role. In the minds of many, 'black African' meant one type of character portrayal was required, usually very stereotypical, as did 'West Indian calypso singer', or 'native sergeant'. One fellow actor recounted being 'directed' with the words: 'Well, you must understand, dear boy, that I have known West Indian people all my life and they do it this way!' and the actor's retort was: 'Well, I have been a West Indian man all my life and I have been doing it this way.'

One of the things I noticed while watching my fellow actors on television was that not many of them bothered to imitate African accents or mannerisms. So, if they were asked to play a Nigerian chief, their delivery would come out with a strong West Indian accent, cockney, or Oxford English, depending on where they were born. Even two brothers might have different accents! But if the director didn't care, why should the actor? They should have! I was probably one of only a few who took the plunge and tried to get some sort of a semblance of a particular accent to suit the role. A Nigerian accent is nothing like a Jamaican accent, for example. I also never used gibberish when called upon to say something African either, as a number of actors did in those days. I would always use my initiative and try to learn a few words of Yoruba or whatever language I was supposed to speak, but for many directors of the time, there was still the view that the average African was an 'uneducated native', only able to speak simple sounds. How little many of the British knew about African history and heritage!

A part of the problem facing black actors was that many had to take unsuitable roles – and play them in the stereotypical ways the director asked for – simply for the sake of earning some money. It was all that was on offer. I could not criticise this, because some had families to support so had little or no choice if this is what the director wanted. But it could be likened to the way some American actors of the 1930s would, when asked to, roll their eyes and become the butt of jokes. They were still trailblazers though – black actors appearing in movies: a big part of why I am where I am today. But I was determined to resist the temptation of putting money before my artistic integrity. For me, I felt it was important to use my talent to challenge stereotypes and prejudicial portrayals. I did not want to reinforce negative and outdated stereotypes.

Additionally, some of the European directors and casting directors were often not sufficiently culturally knowledgeable when casting African or Caribbean roles. I turned up once to an audition with many other actors for a role as an 'African President'. The choice finally had to be made between a friend of mine – Willie Jonah from Sierra Leone – and me. I got the nod because in the eyes of the director and casting director I looked more African than Willie. The accent didn't matter at all in this case, just appearance. Suffice it to say, Willie and I had a good laugh afterwards.

I had no problem with playing an African, because as a West Indian actor I did not want to play only West Indian roles; to be versatile in all other areas was my ambition. Those casting sessions just tended to highlight a lack of research and the lack of respect black actors had in the industry.

When I got a review from the critics, I was also always referred to as Jamaican. As far as they were concerned, every black man in the UK was either from Africa – the whole continent, no specific country – or Jamaica. Even if you had a strong Barbadian accent, you were still described as Jamaican. The public had a different twist; I would say to someone that I was from Trinidad and that person would want to know where in Africa it was situated. I like to think that my sense of purpose, my upbringing, my spirituality, my sense of humour, my heartfelt desire to see us all as one race – the human race – was what got me through those early years. But these obstacles also fuelled my determination to succeed, on my own terms.

However, it is very sad to realise that there were individuals who had been put off from pursuing a career in acting when they could have become truly great icons in the British theatre. For instance, there was the late Charlie Hyatt, a Jamaican actor, who went back to Jamaica many years ago. He was a very talented actor, who just could not cope with the lack of roles and opportunities. Leonie Forbes was also another brilliant actress who could have been a star but decided to return home. In fact, there were quite a number of actors and actresses who, as a result of the lack of opportunities, decided to opt out. Some returned to the Caribbean or Africa, while others sought fame and fortune in the USA. Many, however, did stay and try to make a success of their career but more than a handful of them found the going very tough and frustrating and I have heard of a few who even committed suicide out of despair.

We were such a mixed bunch. Among my fellow-actors were Bari Johnson, who hailed from Jamaica and returned home; Norman Beaton and Carmen Munroe from Guyana; Johnny Sekka from Senegal; Willie Jonah from Sierra Leone; Earl Cameron from Bermuda; Horace James and Oscar James, both like myself from Trinidad. Others came from all over the continent of Africa and the Caribbean, and I got along with them all – with the odd exception. The biggest problem, however, was the cultural divide and the negative attitudes displayed by some of the black American actors we met, who had not done the volume of work we had done – especially on stage – yet they felt superior. This was because, on the basis of a few appearances on screen in the USA, they'd been invited to come over and play certain key roles. No audition necessary. Hence, they often felt they arrived with higher status, regardless of what work they had actually done. This sense of superiority they then extended to how they conducted themselves generally, and they often came across as more aggressive in their approach, and on a completely different wavelength from us.

Basically though, finding work for any actor, let alone a black and unknown actor, was extremely difficult and challenging and these early years when I was trying to establish myself as a full-time theatre professional were not easy. Whenever a part was available there were just a handful of black actors among us who tended to be employed: Johnny Sekka, Bari Johnson, Alaba Peters, Clifton Jones, Oscar James, Earl Cameron, Lloyd Reckord, Thomas Baptiste, and even then, parts were few and far between.

I relied on my agent and word of mouth from other actors to be informed of possible roles, although by the time one got a tip from another black actor, the actor had either already been turned down or the part was already cast. The other source was the casting section in The Stage, which was published every Thursday. Although the advertisements were mainly for dancers, singers or musicians, nonetheless I read them, even though they were of no use to me since I wasn't a trained singer and although I did ballroom dancing, I just didn't see myself in a chorus line doing that kind of disciplined dancing. So, I just ignored those adverts.

Personally, things were changing for me too. I liked the ladies but was never someone who jumped from one relationship to another. When I had a relationship with a girl, I was nearly always faithful to her, hoping that it would develop into something serious, and there was generally a good reason why we would eventually part. It certainly wasn't because I just met somebody else, sometimes it related to my work; it could be difficult for a girl to have a boyfriend who would suddenly be working every evening and at weekends, or – once I had left printing – might have to move elsewhere for a couple of months if a job came up. Obviously, I met girls from the West Indian community at dances and parties, but some of the girls I dated were also white and I don't recall ever really having any problems with a girl's parents.

Around 1964 I became a member of what was one of the UK's leading theatrical companies, the Amateur Theatre Company, Mountview Theatre Club in Crouch End, North London, run by Mr Peter Coxhead. It had a reputation of having as its members ex-professional actors, some of whom felt that they were not making any headway in the profession and had dropped out to pursue another career but still wanted to display their skills. I was not at that stage, but I felt that by joining the company I could learn from those experienced actors.

The stage manager on one of the productions I did was Miss Ricky Tucker, who was very warm and friendly, but firm when having to perform her duties, and within a few months we developed a very strong relationship. She was my first white girlfriend, but I had no problem dating a white girl – Aunt

Millie had taught me as a child that there should be no issue about skin colour when finding someone to love.

Ricky was from Norfolk originally, slightly older than me, and worked as a top secretary at St Godric's College in Hampstead, London, and lived in a rented flat in Kilburn, within walking distance to where I lived in Willesden Green.

She was instrumental in introducing me to some of London's experiences; in particular, she was the first one to take me to a theatre in the West End of London. What an experience! First, we were ushered to our seats in the circle, at which point I realised we couldn't just sit anywhere as I did back in Trinidad – this was all very organised. I noticed on the back of the seats in front of us were these red objects which Ricky said were binoculars. I said that must be for people who could hardly see, and she said not necessarily, then used a couple of coins and released them. I was amazed at the extra clarity it gave to the surroundings, the beautifully designed ceiling and boxes.

The show was supposed to start at 7.30 p.m. and at 7.30 on the dot there was a blast of the National Anthem, and everybody started getting up. For a split second, I remained sitting, wondering what was going on: was the Queen in the audience? Where was she? I started looking around. An instant tug on my jacket from Ricky and I was on my feet. That was the custom of London shows at the time.

Another surprise was to follow. The Interval arrived and within a minute or two ushers appeared with trays of tea and biscuits and were passing them along to various people in the audience. What was so special about them? I asked Ricky. She said it was nothing, but they'd ordered the refreshments before the show started. Then I saw a tray with two cups, a pot of tea and biscuits making its way along our row of seats, and I was just about to pass it on to Ricky when she said, 'No, that's ours.' How I didn't drop the tray, I'll never know! This was a very British thing, not a Trinidad thing, so I was a little uncomfortable to start with, and especially as I was the only black face in the audience, and it was like all eyes were on me. I don't think I have ever eaten a biscuit with such delicacy or drunk a cup of tea with such grace. I also saw some people dipping their biscuits in the tea, and when I asked Ricky what that was all about, she said it was called dunking. I found it hilarious, as the biscuits – two of them – were tasty, so why on earth would anyone want to make them soggy.

Later, I went back to the theatre on my own, and ordered tea and biscuits, mainly for the biscuits, but somehow it wasn't my style, especially when more eyes were always steering towards me. 'What were they thinking?' I asked myself. 'Who is this black man, well-dressed and ordering tea? Is he a diplomat? Or some African prince studying at Oxford or Cambridge University?'

I still love the theatre today and whilst I'm not able to go as much as I would like because of the distance I have to travel to get into London, I enjoy the atmosphere as much as I ever did. I am recognised, that's to be expected, and I often find myself signing autographs during the intervals and after the show, a very small price to pay for pleasure of a West End show.

During our relationship Ricky spoke of a brother who was in the army, and at one time stationed out in India – she admitted that he wouldn't like me because of his racist views. However, I was surprised when she invited me to spend Christmas with her mother in Norfolk who lived alone, and other members of the family who were likely to be there.

The brother according to Ricky might or might not turn up, but Ricky being Ricky she didn't care, and I guess would be more than a match for him.

It was Christmas Eve when we arrived. Her mother, a very short lady, grey-haired, greeted me with a little smile, and I did what was natural for me and gave her a gentle kiss on the cheek. Her reaction was controlled shock, no hostility or anger. Ricky did tell me in advance that her mother was not used to black people and had probably never been face to face with a black man in her life. Her reaction did not make me feel uncomfortable, for there was no hint of racism.

Christmas morning, two of Ricky's nieces were dropped off; they appeared very shy and unsure how to react to any questions. To break the ice, I started singing a Christmas carol and that seemed to have broken the ice, because I got them all singing, exactly as I had done when I lived in Northchurch Road when I first arrived in the UK.

We stayed there Christmas Day and returned to London on Boxing Day. On our way back Ricky revealed that her mother had gone to check the bedding after I'd slept that first night, to see if I'd left any marks on the sheet! As if skin colour could rub off. We both found it hilarious.

We were known as a couple – Rudy and Ricky – amongst our friends, and were very comfortable in each other's company, going to parties together, the theatre, getting the odd raised eyebrow from some white people, but it didn't bother Ricky and certainly not me, but all that was to change unexpectedly. There was growing tension in the community between a group calling themselves 'skinheads' and West Indians in Notting Hill Gate, fuelled in part by the Conservative MP Enoch Powell.

One day a riot had broken out in Notting Hill Gate, and we were watching the events unfold on the TV news. Ricky in the middle of the coverage said, if there was to be a war between blacks and whites, she would fight for the whites. I looked at her, and she repeated her statement: 'Yes, if there is war between blacks and whites I'll fight for the whites.'

I found it an odd statement to make, though at the time I did not challenge her or question her reasoning behind it. It was to spell the ending of a beautiful friendship, however. It was something that stuck in my memory, but, realistically, if such a situation had occurred, what side would I fight for? Not a scenario I wanted to dwell on, and I hoped would never happen.

I know Ricky thought we had a future together – at one point she was thinking of buying a flat for us to live in – but I had decided by then that the relationship had run its course, and so we parted. She stayed single and never married, but about three years ago, I had a letter from her niece who told me how she and her siblings all had fond memories of my visiting their grandma's house at Christmas – especially when I had begun singing Christmas carols to them. She also told me that when Ricky – her aunt – died, they sorted through her things and found a collection of programmes from plays I had appeared in. Suddenly I realised that she must have come to watch me over the years, never revealing herself. Probably because, by then, I was married, and she felt it would not have been appropriate, but I wished she had, and she died without my saying thanks to her.

1965, and it was now five years since I had arrived in England and although I hadn't forged my way to any level of recognition, I felt confident enough when working alongside seasoned actors, felt I was holding my own, learning all the time through observation. It was a work in progress, and still is.

In November 1965 I was invited to audition for the part of Larry Presday, a young footballer in *United*, a football series that was running on BBC Television, and the character was to appear in four episodes.

When I arrived in the UK in 1960, and living in Islington, the conversations about football in the barber shop focused on two clubs: Arsenal and Tottenham. The support for both teams was equal, but because the names of Danny Blanchflower and Dave Mackay kept coming up as exceptional players, I decided that I was a Spurs supporter without even having seen them play.

Football had not featured much for me as a player before coming to the UK. I supported our local amateur football clubs, like Maple Casuals, and frequently attended the annual football clash, called 'Intercol' between St Mary's College and Queen's Royal College. I didn't participate much when the boys were playing at the street corners as I didn't like the physical aspect of the game. However, I was roped in to play a few times for the school team, because I was athletic, to play full back alongside my friend the late Fitzroy Hoyte, who was our opening fast bowler, and he was quick and very strong. Early on in what was my final match, an opponent deliberately chopped Fitzroy down at the knees, making him double up in pain and was unable to continue, so for the rest of the game I avoided as much contact as possible, and because of my speed I tried to get to a ball first and just belted it anywhere, I couldn't wait for the game to finish. It was the last game of football I played before coming to the UK.

It was not therefore a skill I would put on my actor's resumé, but there I was at the BBC Centre in White City, London, to be auditioned for the role of a footballer in a TV series.

I was ushered into a room of black actors, dancers, singers waiting to be interviewed by Mr Anthony Cornish the director, and a casting director for the one part.

I looked around and thought at the time, I don't stand a hope in hell because there were actors a lot more experienced than I was and looked more athletic and could pass as professional footballers. After an extremely long wait I was finally summoned in to meet Mr Cornish and the casting director. They briefly talked about the role, asked me a bit about football and if I played, and of course I said yes, even though the last time I had kicked a ball was at school aged about fourteen. I quickly steered the conversation to talk about Spurs so they wouldn't challenge my skills. I was then asked to read a scene with the casting director, at the end of which, a friendly thank you for coming with no hint whatsoever of being the chosen one. There were only two added to the waiting list when

I came out so it must be coming to the end of the casting session. I found a phone callbox in one of the corridors and called my agent just to confirm I'd had the audition and they'll be in touch, and her response was that they also saw a few others from the same agency. The importance of being in four episodes of a popular TV series is excellent to have on your CV, especially as a black actor, so the eagerness and tension was immense.

BBC White City had one of the best restaurants and unless you were working there or visiting someone you don't ever get the chance to use it, so I seized the opportunity. Firstly it meant that I didn't have to go home and cook, and secondly to see if any of the actors who auditioned might also be eating, but none were, not on that floor. Maybe the ones who did chose the floor above where you were likely to meet directors and executive producers.

The restaurant covered about three floors, and I chose the floor that appeared to be the most popular, although finding a vacant space at a table was extremely challenging. I tried to avoid tables where people appeared to know each other and were in deep conversation – I didn't want to intrude - and instead chose a table where there were individuals.

Several days and phone calls not only to my agent but also to other actors I knew who auditioned followed. Each day the tension mounted; sometimes an actor would say he thought another had got it, without any evidence. And so it continued until one call to my agent, and as cool as a cucumber she said she had some news for me, then a slight pause, good news. They had offered me the part! I made the call from home and just as

I hung up, Marion my landlady was coming down the stairs, so she was the first to know, and she called out to Jack who was in his office upstairs. They both congratulated me, and we sat in the kitchen for a while over a cup of tea, chatting, but whilst the tea was being prepared, I called my girlfriend, at work, to give her the good news, and she invited me over to her flat for a meal that evening.

I arrived in Birmingham in my old reliable Morris Minor car for the first time the day before I was due to start filming but wasn't pre-warned that I was going to enter what looked like a building site. There were trucks everywhere, transporting cement; the Bull Ring, as it's called today, was being built in the city centre and the area was a mess of mud everywhere. I had past my test when I moved to Melrose Avenue in 1964 and so had only been driving for about a year. It had taken me three attempts all due to simple errors but I was very happy to being on the road and having more freedom the car gave me.

The filming of *United* took place in the BBC studios in Birmingham. It was a city I was visiting for the first time, so that required finding accommodation within a manageable distance from the studio. In those days, the BBC would send actors a list of digs, guest houses and hotels that were available, and those accommodations catered for people working in the entertainment industry so it was expected that courtesy and hospitality would be extended to us. The landlady of the digs I chose was quite amiable. The rooms had the basic minimum requirements, even though my room was small and extremely cold. However, my greatest disappointment came when I was approaching the eating area where the first meal was being served. My experience that first morning, of having breakfast, lives on in my memory and probably in my digestive system.

Firstly, I was greeted with a scent which gave off the odour of something swimming in old oil; then the sight of mushrooms, bacon and eggs, which also seemed to be swimming in blackened, stale cooking oil. I nibbled the toast and fished out a curl of scorched bacon.

The next day, I decided to order just toast and tea, which seemed like a recipe for someone on a diet.

But digs were difficult to get in those areas as well, so when someone got a landlord or, more likely, a landlady who was prepared to have a black actor as a lodger, that person held onto it, even to the extent of tolerating dreadful cooking.

Speaking of food, it is one area which took a lot of getting used to, especially when I was invited to the homes of some of my English friends. It was mainly roast beef and Yorkshire pudding, and I always had to ask for salt and black pepper to give it some flavour and Tabasco sauce if I am lucky, however if it was followed with something like spotted dick and custard then I was in my element. I loved the English puddings. I can honestly say that one of the things I have found most satisfying over the years, is seeing the UK embrace new cuisines, using spices and flavourings from around the world. Today when I am invited to the home of most of my English friends for a meal, a richly flavoured stewed lamb chops with sweet potato, green banana, vegetables and maybe a few Yorkshire puddings thrown in wouldn't come as a surprise.

The floor manager on *United* was a Mr Stuart Allen, a very relaxed and friendly gentleman who went about his responsibility with a very subtle firmness and was respected by all. I did not know at the time that Mr Allen was to play a very important part in my career.

I was relieved to discover that most of my scenes were done in the changing rooms, immediately before or after a match, or in the players' canteen, so I was called upon to play very little football. However, we always had on hand as a coach and advisor the late Jimmy Hill.

I had completed about two of the four episodes with a small gap to follow and with the promise of bringing back the character within a few weeks, when I got an offer in February 1966 from Mr John Ridley the director of the Malvern Festival Theatre to play the title role in Shakespeare's Othello. It was very unusual for black actors to be offered the role, but it transpired that Mr Ridley was one of the directors I wrote to a while back and he had kept my information on file.

At the time, students at the Malvern college were preparing for their O-level exams and were studying *Othello* for their GCE in English. If I said yes, it would be my first professional classical role. And Othello was a very meaty role too. In the play, Othello – a Moorish general – is married to Desdemona, and when fellow soldier Iago is overlooked for promotion, his revenge focuses on making Othello believe his wife has been unfaithful. Jealousy, murder, and then suicide follow.

I was warned by the producer of *United*, Mr Anthony Cornish, that if I accepted the role, I would lose the opportunity of getting back into the series for further episodes. I weighed up the advantages and disadvantages. This was typical of the tough decisions I found myself making quite early in my career. To play Othello, I would have to forgo the bright lights of London and set off for 'the sticks', Worcestershire, a remote part of the country.

I told myself that I had to learn my trade – having a wide range of experience was vital for any actor – and this was how it needed to be done. I would have to leave the city and perform in plays all around the country: in the provinces, Birmingham Repertory, or wherever the parts became available. It was a strategic manoeuvre on my part that I hoped would pay dividends in the end. I mentioned the offer quietly to Stuart Allen because in that short space of time I felt I could trust him, and his response was immediate: 'Fantastic.'

'Man! You stupid,' a black actor friend told me. 'I wouldn't leave a TV series and go out to the sticks to work for peanuts.'

But in those days producers were often happy to 'black up' white actors to play parts like Othello. Might they cast a white actor if I turned down the role? This was a time when one of the most popular shows on TV was The Black and White Minstrel Show, in which white dancers and singers all 'blacked up' and behaved like caricature black people. A lot of black people were among their audience too, but slowly reality stepped in, and as attitudes changed for the better, the show was cancelled. At the time, however, it would regularly pull in over 15 million viewers. So I took the decision then that a chance to play Othello was too good an opportunity to miss. And no casting director or producer casting a classical play could then say to me, using a traditional excuse: 'Sorry, Rudolph, you lack experience.' Looking back afterwards, it was absolutely the right decision. No young black actor would turn down such an opportunity.

I had, in fact, played the role once before, which gave me a working knowledge of the part. But it had been only one or two performances in the early Sixties for an amateur theatre group in North London – the Stanhope Institute. Not professional.

Going to Malvern, however, meant looking for digs - for the umpteenth time, so that was nothing new to me. And it was there in Malvern that I experienced first-hand the joy of living in a bed and breakfast (B&B) accommodation with a fantastic white family, the Kilwicks, who really looked after me, also later the Smithwoods. As a result, playing Othello in Malvern turned out to be one of those dream jobs that come along only once in a lifetime.

There was a three-week rehearsal period, which was pretty standard; and the production was to be along very traditional lines. Most of the audience every day consisted of students from the college. They reacted very well as a whole, although I do recall them starting to laugh when the actor playing Iago came on stage, as he had a very effeminate way of walking and talking. He was, in fact, a very supportive fellow cast member, and extremely helpful to me, and so did a beautiful actress Narissa Knight who played Desdemona.

The Malvern Hills, with the spectacular views, also offered me the opportunity to go for long walks, especially in the early mornings when I would learn my lines, while I admired the beautiful surroundings. I find that walking gives me a great peace of mind, I have always been an early riser, and the English countryside is a beautiful place to watch the sunrise.

Throughout my life I have often jumped in the car, not knowing where the road would take me, just to enjoy new landscapes.

After 64 years here in the UK I still find great peace and happiness in walking along a riverbank and watching the scenery go by.

Once I even signed up for further horse-riding lessons with a local stable. I had learned to ride a bit a few years earlier, primarily because I had been offered the chance of a part in France. At the interview I had been asked if I could ride and, of course, my immediate answer was, 'Yes, I can!'

A total lie, so I immediately went and enrolled with a riding school on Hampstead Heath, signing up for some lessons, and on the third or fourth lesson, for some reason the instructor's horse took fright and bolted – and the other horses just shot off after it, so we were galloping through the Heath while I held on for dear life. Would I be thrown? Paralysed by a fall? All sorts of horrors ran through my mind, although it must only have been a few minutes before the horse eventually stopped and the instructor told me, 'Well done.'

Clearly, despite my fright, I had to continue, and I had learned the basics before I went to Malvern.

I didn't get the part in France, but at least I was able to add another skill to my CV. The episode had also led to another change at that point. To work in France, I needed to update my British passport, which was running out and would take many weeks to renew through the Trinidad Embassy which was only recently established in the UK. I couldn't wait, so it was suggested I should apply for a proper British passport and citizenship; as an actor based in the UK it would make travelling to various parts of the world for filming purposes a lot easier. I applied and within a short space of time I was given a British passport. Now I sometimes wonder; if I hadn't done this, might I have been in line decades later to be deported as part of the Windrush scandal in which many Caribbean people were sent back to islands they barely knew, and had sometimes left as small children, as they were unable to prove they had arrived with the correct paperwork.

I made many friends in the area, in particular a girlfriend who I felt might have become someone permanent in my life. She was a farmer's daughter, and I had even met her family. But I was being a bit naughty, as I still at that time had my girlfriend Ricky back in London, though I was already sensing that the time was coming when Ricky and I would part.

I stayed with the same family in Malvern again in the summer of 1966, when I had a part at the Swan Theatre in Worcester in *Sergeant Musgrave's Dance* – a play about a group of British army deserters coming to a mining town in the middle of a coal strike. It was interesting to note that the character I played was not written for a black actor. It was that of a miner, so I could safely say that it was the first time in my professional career in England that I was asked to play a non-black role. However, there was quite an exchange of banter among the white actors and me, since those who had to show they had been working down the mine had to blacken their faces and hands, and I simply could not put enough black on my skin to make it look like coal dust to the audience.

This play became the first time that I had to miss a press night or opening performance – something every actor dreads. Two days before the play opened, I caught chicken pox from one of the children at my digs and the director had to take over my role until I was able to resume a few days later. The family really nursed me well, I was pampered. I sometimes reflect on the picture I must have cut, lying in their garden with just a towel over my private parts and covered with calamine lotion! I couldn't help wondering what a neighbour would think if they looked over the fence. Thank goodness no one had smartphones at the time or I'd have been all over the internet!

However, there were other changes ahead for me now, not based on my career but in my personal life. As a young single man I had been playing the field and some of my friends suggested that we should go to the Young Women's Christian Association (YWCA) on Russell Street, London, where they usually held the odd dance, and it was where single guys like me were most likely to meet fellow West Indian women.

I had come to the realisation that I wanted to look for something more permanent than the short-lived romances I and many of my friends, other black actors, had been enjoying. I felt that if I was to get ahead in my career, some background stability would be invaluable – I also began to want a family of my own. And a big role model for me was Earl Cameron, who was married and had a family. I could see that this was the sort of life I aspired to.

And so I went to the YWCA with my friend and it was here, in 1966, that I met Lorna, a very attractive young lady from Trinidad. She was with her friend the late Miss Bessie

Carrington, who went on to become Solicitor General of Trinidad and Tobago. Both had rooms at the YWCA, and Lorna and I immediately hit it off. We found we had lots in common, both being from Trinidad, both coming from strict families, and I gave her my number and got her room number so we could meet again.

We took it slowly, building a strong friendship first, with meals out together in a restaurant just around the corner, chatting about everything – and discovering that we agreed on a lot of things about how we hoped our futures to develop. The romance was therefore built on a strong foundation of shared values and expectations, and we continued seeing each other, eventually getting married in 1968.

Neither of us were a hundred per cent keen on a church wedding, so we were able to get a slot at Westminster registry office near Scotland Yard. That particular registry office was very trendy at the time. Neither of us either had much money either, so holding a reception anywhere was going to be difficult, so in stepped the YWCA management who offered to give us one of their reception rooms, and their caterers supplied us with refreshments. I doubt there were many people who could boast of having their wedding reception at the YWCA in Central London.

The majority of people who attended the wedding were friends of Lorna's along with Marion and Jack Cassin-Scott, they were the people that meant a great deal to me at that time.

Our first home as husband and wife was a one-bedroom flat above Clapham South Tube Station, with easy access to central London for Lorna going into work, Clapham Common across the road, and Brixton market where we did a lot of our shopping a short drive away.

I loved challenges and playing pranks on my family, and one of the challenges I completed for Lorna one day was for myself to walk down the street wearing only my dressing gown and buy a loaf of bread and some cheese. It was summer, but typically, no one batted an eyelid, not even the shopkeeper. Not an act I would undertake today.

I was the proud owner of a Ford Anglia at the time and parking in the area was at a premium, so many of us had to compete for the few spaces available on the side streets and along Clapham Common. One space I occasionally found was on a side road opposite my block of flats, about a car length to the left or right to the entrance of a sweet shop, and sometimes directly in front of the shop. One day I had just pulled into the spot and was about to get out when the owner of the shop came out and started banging on the car and demanded that I move my vehicle. I stepped out and quietly asked him why, it was no business of his, and he said to just move it. I politely asked him again why, and that seemed to annoy him even further. 'I'll call the police on you,' he threatened. I said, 'Go right ahead!', locked the car and left. I was in the UK long enough to recognise most forms of racism, because I knew for certain other drivers, who were white, parked on the same spot and he never challenged them.

A few days later I received a summons to attend court in Clapham, London, to answer a charge of public nuisance. I was petrified, never having been to a courthouse before - the only experience I had was watching American movies, so I put together all sorts of questions to put to the shop-owner when called upon to do so. and I walked up and down my small flat rehearsing them over and over again so that I would sound like a proper barrister just as in the movies. I arrived at court dressed in the suit I wore for my wedding with a folder under my arm and in it was a sheet of paper with a few questions I was going to ask and a lot of blank writing paper to make me look like a professional. When I arrived at the courts, the receptionist said to wait outside the court, and I'd be called. The shop-owner was already there seated, and the look on his face when he saw me, can only be described as smug, as if to say, I got you, mate. It unsettled me a little bit, so by the time my name was called and I walked into the courtroom I was sweating.

We were told to be seated, then the magistrate took a quick look at his notes, identified who brought the charges, asked him no more than a couple of questions, and just said there was no case to answer, case dismissed. I was confused, as it happened so quickly, so I didn't move, and I'm sure when I hesitated the magistrate asked if I had anything to say, to which I said, 'No, Your Honour.' The shop-owner stormed out without looking at me.

When I related the episode to some of my friends, they all said that maybe the magistrate was waiting for me to make a counter claim against the shopkeeper. But all I wanted was for the incident to be over. In fact, although I had won the argument, I thereafter avoided deliberately parking on 'his' spot, only doing so if I got home really late and there were no other spaces. I simply didn't want to rub salt in the wounds. Who needs trouble?

Top: A parlour I frequented just around the corner from my home; Middle right: Print office going away party aged 18
Middle left: Me in Trinidad age 4; Bottom left: Third from the left top row next to the teacher Barataria EC School Cricket Team age 12; Bottom Middle: My mother Carmen Bishop; Bottom Right: With Veronica my sister in Trinidad 1948

Top right: As an apprentice on Trinidad railway aged 17 Top left: With two friends in Trinidad aged 18; Middle Left; Dressed to come to the UK 1960; Middle Right: Performing on Ship on way to the UK; Bottom left: Off to work, my first job 1955; Bottom Middle: My two sisters Aliena and Veronica in Trinidad 1957; Bottom Right: Dancing at a wedding in the UK 1961

Top : Bristol Old Vic, And People All Around 1967;
Middle & Bottom: As OTHELLO at The Space in London;

Top: BBC live Thirty minute Theatre - Thank God For UDI 1968
Middle: Love Thy Neighbour London promo picture;
Bottom: Scenes in the Love Thy Neighbour movie

Top: With Mohammed Ali at Tulse Hill School;
Middle left: With Liz Taylor & Richard Burton on the set of the film Divorce His Divorce Hers; Middle Right: Addressing the pupils at Dick Sheppard School; Bottom left: Behind the scenes on set with Baden-Semper; Bottom Middle: With head teacher at Dick Sheppard School inter-school drama 70s; Bottom Right: With Lorna & The Mighty Sparrow - Calypso King of the World 1972

Top: With Lorna and Darren aged 18 months;
Middle left: With Lorna, Darren 7 and Sheona 3; Middle Right: Christening of Sheona. With Sir John & Lady Carter;
Bottom left: Darren almost 4 and Sheona about 4months; Bottom Middle: With Lorna, Darren, Marion and Jack Cassin-Scott; Bottom Right: With Sir Clive Lloyd

Top: Celebrity Cricket match for the Vic Lewis Celebrity Eleven - I missed the ball!; Middle left: Photo taken when being interviewed in a studio in Ghana in the 80s; Middle Right: Charity Cricket Match with the Vic Lewis Eleven; Bottom left: Playing tennis in a court in Nottingham back in the 80s; Bottom Middle: Dayroom - at Croydon Warehouse 1981; Bottom Right: With Mona Hammond from Two Can Play at the Tricycle Theatre 1984

Top: One of the carnivals in Trinidad taken by The Queen's photographer at the time, Norman Parkinson; Middle: With the cricket team on This is Your Life; Bottom Left: Michael Aspell & Eddie Grant, This Is Your Life; Bottom Right: With Eddie Grant & Sheona

PART THREE

Making My Name

THE RAINY DAY

The sky was dark and gloomy,
The air was damp and raw.
The rain came slowly and doggedly
As if it hadn't the spirit to pour.
A game cock in the stable yard
Balanced disable on one leg,
A donkey under an outhouse
Stood moping with drooping head.
The smoke above the chimney tops
Hung sluggishly in the air,
As if lack of courage to rise
Caused by the frosty atmosphere.
Suddenly there rolled a thunder
Which sounded like a machine gun.
It seemed to split the heavens
And open the helpless ground.
Then after all that heavy rain,
The sun pierced mortally its glowing rays,
Running the lingered clouds in its flight
To reveal the bright blue sky.

by Malcolm Walker, aged 15

CHAPTER 9

Rep, The West End and a TV Pilot

'. . . talent is everywhere . . . opportunity is not'
Darren Henley, CEO, Arts Council England

It is the dream of most British actors to one day appear on a West End stage and to see your name up in lights. On 15 July 1968, I fulfilled my dream and made my very first appearance in the West End at the New Theatre, St Martin's Lane, as Bart Williams in *Janie Jackson*, directed by Peter Coates. I was to work alongside Earl Cameron, someone who I regarded as one of my mentors, Horace James from Trinidad, a close friend and also my mentor, and a great singer, Miss Adelaide Hall. A stellar cast indeed. And the first time both Horace James and I would be on a West End stage together – two Trinidadians.

The play was set in the Deep South of the USA, and the young character that I was playing was meant to be a stud, having an affair with the lady of the household, Janie Jackson, played by Miss Marlene Warfield from the USA. No disrespect to Marlene, but this was an example where producers felt that using an American actress instead of one home-grown would be better and guarantee success – even if it deprived someone here of a great chance to advance their career. None of us at the time knew anything of Miss Warfield, and there was a general feeling amongst we the black actors that the part could have been played just as brilliantly by Miss Carmen Munroe.

The rehearsals were not without minor disagreements. The plan was to take the play on tour to various venues and, depending on the reviews and audience reactions, it would then move to one of the West End theatres. So, there was real incentive to do well and making it work for the audiences was of paramount importance.

I still considered myself a learner in the industry, absorbing everything possible, from the solidness of Earl Cameron – nothing ever seemed to get him angry – to Horace James – who brought humour to the most difficult situations. I also found Miss Warfield's self-assuredness very helpful. But one of the lessons I had learned before doing this play was that unless a play was a farce, the less you do is stronger and makes the message you want to convey to the audience more effective. In my part, I felt it wasn't necessary to display myself as a stud every second, every movement, or it would become boring to watch.

That was where I disagreed with the director. Earl and Horace agreed with me totally; however, the last thing I wanted was to be replaced by another actor, and knowing I could deliver what Mr Coates wanted, rightly or wrongly I went along with his direction, with my mother's saying ringing in my ears: 'There are different ways to skin a cat'.

And while this was happening, my agent was dropping hints that I might do well in America, and he was talking to his contacts there. I was also still at this stage courting Lorna, though it was early days. When I mentioned we might possibly get married, my agent's reaction wasn't as supportive as I expected. Instead, he tried on several occasions to set up meetings with Miss Warfield and myself at her hotel, of which I don't think she was aware; I was under the impression that he felt that if we got together, it might mean he could pursue his contacts in America for me.

My agent also loved and played tennis, and so did I. So as Wimbledon was on, I went to an outside court specially to see a player whom I viewed as one of the most beautiful and graceful players at the time. When she passed close by after her match, that only reinforced my views and I thought, Wow. I mentioned to my agent that I'd like to meet her, because he moved in that circle, but his response was that she wouldn't be interested in me. His focus was still on Miss Warfield!

I did visit Miss Warfield at her hotel once, but there was no real chemistry between us, so there was no point in continuing to meet her socially. When I mentioned the episode to Horace, he said, 'American visa? You could get that without being hitched.' And he knew Lorna from her time at school in Trinidad.

We were playing at Portsmouth when we were told that the play was going into a West End theatre. There was joy and relief all round and getting off the tube at Leicester Square and walking towards the theatre just around the corner for our first rehearsal there felt like I was walking on air. Going through the stage door and making my way to my own dressing room, knowing that many famous actors before me had done that same walk . . . Simply thrilling!

We had the usual previews, with friends and industry professionals seizing the opportunity to get complimentary tickets and tickets at reduced prices. Little bits of tinkering took place the day after each performance, and it was noticeable that Peter Coates was trying to get me to increase my character's emphasis on his sexual prowess, but each time I walked on stage I resisted taking it any further than I had already done. Anyway, I knew it was too late for him to recast.

It all came to a head on the press night. I walked into my dressing room to find a cricket box sitting on my table. I suspected that it was for me to wear. My plan was to ignore it – but shortly after there was a knock on the door and in walked the stage manager, the director's mouthpiece, and he told me that the director wanted me to wear it. The reasoning was that the character was supposed to be well-endowed, so the cricket box would exaggerate this, making the audience really notice the region of my private parts. How degrading! And so stereotypical. I told him it wasn't going to happen, and when he realised I wasn't budging he left. A few minutes went by and in stormed the director without even knocking on my door, furious that I was going to ignore his instructions. With less than half an hour to go before the curtain went up, I stood my ground and refused to conform. Horace James was the Equity rep at the time and he, together with most of the other members of the cast, supported me.

Mr Coates angrily left my room without getting his way. I played the character exactly the way he wanted – stud all the way, but minus the cricket box.

The reviews came out the next day, and B.A. Young of the Financial Times slated me simply because of the way I had played the character. Of course, this had been exactly the way I hadn't wanted to play it, and not surprisingly, I felt great. The play closed after a short run – and Mr Coates avoided me when he saw the review – but this incident did confirm to me that my instincts about how I had wanted to play the role, my research, and my limited training, had been right. So rather than feeling negative about the poor review, I was quite positive and buoyant for the rest of the short run. What a way to start my career, what a way to make my West End debut with reviews like that and be able to turn the negative into positive.

Sometime afterwards, I did a play at the Arts Theatre and the same critic B.A. Young gave me a glowing review this time. I sensed then that the critics' reviews could be very helpful – bringing me to the attention of other directors and producers. At the same time, I resolved not to allow reviews to influence me to the extent that I would alter my style of performance, depressed when they were awful, and over-excited if they were excellent. I brought my instincts and integrity to each role I played – this was what an actor did – so if I knew I had given 100 per cent, knew I had played the character the right way, no negative review should make me change this. It would not have felt honest to me.

When I joined the acting profession I just missed out on the weekly and fortnightly repertory theatre system: an excellent form of training on the job. It meant rehearsing during the daytime for two weeks for one play, whilst simultaneously performing another play at nights. You didn't want to get the two mixed up!

Different productions brought different challenges. And I loved this; variety is great for an actor. I never wanted to be typecast and the only way to get better was to always try new things. But it didn't always fit in well with married life . . .

Christmas of 1969, for instance, I was cast in a musical play as Jim in Huckleberry Finn at the Nottingham Playhouse Theatre. For that role, I had to learn to play a concertina and do a little bit of singing for the first time on stage. Then the day the play opened, I developed a really high temperature and was taken to the theatre doctor.

His words to me were, 'Well, look! You are an actor, and there is no point in my telling you, do not go on stage tonight, as you will go anyway. Any other job and you would be off for at least two days.' Having said that, he gave me some pills. Just before the performance, however, I suffered a nosebleed as well, so that night I did the entire show using a red handkerchief to stop the blood and not allow the bloodstains to be too obvious. Luckily for me, I was able to smoothly incorporate that into the performance!

This offer to perform in Nottingham was the first time I was going to be working away from home a year after Lorna and I had got married. Lorna was working in Westminster in the private office of the Labour MP George Brown, so was busy during the day, and by a stroke of luck a fellow Trinidadian who was the brother of Lorna's best school friend occupied one of the flats in the same block with his wife. Lorna's job as I gathered meant she was circulating with a number of the ministers, reading documents that are not meant to be public, so it wasn't a surprise that after we were married, I found out that before the wedding enquiries had been made about me – as far away as back in Trinidad, a security check that, if I'd failed, she'd have been told not to marry me!

Luckily, I'd be able to get home for us to spend Christmas together as one of the actors in the company was driving back to London on Christmas Eve after the show, returning in time for the performance on Boxing Day. It was a taste of what married life for an actor was likely to be, and Lorna totally accepted this - after all, she had known she was marrying an actor.

However, after nearly two years of living in our rented flat, we thought it was time now to purchase a house of our own with the plan to start a family – we both very much wanted children - and someone with contacts at the London Council suggested a property in Goodmayes that was up for sale. Lorna, of course, had a full-time job but I had no savings and getting a mortgage for a relatively unknown actor proved difficult. At the time, of course, the husband's income was routinely used for calculating a mortgage; the wife's income was considered secondary. Fortunately, I was appearing at the Mermaid Theatre at the time in *Benito Cereno*, directed by Dr Jonathan Miller. The theatre was run by Sir Bernard Miles, and I was able to get a glowing reference from him, which seemed to tilt the application in our favour, so we were able to move into our first home: a three-bedroom terraced house in Goodmayes, Essex.

The back of our garden overlooked a large park, ideal later for taking our children for walks, and a tennis club. It was also easy to get into Central London from there, and I was gradually getting more and more roles in London theatres, where the roles varied from Caliban in Shakespeare's *The Tempest* to Babu in *Benito Cereno*. Great variety.

There were also many memorable experiences – not all of them good either. On one awful occasion I totally forgot my lines. It was rare for me to get a complete blank on stage, or need a prompt, but just as travelling the same route every day can become automatic to the point of even going through a traffic light, so too on stage there is the danger that one can miss out lines when acting in a long-running performance. For this particular play, I shared the stage with an American actress, whom I thought should not have been cast for the play. Perhaps she knew this, as she was no help to me at all on the night in question when I was absolutely certain that I had said the right lines before realising that there was suddenly a very long pause. I thought my co-star had dried, so I decided to improvise and bring her back into it. When we came off stage, it was only then I learned that I was the one who had forgotten the lines. She remarked that there was no way she was going to help me and make a fool of herself!

My only other nightmare on stage during this time was at the Lyric Theatre in Hammersmith, in a two-hander – a play with two actors – that was written by the brilliant writer, Caryl Phillips. I had to deliver two speeches, both with similar beginnings, but one was to be delivered one third of the way into the play and the other was towards the end. Twice during the latter stages of rehearsals, I had jumped from one passage to the other, so during the first week and a half of the public performances, my adrenalin seemed to pump even greater when I approached the first passage. For some reason one night, I went straight to the second passage. My co-star went along with me, but I realised my mistake too late, so a play that should have lasted one and half hours ended in forty-five minutes. The audience sat with a dazed expression, wondering what had happened!

It showed me how important rehearsal time is for any actor. Later in my career, when I was living in Berkshire, I had a very big garden, access to playing fields, woods and a river, all within walking distance. It remains the ideal environment for me when I am preparing for a major role. Being near the natural world – in the garden, walking along the river or in the woods – relaxes me and I think clearer. The house in Berkshire gave me those surroundings and I could step out and walk for about five minutes and I'd be on the river and within ten minutes, in woods. Just sitting outside, looking at the lines I have to learn, helps the words sink in much better.

In the early days, in the theatre, we'd have the luxury of a few weeks' rehearsals before an opening night. To begin with, we'd be doing read-throughs, with the scripts in front of us. This gave me the time to develop the character, learn my lines and then use the previews to further fine-tune my performance. For me, my lines sink in far better when I am actually on-stage, rehearsing with the other actors. I have continually surprised myself whenever I get a script for the first time, look at the volume of dialogue I have to learn and manage to achieve it by the opening night. In most TV series today, one must arrive on set knowing his/her lines, and with his/her character set in stone. Theatre companies try to allow sufficient rehearsal time, but there seems to be a growing trend nowadays for directors to expect their actors to know their lines from the very first day of rehearsals. Over the years, I have discovered that if actors arrive on the first day word-perfect, they are more likely to dry on stage, within the first week or two of the performance.

It's one of the worst nightmares for any actor – to totally dry up on stage. And fortunately, it has only happened to me a few times. Even when I was a very experienced actor. In June 1997, I walked on stage on a press night knowing only three quarters of the play and needing the stage manager to prompt me throughout the evening – an almost unheard-of event in the theatre world.

The play was called *Disappearances* and premiered at the Salisbury Playhouse in Chichester England. I sometimes look at the cast list of a well-known stage play and become fascinated by names of the actors who first did it professionally. The chances are that if and when *Disappearances* is published, my name too would now be credited. It was a very political new play and, for an actor, a real challenge to ensure that the audience would stay engaged with the drama as it played out – this sort of play always needs extra effort and always feels very satisfying when it works. My character Kaman was on stage from beginning to end, with some beautiful lines. It was a very wordy play, and I had very little time to prepare as we only had about two weeks of rehearsal. I knew well before the press night that I was going to struggle, but it was too late to fix an alternate date. *Disappearances*, however, remains one of my favourite and most challenging plays as we were able to capture something very magical, and I still hope to do it again one day.

One of the young actresses in the company had just left drama school and she was amazed and full of praise for my ingenuity as I managed, despite needing prompts, to sustain the role and hold the audience throughout the evening. The press recognised the difficulty, and collectively praised the production.

One critic even told me that he was mesmerised, saying, 'It was a fantastic performance, and I am looking forward to the time when you will be completely relaxed and have full command of the language and your lines. It will be quite a tour-de-force!'

How did I do it? I still don't know. I just always say that when a situation in my life is critical, I have to struggle to the end. It was terrifying in the middle of a long speech, when I did not know what was coming next, so I developed a system where I said, 'Yes', and the prompter came in straightaway and I just carried on in character. Within a few days I was in full control and thoroughly enjoyed the rest of the run.

It has never happened since, and I hope it will never happen again!

Some actors prefer television and films, and the idea of doing and saying the same lines every night, for a long period, does not appeal to them. But I love acting before an audience. It is like being on a high. Every audience is different, and I am able to make them laugh, cry or be absolutely silent when I want to. Audiences in different countries react differently or have different ways of showing their appreciation. Even here in England, when I perform in places like the Tricycle Theatre or Stratford East, where there is a predominantly West Indian audience, the comments that fly left, right and centre during a performance, are exceptional. One must have that strength of personality and focus as an actor and know what one is doing to be able to cope with it. There are some English actors with whom I have worked who could not cope with that and have found it very annoying and distracting. The parallel for me is when I watch cricket at Lords today – in the Caribbean, at a cricket match, there would be major enthusiasm, clapping, the sweet music of a steel band, the banter and the noise that West Indians make. Here in the UK, it is all very polite – that atmosphere of euphoria is absent. That doesn't stop me going and fully enjoying the day.

On the flip side, even a single audience member can throw everybody off their stride. Once, in October 1969, I was appearing in Barry Reckord's new play *Don't Gas The Blacks* at the Open Space Theatre on Tottenham Court Road. A one-act play with only three cast members, I was on stage for almost all of the performance so any hesitation would be noticed immediately and there would be no time offstage to refocus. It was a small theatre with a seating capacity of only about seventy, so it was full. In one scene, I had to talk at length about illness and death, and as could be expected, the audience usually remained absolutely silent. But one member of the audience, a West Indian in the front row, began laughing loudly whenever death was mentioned – it certainly made my partner on stage, Mary Peach, feel very uneasy as did the rest of the audience, who were leaning towards him with a whisper or two, asking him to stop laughing. In an effort to connect with him, I chose a passage of the speech and delivered it straight at him; slowly I could see him getting a little emotional and, in the end, he was more tearful than any other members of the audience. I found out later that he had lost his father to cancer and his laughter had been his way of dealing with this.

As well as these theatrical productions, I also had an early opportunity to film alongside some legendary actors. In 1972, I spent two weeks with Richard Burton and Elizabeth Taylor on location in Germany and Italy filming Divorce His - Divorce Hers, a movie made for television. It was a wonderful experience with both Richard and Elizabeth being very friendly and relaxed throughout the shoot. On the first day, Elizabeth made a special request to have a photograph taken with me. I was surprised and most flattered. And Richard, whose reputation as a somewhat mercurial character preceded him, turned out to be easy-going and well-behaved. It might have been expected that they would keep to themselves, but quite the contrary. On about the third or fourth day, Elizabeth approached me and asked, "Would you like to come over to have dinner with us?". And she arranged a small, informal dinner at their apartment that only included two other fellow cast members, Barry Foster and Thomas Baptiste. I was sat next to Elizabeth – something of a pinch yourself moment – but what happened next was a perfect example of how down to earth a couple they were. At some point Elizabeth started choking and asked me to tap her back. I dutifully complied, but gently, almost gingerly - this was Elizabeth Taylor after all. My attempt to assist proved unsuccessful as she was still coughing when from across the table Richard commanded in that booming voice, "Thump the woman, for damn sake!". A startling but good-natured moment in what was a truly memorable evening on so many levels.

An amusing incident, involving my insurance company, happened many years later. I was discussing options for vehicle insurance and asked the assessor on the other end of the phone why the quoted estimates were so high. His answer: "Well, you're an actor and could have any accident at any time with some big star in your car such as, erm, ..." And after casting about for a suitably starry name he alighted on: "Elizabeth Taylor!". How random, I thought, if only he knew. That gave me a good laugh.

Whilst I enjoyed those one-off projects, as well as my stage work, I was still interested in working in TV, especially if there was a series in the offing, I was still interested in working in TV, especially if there was a series in the offing, as a series meant regular work, and regular hours, plus being based in one place for the duration and usually being at home in the evening. And Lorna had been making noises about starting a family and had just confirmed that she was pregnant. I was going to be a father!

I rang Trinidad immediately and told my mother. As always, she kept her emotions under wraps, but she asked me if we'd thought of any names yet. We had no idea if the baby would be a boy or girl – I wanted both! And I was determined to be there for any child of mine; although there are many successful single-parent families around, and lots of different sorts of families, as a father myself, I wanted to do it the traditional way. To avoid my own father's mistakes. To be in my children's lives one hundred per cent.

Just at the right time, I had a call from my agent to head over to Thames Television in Teddington for an interview in which I'd meet writers Vince Powell, Harry Driver and Producer/Director Stuart Allen for a part in the pilot of a new comedy series.

I had no idea then about the nature of the project, or that it would turn into a show that was immensely popular, running for eight series and make me a part of TV history, but a TV series would be perfect for this stage in my life. I arrived early as usual and had to wait in the restaurant overlooking the Thames, a really beautiful setting. As was expected, nearly every other black actor was there. We often described these interviews as a cattle market as one would rub shoulders not only with excellent black actors, but also with models, dancers, extras or supporting artistes, and others: those who could act and those who could not. All were being auditioned for the same part. That was understandable because good parts were few and far between, and the odds against landing one was fifty to one. If it was a major role, there was always the possibility too that the producers would import an actor from the USA.

I had worked with Stuart Allen twice before – when he was floor manager at the BBC in Birmingham when I was in the first series of the football series *United*, and again with him as Producer/Director of *On The Buses*, but this did not mean I would be an automatic choice. I also remembered an incident that happened while filming *United* when I had been doing a scene in the players' changing room; I had to hold one side of my football boot. A note came down from the director in the box that when they called action, I should lift the boot closer to my face. After a couple of takes, Stuart whispered to me that I should try licking the tip of the lacing and threading it through one of the holes. It was a fantastic suggestion, making total sense of why I was picking the boot up, and instantly my confidence drained for having to be 'directed' to do so. I should have thought of that myself! But I learned from this. Even to the present day, if at any time a director asks me to make an extra move or action, I look for a reason to justify it.

Now I wondered: would Stuart remember that incident in the early part of my career and use it against me? I was already nervous anyway, since I had been told I was being considered for one of the four principal characters. But a lesson I have learned and have heeded over the years is the saying that 'whatever is meant to be for you, you will surely get'.

The series *Love Thy Neighbour* was to be written around Jack Smethurst, who had already been cast. He had worked with the writers before in the other successful comedy series Bless This House and For the Love of Ada. Stuart greeted me as only he could, with a joke about cricket, which was not funny, but I was so nervous that I smiled appropriately. I then read a couple of scenes with him, after which he thanked me for coming.

I had to play the waiting game while they considered whom they wanted. A week went by and during that time, I phoned all the actors I knew to find out if they had heard anything. Soon after, I received a call requesting my presence as I had been shortlisted. On this occasion, I was required to do a scene in front of the camera, and that only increased the tension even greater. Would it be a case of so-near-and-yet-so-far?

Again, a few days passed before I got another call informing me that I had been selected to do the pilot, together with another fellow Trinidadian, Nina Baden-Semper, with whom I had acted once before, Jack Smethurst and an actress playing his wife – they wanted Kate Williams, but she couldn't do it due to pregnancy.

The pilot was taped in front of a live audience at Thames TV. The purpose of doing a pilot is for the producers, writers and director to check if the script worked, how well we blended as couples, and the audience reaction to us. In the audience were friends, industry professionals and members of the public who were lucky enough to get a ticket.

There was another long spell of waiting to find out if this would lead to a series, as planned, and if I'd be offered the part. During that period, I began to have little doubts about wanting to be involved in a comedy series. I had until then considered myself a serious actor, having already chalked up a number of good roles, both on stage and on TV. But a friend who was a well-respected casting director, the late Maureen Risco, and had been my agent for a time, thought I should do more comedy. She believed I had a gift for it: excellent timing, good characterisation.

The call finally came from my agent that I had been contracted to do seven episodes! The writer Vince Powell and Harry Driver had a string of TV hits, and *Love Thy Neighbour* had a chance of adding to their success; should that happen it would make a significant impact on my career.

Kate Williams had been chosen as the fourth principal, despite not having done the pilot. I was pleased, as Kate and I had a lot in common; she was pregnant at the same time as my wife and both of our first children were born around the same time.

Yes, I was now a dad! Sadly, I missed the actual birth, though I had planned to be there. Growing up in Trinidad, traditionally men are hardly there for the birth of their child - it's a woman's thing. I wanted to break that cycle, because I feel it's a very bonding moment, so I was gutted when it didn't happen.

When Lorna's labour started, I went to the hospital with her. But I was then sent home since 'nothing would happen for ages yet' and they promised to call me when it did. A change of staffing? A sudden rush? I don't know why, but I wasn't called. This wasn't what I'd aimed for. I was determined to be there as a father as my own father never had been for me, so I was extremely disappointed that I'd missed my son, Darren's arrival.

My son. I had been sure the baby would be a boy, although no one knew for certain until the birth in those days.

It was a fantastic feeling when I was at the hospital a couple of hours after his birth and I was there, holding him in my arms. My first-born. Our son, Darren, had come into the world.

We were now a family.

CHAPTER 10

TV Comedy History

'My favorite kind of comedy comes from the awkwardness of living, the stuff that makes you cringe but borders on tragic – that is more interesting to me. It resonates; it comes from emotional truth.' Taika Waititi, award-winning filmmaker, actor and comedian

Love Thy Neighbour revolves around the characters of Joan Booth played by Kate Williams and Eddie Booth, a working-class socialist played by Jack Smethurst, who is horrified when a black man Bill Reynolds played by myself and his wife Barbie – played by Nina Baden-Semper – move in next door. The two wives are friendly and are appalled sometimes at their husbands' behaviour. The big feature of the programme is the banter between the husbands - they take the mickey out of each other continually.

However, this was made in 1970, when both attitudes and everyday language (much of it extremely derogatory, from both sides) were very different, so if watching it today, many would surely feel uncomfortable or outraged. As a result, it is rarely screened nowadays as it has become understood that allowing youngsters from a new generation to hear the racist expressions is inadvisable, given that they might then start to use these terms themselves. Storylines, too, reflected the times. In one early episode, for instance, Eddie Booth asks an estate agent to value his property and then learns that having 'coloured' neighbours would decrease its value by around thirty per cent. This was no surprise to me. And I believe it is something that can, sadly, still happen.

Some people at the time did in fact take offence, but that sentiment was not generally widespread. Mostly it was seen as the comedy it was, highlighting the stupidity of prejudice – from both sides. I do still believe that jokes and banter can break down a lot of boundaries. We are all in the same boat, all have problems, whatever our skin colour – brown, white, black or green! As a great illustration of this, for many years I used to go down to Smithfield market very early in the morning to buy fresh fruits and vegetables, – boxes of mangoes, for instance – and would get together regularly with a group of guys there from all sorts of backgrounds: Cockney, Pakistani, West Indian, Asian, Middle Eastern. The banter between us would be unbelievable today – especially the name-calling – and all done with immensely good spirit. An outsider listening in – even more so today – would be horrified.

I also remember Jack Smethurst jokingly saying to me that some of the dialogue in *Love Thy Neighbour* was similar to lines in For the Love of Ada; the only difference was that a black guy was saying the lines instead of a white guy. Apart from the times when we called each other derogatory names, it could easily have been either two white guys or two black guys making fun of each other. The only new aspect that I introduced was a famous laugh, that high-pitched cackle that we have in the West Indies and which became the trademark of my character, Bill Reynolds. Apart from that, I took the script as it came. It was only on the very odd occasion that they might have written something with which I disagreed, and I would always then have expressed my preference as to the way it should be said or done. They wrote the script in straight English, not in pidgin English, and as an actor I added my Trinidadian accent to it.

I am convinced that most of the show's success had to do with the whole nature and timing of the series. It was controversial and people who watched it either loved it or hated it. There was no middle road. And, of course, in the early 1970s, there were no video recorders, no streaming services – when a show was on, you watched it or you missed it. And *Love Thy Neighbour* was clearly one of the shows people stayed in for; notably, it was never out of the top three in the ratings throughout its run.

The series had an immediate impact everywhere it was shown. It was an instant success, far greater than any of us anticipated. It became a major topic of conversation the next day in schools, clubs, hospitals and on the buses, but its greatest impact was in Nigeria, Australia and the Caribbean, especially in Trinidad. It was an established fact that in Trinidad the streets became empty whenever the show was being transmitted. I was the first British-trained Caribbean actor to be included in a successful prime-time television show, made in England. My mother was very cool about the sudden national attention I was receiving – from the national press, her friends and neighbours. In her usual way of not showing her feelings, unless someone said something to her about me, she remained silent – that was her way – but I knew she was immensely proud.

The relationship among the four of us – Jack Smethurst, Nina Baden-Semper, Kate Williams and I was good – although we never lived in each other's pockets and we all went our separate ways after rehearsals, except for Kate who lived not far from me, so occasionally when we were using public transport we'd arrange to travel together, which was always a joy. Many actors also made guest appearances on the programme, one being a very young Floella Benjamin, now a Life Peer and Dame Commander of the realm. I remember that she looked a bit lost when she arrived so I took it upon myself to take her around and show her the location of the dressing rooms, the studio and make-up rooms and ensured that she was all right – it could be very nerve-racking coming into a successful, smoothly running show. It had certainly happened to me, and by now I was an established and experienced actor.

Love Thy Neighbour brought me a lot of fame – suddenly I was a household name – but I accepted this as just another step towards fulfilling my purpose on this planet Earth. I was not overawed, nor did I feel that I could not cope with my new status. Life, in fact, continued to be normal: I still enjoyed the same sort of fun, went out and played cricket for entertainment and remained the kind of friendly guy who would talk to anybody. Lorna, because of her upbringing, also helped to keep me grounded, never attempting to portray herself as a celebrity wife.

I was still living in Goodmayes Essex, at the time, an eastern suburb of London. Our house was terraced, with a short walk from the gate to the front door, and we would often have youngsters banging on the door and calling for me, especially young schoolgirls. They would either shout out 'Rudolph', or more often 'Bill'. One afternoon a group of them turned up and kept banging for a while, so I crawled down the stairs with my son Darren behind me and began barking like a dog. They scattered in seconds! My son could not contain himself with laughter – his sense of humour from that early age was very apparent.

My character certainly seemed to appeal to young girls. One event that all four of us – the main characters in the show – attended as special guests, and which stood out because of its sheer scale, was the Vauxhall Motors open day party in Luton. There appeared to be thousands of people in attendance. What should have been a simple walkabout for me, shaking as many hands as possible and signing autographs, almost turned into a stampede, with a heavy contingent of young girls – mostly white - all wanting to get hold of me as they screamed, 'Bill, Bill, Bill!' It was exciting, but took me back – I was an actor, not a pop star. Somehow I'd become a sex symbol of the show for these girls, totally unexpected given the nature of the role. I was, after all, playing a married man. I had to be rescued by the security guards and taken to the marquee. A few of the girls climbed up on the marquee and managed to get in somehow.

One of them even became so hysterical that Kate Williams had to go over and talk sternly to her.

So, recognition was inevitable. Even if they didn't seem to know my real name! But sometimes the attention felt very unnecessary; the odd individual might feel that it was not enough to say 'hello' or 'good morning' or simply acknowledge me. If they tried to turn a spotlight on 'Bill Reynolds' in a local shop or supermarket, claiming acquaintance, I could feel rather uneasy.

And it didn't stop there. At the height of Love Thy Neighbour, I had a call one evening that was totally bizarre.

'Birmingham Criminal Investigation Department (CID) here.'

There were no skeletons in my closet, but a call from the police… For a split second, I wondered if someone had framed me for something I hadn't done. After all, in the 1970s, the British police, especially in London, were known for unfairly targeting the black population – the 'sus' laws meant that they could stop, search and arrest anyone just on the basis of 'suspicion' that a crime had been committed. African and Caribbean people made up less than one in ten of London's population, but they accounted for over 40 per cent of those arrested under this law in the late 1970s. My celebrity status almost certainly protected me to a degree, but no call from a police officer would ever be welcomed by any West Indian at that time.

'It's nothing to worry about, sir.'

Well, they all say that before they turn the screw… However, he went on to say that they had a gentleman in custody for robbery with violence, and in possession of illegal substances, and he claimed that I was his friend and that we once shared a flat in Birmingham. They did not believe his story, so they thought it best to verify his statements by questioning me. The truth was that I had never met or known the man, nor did I ever share a flat with anyone in Birmingham.

I never knew what happened to this man – or why he had thought it would help him to name me as a friend. Perhaps he thought some of my status would rub off on him and he'd be freed as a result?

At the same time, however, there were other things happening in the neighbourhood that made me feel uncomfortable.

Like any actor who had become well known, I received invitations to open local fetes, cut ribbons at ceremonies and similar. But these occasions were not always as pleasant as they sounded. One example is when in my new role as a 'celebrity' the hospital matron at Plaistow invited me to open their summer fete. After I had done so, music was played and my wife, my son and I were milling around with tea and sandwiches when I was approached by one of the guests, a local Englishwoman, to have a dance. This was a request that I very politely declined. I was quite happy signing autographs, talking to people, shaking hands etc., but I did not feel like dancing.

The good lady walked away without a fuss, but within a few minutes, a burly, rough-looking white guy came over and verbally abused me: 'You f**ing so and so, is my wife not good enough to dance with you, who do you think you are?' He was very angry, and the atmosphere was getting very unpleasant, so although I had no need to do so, I apologised to him, just saying that I was sorry.

Then I instantly moved off, taking the members of my family with me. I found the matron and told her, without giving her the reason, that I had to leave immediately. But this incident felt like a final straw, making me realise that my stay in that area was nearly over. For the man had clearly been racist, and I had noticed elements of racism slowly creeping into the area. Travelling through Stratford and surrounding areas shortly afterwards, I noticed the words 'National Front (NF)' written on shop doors, in the park and on the tube trains. The National Front were a British Neo-Nazi whites-only political party, so once we saw that, Lorna and I said to ourselves, 'Oh no, we are not going to bring up our children in this place!'

That is why Lorna and I decided to move out of the area. It wasn't important for us to have a bigger property but to find somewhere we wanted to live, and one where our son and future children would not be targeted for their race. And so, we found our house in Caversham, on the outskirts of Reading. After our terraced house in Essex, it was huge! And it had the most fabulous garden. It was one of those serendipitous moments, we visited the house and found it was owned by another Mr Walker – Sid and his wife Elsie. They had purchased it for his mother, but she had moved in with them and they were keen to sell. They offered me the chance to go home and think about it but I said no and we shook hands there and then.

Over the years we became very good friends with Sid and Elsie, they were wonderful neighbours. I considered Elsie as a mentor and sister in all things relationship, and I would often call and see her if I needed advice. Sadly, both have now passed away, but I recall our weekends and days together with great fondness.

Despite being a very recognised popular face, I actually did very few interviews or celebrity functions simply because I wanted to get on with my work. And I did not want to be some kind of spokesperson for the West Indian community and black people. I had to make it clear, at the handful of interviews I gave, that I spoke only for myself, and it was always my view and my view only. Not the views of all black or West Indian people! I had not set out to be a role model, although people liked to pin that label on me. And surely, being on the TV and doing the work I did, should be enough to expand perceptions. The celebrity interviewers weren't usually interested in my work, either – they just wanted to know more about my private life, even down to such trivia as what I'd eaten for breakfast. And given that I had so much attention from young fans, I wanted to protect my family, have my children grow up with their feet on the ground. Either I'd court the press, and they'd be knocking on my door, involving my wife and children, or I'd just avoid such interviews. There was no middle ground really.

I had seen other actors utilise the press to gain attention or notoriety; this was not something I was interested in. As technology has evolved over the decades, I have seen how comments made years ago have come back to haunt celebrities today, for this reason I am grateful that I stood by my decision to not court the press. Today it feels as though you have to be far more cautious in how you speak to the press as words are very often taken out of context and used against people in order to contrive a reaction. I did take part in some excellent interviews; these were the ones that I chose to take part in, journalists such as Mike Reed and others always took the time to ask thoughtful questions and I knew that these would be thought-provoking and well-presented conversations.

I was not alone in wanting my privacy; Kate Williams, who played Eddie's wife on the show, also tried to keep away from the press or celebrity hype surrounding the show. It didn't need publicity stunts from us as it remained highly successful. But journalists could be most insistent, and I remember one particularly unpleasant incident whilst I was still living in Goodmayes. I had just walked through the front door from rehearsal, when I received a call from a female journalist who worked with one of the tabloid newspapers. My number was ex-directory, and she wanted an immediate interview.

'How did you get my number?' I politely asked.

'Well, we have our ways and means.'

'I don't give interviews, especially to someone I don't know.' Again, not aggressive.

I was stunned by her response – 'Who do you think you are, don't you realise I can build you up and I can also pull you down and break you?'

With that reply, I put the phone down. It was very unpleasant, very threatening and scary. I half expected to open the papers the next day and find an unpleasant article about my family and me. To my relief, none ever appeared.

On set, however, I was happy to give my views.

I remember doing so just by laughing, when the director, Stuart Allen, came into the room at the first episode of *Love Thy Neighbour* and told the make-up artist that I looked too African and she should lighten my skin to match Nina Baden-Semper, a fellow Trinidadian, who played my wife Barbie. He thought she looked more West Indian than I, because she had a lighter complexion. I just burst out laughing. However, all credit must be given to Stuart, as he never mentioned it again and did accept the fact that like all other nationalities, people from Trinidad and Tobago come in all shades.

It was customary in those days, for the casts of most of the popular TV comedy series to do a summer season at one of the seaside resorts. Blackpool was the biggest. So, in 1977, the *Love Thy Neighbour* cast was invited to perform there.

The person responsible for producing the show was Mr Leslie Grade, and I was invited to a few meetings at his home, which was near Kensington Palace in an exclusive area, where there were guards at the gate and you had to give them your name before you could drive in. I thought I was entering Buckingham Palace!

A summer season could be tough and tiring, as sometimes it meant doing two or three performances a day, six days a week, for a period of approximately three months. I didn't want to go – weeks away from my family, and no chance of doing anything else in the theatre over the summer. Kate had already refused to go, and I had told my agent that I'd prefer not to go. But *Love Thy Neighbour* on stage for the first time with only Jack Smethurst, and no Rudolph Walker, would not have been *Love Thy Neighbour* – the banter between the two of us was so integral to the show. It was staged again the following year, on tour in places like Portsmouth, as well as in London venues like Kilburn, and some overseas, but I was in a position then to decline the offer and Oscar James played my role on the tour. I only toured in Australia. This season, however, I realised halfway through my conversation with Leslie Grade that I had no alternative but to do it.

This type of audience is different from the usual theatre crowd – most people in the audience would be there on holiday, many from other countries. So, we were not sure how it would be received. Jack said at the time that he thought it could be a bit of an eye-opener for tourists, especially those from countries like South Africa and the American Deep South. They'd never see a show at home where black and white characters traded insults with each other in a comedy.

We rehearsed in London for about three weeks before moving to Blackpool. The theatre management selected various types of rental accommodations, from apartments, family houses, digs etc. I chose a detached two-bedroom bungalow about three miles outside the town centre in anticipation of my family joining me. The opening night was a tremendous success, with the show overrunning several minutes because of the laughter. That continued for the entire run with packed houses for every show.

In between performances, alone in Blackpool, I began to search for things to occupy my spare time – and discovered the joy of looking round antique shops and warehouses. So I spent much of my time driving around in my old Rover 110, looking at old furniture. I discovered warehouses in some far-out places and bought several pieces and had them transported back to our home. Later, when selling the house in Caversham and moving back to London, some of the pieces went into storage but I ended up selling most of the pieces I bought over the years. Lorna, however, still has some of them. Although I enjoyed this for a time, it did not become a lifelong interest.

Later in the season, my wife Lorna and son Darren, together with my younger sister Veronica, joined me; their presence helped tremendously to ease what could have been a boring period, but I still could not wait for the summer season to end. Darren enjoyed the show very much indeed though! At the tender age of five, he sat with his mother in one of the boxes at the Grand Theatre in Blackpool to watch the live performance. Throughout, whenever I got up to any antics on stage his laughter was always a split second before the rest of the audience and even louder and more distinctive, to the point that Nina remarked in the interval, 'There is a little bright boy up there in the box really enjoying himself.' I proudly admitted that he was my son.

Blackpool, however, was where I also had a very unsettling experience with a woman and her daughter. The minute you become famous, all sorts of temptations pop up to challenge you, and one obvious one for any male actor is the sudden interest from women. This did not appeal to me, but even so I was accustomed to approaches. Though I was totally unprepared for an offer that was made to me when I came out of the stage door after one evening performance. All the fans had already gone, and I was about to leave for my car when a woman who looked as if she was in her late thirties came over to me, accompanied by a young girl who seemed to be no more than about fourteen years old. We shook hands, I signed her programme as was normal and the older woman suggested that the young girl give me a kiss, so I offered her my cheek, then to my horror, the woman whispered that the girl was her daughter, and I could have her if I wanted.

She said it so quietly that no one else coming through the stage door could have heard. It took a few seconds for the impact of that statement to sink in. I think I might have said, 'I beg your pardon?' but there must have been something that registered on my face, because she quickly snatched her daughter's arm and said, 'Come on! let's go!' To this day, I do not know if it was a set-up or if she was genuinely selling her daughter's body. Either way it was shocking.

I am now the proud father of not only a son but a beautiful daughter and the thought of a parent handing over their daughter for sex is beyond belief.

In my 'downtime', during this stage of my life, my celebrity had one extra advantage: it meant I got to play a lot of cricket! There were often matches arranged, to raise money for specific charities, between a club or county team and a celebrity team. Celebrities didn't have to be great cricketers – but most of those who turned up were pretty capable, and the teams even included a few ex-professional cricketers like fast bowler, John Snow and Gary Sobers. Michael Parkinson (his local club hosted a match every year), the Gibbs brothers from the Bee Gees, John Alderton, Robert Powell, Wes Hall, . . . I'd do a bit of bowling, and as a batsman go in to have fun, scoring a respectable fifteen, twenty or thirty – that sort of score. We played at Lords, at Edgbaston, at the Oval, and the ground would always be packed. Lorna and I would get in the car, a nice family Volvo estate, pop the kids in the back and drive miles to get to a match. If it was particularly far away, the team manager would arrange a coach from London, and we'd all head off en masse. It was hugely entertaining, both for us and for the crowds who watched us, and we made a lot of money for charities at the same time.

I loved taking the family to the beach too, we spent a lot of time there when I was in Blackpool, I do find the sound of the waves very relaxing. Although you won't catch me paddling or swimming, I'll save that for the warmer Caribbean waters.

Love Thy Neighbour was finally cancelled – and I was not sorry. I had wanted to move on earlier; after one of the script writers, Harry Driver, died, I had not felt the following scripts were as good. However, I had been persuaded to continue into the final series.

I am proud and delighted that I was the actor chosen to star in *Love Thy Neighbour*, despite the criticism it got later on. I played the part with all the dignity I could muster, and it made my name, for which I'm grateful. There are many who do feel it is one of those roles I might wish not to acknowledge, but far from that, for it was a big stepping stone for me and although I can respect – and share – other views today, at the time it was a great opportunity for me. I am where I am today because of *Love Thy Neighbour*, because of actors like Earl Cameron, Errol John, Bari Johnson, Sidney Poitier, Paul Robeson, Carmen Munroe, the actors who held spears for years at The Royal Shakespeare Theatre, the ones who rolled their eyes and said,

'Yes mum, no mum, yes massah, no massah', they all built a foundation, a ladder for me to climb and to be where I am today.

I salute them all.

CHAPTER 11

Onwards and Upwards, via the Bard

'I think the crucial thing about being an actor is to be doing it'
Chiwetel Ejiofor CBE, award-winning British actor

My success in *Love Thy Neighbour* meant that more roles were offered to me. I was now, for better or worse, a 'name'. I had continued to perform on stage whilst filming the series, but after it ended, I focused more on-stage work for a bit. One landmark performance, I felt, was playing Idi Amin, the President of Uganda, in Michael Hastings' play *For the West* at the Royal Court Theatre. Amin was usually shown as a buffoon – a caricature of an African leader with a love of medals, who exercised his power to terrorise the people whilst he himself lived in Western luxury.

The audience and critics probably expected me to play the role with a comical representation of this 'Butcher of Uganda' – after all, I was now known as an actor from a comedy series.

I chose the exact opposite! *For The West* was a serious play, and the character of Amin needed to generate a sense of tremendous power. The sheer magnitude of the part was an enormous challenge, a test for me as an actor, and I had to wear a body suit to make me appear much larger, with latex padding used to enlarge my face and nose! The process took over an hour, so I had to be in the theatre long before the actors' half-hour call. The most amazing thing was that in the beginning we played in a small space which was upstairs at the Royal Court, where the audience was right smack in my face. I felt the reaction of the people sitting that close to me – at times I could feel them cowering or just being nervous. It was a super role to play.

Both the writer Michael Hastings and the director were extremely encouraging and supportive during the rehearsal period and very complimentary about my performance. I am totally aware that actors can be very diplomatic when talking about another actor's performance - not always truthful - so I have learned to take most compliments or criticism with a pinch of salt. However, a letter I received from Michael Hastings sometime after that showed his compliments were very genuine.

Letter from Michael Hastings who wrote *For The West* Dated 14-11-81

Dear Rudi,

V and I were sitting around gassing with Rudman, Bryden and some others, and all together in the midst of comparing actors it became unanimous you are one of the finest actors of our generation; 'Well then, why don't you give him the parts to show it true?' And they had no answer. It was like Nic Wright saying at

*Theatre Upstairs, after watching the first week - "You forget how f***ing good he is - we take it for granted." And yet when it comes to the next play they won't try hard enough to act on what they say. It seems it will be a fight, over and over. How it is made necessary to always remind them of this depth and range which you possess. One day the parts will be written. It will then seem so effortless. This long uphill war of a grind falls away into legend. And yet when it comes to the next play they won't try hard enough to act on what they say. It seems it will be a fight, over and over. How it is made necessary to always remind them of this depth and range which you possess. One day the parts will be written. It will then seem so effortless. This long uphill war of a grind falls away into legend.* **

Then an opportunity to appear in another ground-breaking series came up in the summer of 1979, when I went up to Birmingham to film a few episodes in a BBC sit-com, *Empire Road*, starring the late Norman Beaton, who later went on to star in the Channel 4 series *Desmond's*. The series, a soap opera about the lives of African and Caribbean, South Asian and East Indian characters living in one street in Birmingham, was the first British TV series to be written, acted, and directed by mostly artists of colour, transmitted once a week.

The late Rudy Narayan, a barrister and civil rights activist from Guyana whom I had known for several years, invited me to stay at his home in Birmingham, and staying there led me to yet another TV series.

One day, he presented me with an envelope: 'Look, Rudolph, I have written this stage play that I would love you to read. You are the only one I know who could do something with it! If you like it, it is yours. Do what you want with it.'

I took it and read it that day and I just loved the idea. It was about a barrister, who I knew immediately was about Rudy himself. It would make a fantastic TV play, I thought. Having once before had the rug pulled from under me with an idea I took to a TV company, I showed it to no one, not even my agent, until I met a producer or director whom I felt I could trust. That person was the director Mr Barry Davies, whom I had worked with before and thought trustworthy. He called me within a couple of days to say he too loved it and it would make an excellent TV series, and he knew exactly which BBC producer would be interested, a Miss Ruth Boswell. I somehow expected a call within a few days, but when a week went by then two, I began to fear the worse.

A call to Barry reassured me, but it was still a month gone by before I had a call from Miss Boswell's office to come in and see her. This was a producer who could pull strings, have the final say, so I was conscious of the importance of the meeting.

And that was how the 1985 series *Black Silk* came about.

The decision to go with the series took very little time, probably because it was a period when Equity, the actors' union, was campaigning for many more black actors to be used in the media, so the BBC were very keen to demonstrate their commitment. It was the first time in my career that I found myself sitting alongside a producer and director to discuss who I wanted to play opposite me in the series – a decision I knew could really make an actress's career if the series did as well as we hoped. Miss Kika Markham was chosen and it could not have been a better combination. She was a warm and generous person to work with and possessed a terrific sense of humour.

Black Silk revealed to me the attitude of the press. They had frequently asked for interviews when *Love Thy Neighbour* was transmitted, but for *Black Silk* their absence was really noticeable, even part of the Black press failed to support it.

It might seem that having a series made around me as the central character would be something that would mean I could feel I had truly 'made it' in the TV world. But I never entertained that thought, because as a black actor I knew there was still a hell of a long way to go. I'd made inroads, but I knew of actors who had been involved in a couple of jobs, one after the other, and then projected an image of being a bit aloof, above the need to go to interviews or auditions. But everyone was only as good as their last job. A precarious business! And those actors might never get another job on TV. It's only now, when I'm in my eighties, that I do feel secure in such an insecure world; now I can be sent a script and say if I like it or not, and I won't answer a 'come and read'.

After *Love Thy Neighbour*, I did a string of work in the theatre, but it took me some time to get back on screen. *Black Silk* was therefore a terrific opportunity for me to do some quality TV work again. The series also taught me a lot about the workings of the legal system. With the help of Rudy, I visited prisons, and attended meetings and functions with black lawyers, and discovered the depth of racism that existed within the legal profession. A black person wanting to go into the law faced serious challenges getting into chambers or pupillage – the final stage in becoming a practising barrister.

Sadly, I don't think this has changed as much as it should, even today. I seem to remember reading in the news not too long ago about a black barrister who turned up at the court and was assumed to be a defendant! I do know that during its transmission, *Black Silk* became a topic of conversation in legal chambers as young Afro/Caribbean and Asian lawyers told me that their white counterparts, who had often ignored them previously, had begun speaking to them in the corridors. That said, I cannot dispute the fact that we are seeing more and more black people in positions of power, something that in the early days here I might not have thought possible.

The series tackled several controversial issues – storylines included a tale of a black man hit by a car, with nobody caring until his brother raises the issue; or a reggae singer being prosecuted after attacking a right-wing racist; as well as a problem for an Asian pupil barrister getting a place in chambers.

Today I look back on these episodes and realise how these same sorts of issues keep coming back again and again in society. A black man hit by a car. A Pakistani woman detained by Immigration. It is hard not to see parallels sometimes. And, of course, it brought it home to me then how those attitudes could affect my own family. My children Darren and Sheona when they were teenagers and now my grandchildren Josh, Loveday and Latimer, how vulnerable are they? If any of them should get stopped and questioned about something, how sure was I that they wouldn't be treated with more suspicion than one of their young white friends? Luckily, while there were plenty of other black families around the Reading area, there were no reports of any incidents between the police and the Black community. I try very hard not to allow any reverse prejudice to enter my thinking and I look outward with positive if realistic eyes.

Black Silk had all the ingredients to become one of BBC's flagship series – good storylines, strong characters, contemporary issues – but there was no intention from the outset to make it a long-running series. We recorded eight one-hour episodes, but they were then transmitted on BBC2 at 10 p.m. – hardly a time and channel to target the type of audience we felt would want to watch it. And then that was it! In a TV interview just a night after the first transmission, Paul Boateng, Member of Parliament (MP) at the time, and Esther Rantzen, a very popular TV presenter, both expressed their support for the series and suggested that the BBC should continue with it, and in addition, more money should be spent on it. A few years later, I met Miss Rantzen and belatedly thanked her for supporting *Black Silk* and reminded her of her comment back then.

'Maybe the series was ahead of its time,' she replied. When is the right time? I should have asked.

The series also brought to the forefront for me other issues that needed to be addressed within the industry. Firstly, it was noticeable that I was totally ignored by a section of the media, in spite of the fact that I was the principal actor. Because I was black? And a big regret was not being credited as one of the creators of the series, which was indeed a fact. This is something my agent could have negotiated for me.

It made me reflect on the importance of having the right agent. And how does one determine that? It can be very difficult to distinguish between a good agent and a bad agent, because what might be good for me could be bad for someone else. I have changed a few agents over the years, not because they were terrible agents but simply because I felt they weren't pointing me in the right direction or steering me towards areas that I needed to explore. Perhaps too they did not have the right influential contacts. Or they just weren't asking for me what I deserved? Before the series was given the go-ahead, I got my agent on board, briefed him on how the series had come about and my role in finding the right director for it. When we completed filming the final episode, I was pulled aside by one of the directors and secretly told that I had much more power and influence than I knew and that my agent had accepted far below what I could have been paid for the role. I was not surprised, as most actors always feel anxiety or belief that we maybe ought to get more for our work. But it was not an overriding concern, as my key desire both then and now has always been to critically assess the quality of the parts offered, not the amount of money earned.

In the past, in fact, I had taken on something I regretted later, but I was resolved not to make the same mistake again. I had been offered a guest appearance on the Jim Davidson Show, in which I was to play a doctor. Jim Davidson, of course, was a very popular TV presenter, but his stand-up comedy could include quite offensive jokes, for which he got a lot of criticism. At the time, I badly needed the money as I had not worked for quite some time and had a mortgage to pay. The director, knowing my work, offered me the part without an audition, and I agreed to do it before the script arrived. If I had read the script before saying yes to the part, I might have said no! The rehearsal period was extremely difficult, battling with the image of a character I did not like. When it was transmitted, my daughter's godmother, who was English and white, called me within five minutes.

'Rudy! What on earth was that? You didn't look as if you were enjoying it, did you?'

As before, however, I aimed to work both in TV and on the stage, and to my delight, since I loved playing classic roles, I was once again offered the title role in Shakespeare's *Othello* in May 1984 when David Thacker became the new Artistic Director at the Young Vic Theatre in London. Now I felt justified in having turned down other work before to play *Othello* at the Malvern Festival – the knowledge I gained from having played the role as a young man was very helpful.

But it was a challenge since I was also appearing at the Tricycle Theatre in Mustapha Matura's *Playboy of the West Indies*. The daily travelling from the Young Vic to the Tricycle Theatre was physically and mentally exhausting – and I only had two and a half weeks to prepare for *Othello*. Impossible! So, the opening was postponed for another three days.

David was an exciting director and was very supportive and helpful whenever the need arose. Working with him was one of the best experiences I have had in the business, and we totally agreed on how the role should be played. But he warned me just before the play opened that certain papers – he named them, which I won't do here but I suspect you might have a good idea anyway who he meant – might find my interpretation unacceptable since it was very much from a black perspective. And indeed, a couple of the critics did not care much for my performance. The thrust of the criticism was that the part should have been played by the likes of Laurence Olivier and Richard Burton because their delivery of the Bard's verse would have been better.

I came away from that production feeling that I had grown as a classical actor under David's direction. However, because of the negative criticism, I decided that it was the last time the West End stage was going to see me in that title role again!

But my Shakespearean roles did not end there. Clearly, the 'times were a-changing', and black actors were being considered for roles that a mere twenty years earlier would never have been offered to them. In 1987, David invited me to play Friar Lawrence in Shakespeare's *Romeo and Juliet* at the Young Vic: an important role, this was followed by performances in Germany. In September 1990, I was then the narrator in Shakespeare's *Pericles*, directed again by David Thacker for the Royal Shakespeare Company (RSC) in Stratford-Upon-Avon. That was followed in January 1991, by Trevor Nunn's production of *Timon of Athens*, at the Young Vic Theatre, in which I played Flavius – chief steward to Timon himself, so another important role. And one that had not been written with a black actor in mind.

I did, and do, enjoy performing Shakespeare; as an actor, it adds another string to one's bow, but it also presents its own particular challenges – especially the rhythm and use of language so different from how we speak today. Part of the problem is that the audience, especially those in it unfamiliar with a particular play, might not always 'get' what the meaning is, and the skill is to make sure they understand and appreciate every word you are saying. This is particularly tricky with a play like *Timon*, which is less familiar than, say, *Romeo and Juliet* or *Hamlet* or *Macbeth*.

But there was still a long way to go before we black actors truly gained equal opportunities for the classic roles. In 1999, the National Theatre was doing an all-black production of *Measure for Measure* in 1981, and the director wanted me for that play. At the same time, they were planning a new production of *Othello* and the common prevailing view was that there was not a single black actor in England who was capable of playing the role. As a result, Paul Scofield, a brilliant actor, was blacked-up. So, I was considered good enough to play the lead in *Measure for Measure* because it was an all-black cast, but not good enough to play *Othello* at the same theatre. The same theatre!

I was without an agent at the time, which was an advantage, since I could be forthright in my criticisms of this blatant bit of racist casting and, as a response, my refusal therefore to take any part in the production of *Measure for Measure*. It was clearly risky to stand up and challenge any of the big corporations, be they the National Theatre, the BBC or ITV, especially if you are black, and the theatre tried to pull rank on me and said that I could ruin my career. Who did I think I was? They insisted I should do it, but I wrote to the theatre, putting my feelings in writing. The play went ahead anyway, and I figured that I would probably never work at the National Theatre again. I am happy to say that the climate has changed dramatically since those days.

Feeling angry, frustrated and depressed from the experience at the hands of the National, I flew to my sister's home in Columbus, Georgia in the States after finishing a run at The Bristol Old Vic. I needed a period out of the environment to take stock and decide whether I was equipped mentally to continue this relentless fight with the powers-that-be for some sort of respect and recognition. Interestingly, I received several calls from the National Theatre, including one from the director who also happened to be in the States at the time and was prepared to fly to Columbus to try and persuade me to reconsider my decision. But I stuck to my guns and refused to return.

It was during this stay I received a call in the middle of the night from an agent in Los Angeles, whom I'd met only once before in London, asking me to get on the first available flight to LA where they were casting for a new comedy series and had specifically requested me. The whole trip was to be all expenses paid for by the studio, first class flights, limo at the airport – the works. By the time I hung up from speaking to the agent, my sister and brother-in-law were wide awake, and when I relayed what the call was all about the excitement at the prospect of starring in an American series was just great. When I arrived in LA, I went straight to the agent who called the studio to say I had arrived and began talking fees with whom I guess was the producer. I was to be paid a substantial amount of money to do the pilot, filming to begin in a few days, then there'd be a break of about three weeks during which I would also be paid, and then I'd return to film the series.

I sat there speechless, first at the sort of money that was being negotiated on my behalf - more than I had earned in the UK for the whole of the Love Thy Neighbour series - and second, could this really be happening to me? At one stage of the negotiation my agent was insisting that the company agree to give me eleven episodes instead of ten, and I wanted to say to him, just take what the hell they offer I just want to do the damn thing whatever it is. When the discussion finally ended the agent suggested I go to the hotel they had booked for me to wait for the studio's call. The hotel was beautiful, top of the range. I expected the call to come within about half an hour of my arriving but nothing happened. An hour went by and still no call, so I called the agent who seemed pretty laid back about it all, and reassured me that it'll be okay. It was nearly two hours later that the phone rang and this secretary on the other end of the line gave me the studio address and said I should come straight away. On arriving, I was shocked to see about a dozen black actors waiting in the reception area, all clutching what appeared to be pages of a script. It was just like back in London, my heart sank and all their eyes just drifted to me as if to say "who is this strange dude in our midst?" A female assistant came out and gave me a copy of the scene which I found very difficult to understand immediately because of the confused state I was in. Then a door opened and out came a young producer whom I immediately recognised because I had worked with him in Kenya a couple years before and he was full of praise for my work. He had since become an executive producer of that studio, and apparently had difficulty locating me for some time as I had a new agent. He returned to the room and I felt a little uplifted. A few minutes later I was called into this room with a huge table in the middle, seated around it were about seven people, men and women, all white. I have never had an audition like that before. I was just about aware of someone saying, "it's nice of you to come, Mr Walker", no introduction as to who is who around the table, then straight into a little description about the character and would I like to read. At the end of the second reading, it was once again "thank you, Mr Walker, it's nice of you to come". I left the room feeling I had blown it. In fact, I felt that way as soon as I entered the room. I got back to the hotel and immediately phoned my agent who was surprised to hear they were seeing other actors for the role as the impression he got was that they were prepared to fly me from any part of the world as they were so eager to meet me, and the discussions he had with the producer felt very assured. However, he said to sit tight at the hotel, he felt sure they would be calling with good news, but if I didn't hear from them, just take the flight tomorrow either back to Columbus or wherever I want to go. It was about 9.30pm, it had been a long day and I was extremely tired. I stayed up as long as I possibly could and eventually fell asleep. The next day I checked out of the hotel, and decided to stay in LA for an extra day or two but the only place I could afford to book into was the YMCA. I got out of the bed there the next morning to find rat droppings all over the floor. In less than twenty-four hours I ran the whole gauntlet of emotions from absolute excitement and high expectations to utter depression. I moved out of the YMCA that day and took the flight back to my sister's. The next day I received a call from the Executive Producer to say he was sorry it hadn't worked out for me. He went on to explain that after several actors had been proposed and rejected, he had suddenly thought of me but found great difficulty making contact and by the time he did the company had come forward with another round of potential actors, and it's just my unfortunate luck that the actor who preceded me was the actor they immediately went for, and he couldn't fight my case because he only knew my work as a dramatic actor and not in comedy.

Despite this unsuccessful initial foray, I was still open to Stateside opportunities. About a year later in a conversation with my old landlord Jack Cassin-Scott he revealed that he was acquainted with a successful English script writer based in LA and suggested I should link up with him, which I did and agreed to fly out to LA to meet him.

I took a cab to the office of the writer located near some film studios. I had sent my profile in advance so he was aware of the work I did. He was extremely friendly, said I could do very well out there, but I must be prepared to come and stay for several months, not for the odd week or so, and that the visa wouldn't be a problem. I had with me a beautifully polished stick from the root of a tree that was given to me in Kenya. It was too short to be a walking stick, but I took with me sometimes. He suggested I should take it with me at all times, especially at auditions "so it'll become your trademark". In the taxi going back to the house I wondered, "Is that what I have to do to be successful in America?"

The following morning after breakfast I told my hosts I was going for a walk. They asked, walk where? Just walk, I said, have a look at the neighbourhood. They offered to take me for a drive later. I declined and added, jokingly, "Walker by name, Walker by action." And all they said was be careful. The area was very quiet, early morning sunshine, not a lot of traffic, shops still closed, so I did some window shopping for a few minutes. Then I noticed a road that was tree-lined so I entered it, houses were stunning, few cars were passing and no one was walking, but I felt relaxed. After a few minutes, I was aware of a vehicle slowing down behind me. It was a police car, which stopped. I was then asked where I was going, I answered that I was going for a walk and that I'm staying with some friends not far from here, giving them the name of the street. The policeman's response was not what I expected. "Turn round and walk the f**k back where you came from!" There was no argument, no discussion, I just turned round and retraced my steps as quickly and as dignified as possible. On the way back I made the decision that America definitely was not for me. No way was I going to bring up my family in that environment. I would stay in the UK and fight for what I wanted and deal with the challenges that I knew I'd face. I told my hosts what had just happened, and they said they weren't surprised. I, however, immediately booked a flight and returned to the UK the next day.

One of the personal challenges I revisited was performing in Shakespearean productions. Of course, the National was not the only company producing the works of the Bard. Notably, the Royal Shakespeare Theatre Company (the RSC) put a season on every year and being a member of the RSC looks very impressive on an actor's CV, so most serious-minded actors – especially when young – would not refuse an offer to join them.

At the time, however, there was a widely held view among us black actors that they only employed us to hold spears. In the background, stereotyped as native islanders or common soldiers or whatever. Just as I had found early on when being cast as 'African chief' or similar. None of the good roles. The only exceptions appeared to be Edric Connor and Paul Robeson.

However, possibly with my experience of playing Shakespearean characters, I was invited to meet the artistic director, the casting director and two associate directors at the Dance Studio in London, in what turned out to be an open casting for their coming season. I was kept waiting for an extra half an hour because they were running late, and which did not put me in a good mood.

When finally I was ushered in, the apologies were made, and they thanked me for coming. The artistic director then spoke highly of the work I had done over the years and the parts he had seen me perform. The other directors – including the man who had directed me in *Timon of Athens* – chipped in with their praises and I thought this all sounded very positive.

But their next request was downright insulting. The artistic director, almost in the same breath, asked if I had brought an audition piece with me. When I calmly told him that I had not, he then produced an excerpt from one of the classics and asked if I would like to read it. I laughed because I had to see the funny side of the situation; if I got angry, it could be very damaging for my reputation.

'No. I'm not going to do an audition. You have all said only a few minutes ago how highly you have thought of my work over the years, therefore I can't see the point of an artificial audition, and I'm not any good at sight reading anyway,' I stated firmly. A little white lie.

There was ever so slight a pause and exchange of looks, then the artistic director chipped in with, 'Well, we just wanted to see if you could take directions, and if what we have seen on stage in the past was the finished product.'

I did not think somehow that they expected such a reaction from any actor, let alone a black actor, and then trying to cover up a gross insult only made it worse.

I left the room with the usual smiles: 'We'll be in touch.' I was absolutely fuming. I had to get back home to Berkshire, get on the tennis court at the local tennis club and beat the living daylight out of some tennis balls, which I did. However, there was a further surprise in store. That night I received a call at home from one of the associate directors, who apologised for what I had been put through and said it should not have happened.

A few weeks later, I received an invitation to join the RSC for a year. Their terms for membership were that although they had already cast all the principal parts, they were certain it was possible to find something with one or two of the directors.

I had spent many years producing well-carved out building blocks to erect an impressive building, but each time I erected three blocks, the powers-that-be would come and knock over one and a half. Therefore, I had no intention of holding spears and standing in the wings for a whole year so, of course, I emphatically refused the offer. A doctor friend from the Caribbean who had his practice in Reading strongly disagreed with me, saying I should have joined the RSC as you can only make changes from within not without.

I always thought because of my decision I would end up as one of those actors who could never boast of being a member of the RSC, but that was to change dramatically for me when David Thacker became an associate director of the RSC. In 1989 he invited me to play a major role, Gower, in Shakespeare's *Pericles* – an invitation I could not refuse. It was perhaps one of a handful of times that a black actor played that role in the British theatre. Additionally, although it was customary for most actors joining the RSC to be contracted to appear in at least two plays in any one season, David insisted this stipulation was waived for me.

One surprise for me was how much I enjoyed the number of talks the RSC arranged for us to give to students and graduates. I gravitated towards them, loving how those students related to me and what we shared. When asked the first time to do one of the talks, I had been very apprehensive – an Achilles heel for me. Stand on a stage in front of several thousand and play a character? No problem. Stand in front of a classroom of students and be me? Very different! But the joy and satisfaction that I felt, the rapt attention I received and my lack of nervousness when asked the most searching and difficult questions, was a tremendous boost to my confidence. It left a lasting impression on me.

CHAPTER 12

Ups And Downs

'To grasp the full significance of life is the actor's duty, to interpret it is his problem, and to express it his dedication'
Marlon Brando, Oscar-winning iconic actor

In 1992, I was once again invited to join the Royal Shakespeare Theatre Company, this time to play a character called Billy Blue in Derek Walcott's play *The Odyssey*, directed by Greg Doran. My association with Derek went all the way back to when I was a teenager in Trinidad and a founding member of his Trinidad Theatre Workshop. So once again, I could not let this opportunity slip by. It was also a tremendously exciting play – Walcott mixed Homer's *Odyssey*, with Odysseus heading from the fallen city of Troy to his Greek island home, with Caribbean themes and a host of imaginative characters.

Billy Blue was a blind singer, so I had to sing in the play, which made it memorable for me. We were at least three weeks into rehearsals before it dawned on me that I had to do about four solo songs in the show: a mixture of calypso, ballads, and folksy songs. It was the beginning of a period of sleepless nights for me – I was petrified at the prospect. Did everyone expect me to sing like the great Paul Robeson – 'What a voice! What a man!' – or fellow Trinidadian Edric Connor?

Obviously, with a production this important, I could not expect to just step on stage on the night and hope for the best. Oh no! There was a musical director. My first session with her was a nightmare. I was so nervous, I sweated profusely. I would get the first line of the song right, move on to the second and get it right, but to put them together? No, and to compound it all, the songs were set in a high key, but when the key was changed to suit my deeper voice, I was so nervous that I could not even make the low notes. I tried to look calm at the beginning of each session, but within a few seconds, that calmness evaporated, only to be replaced by inner terror. And each night I went home, instead of learning my lines, or focusing on how I would present the character – which I needed to do – I spent most of the time with a cassette practising the songs. Fortunately, I wasn't driving Lorna and the kids mad by doing so since I was staying in Stratford-upon-Avon for the production.

I had decided very early in my career to forget about singing and just concentrate on acting. There were examples of African and Caribbean actors who had excellent singing voices and had tried to sell themselves both as an actor and as a singer, and it was obvious that the casting directors and producers were not ready for that sort of multi-talented black man. They would turn up for an audition for a play to a disbelieving director.

'But you are a singer, I saw you in a concert last week. You were good, but sorry, this is a speaking part.'

They just could not accept that a black man could be both a talented singer and actor. To me, this is hard to understand. After all, Paul Robeson is one of the world's best bass baritones, but also a damn good actor. And Edric Connor, who concentrated primarily on acting, was a fantastic singer. I didn't have much confidence in my singing, though I was always happy enough to take on a role which involved a song or two. Just not a musical! I also wouldn't want to be typecast as a singer.

I had not wanted to put any unnecessary obstacle in my way, so I'd put all my energies into acting. I also did not mind trying to fool my way through a song, if I had to, which I had done in *Huckleberry Finn*, when I'd needed to play an accordion and sing. Fortunately, I was able to get through it – just squeeze the accordion and sing a bit – but that had been a one-off. This time, the play required a professional rendering of a number of songs.

The remarkable thing about any rehearsal period with the RSC is that it is long – they really are perfectionists. The songs were beautiful and were competently arranged by the musical director. After what seemed like a lifetime, she then announced that the musicians were joining us on the following day.

'What musicians?'

'Didn't you realise that you'll be accompanied by a small band?'

I could have collapsed with fright then and there, not only did I lack the confidence to sing on my own, but the thought of a bunch of guys and or women trying to pull me back to key G when I started in C was never in my actor's manual.

But in any event, at the end of the day the show had to go on. I could not get out of it. And I did feel that there had been a marked improvement since I had started working with the musical director. But there was one song – a love song – that my instinct told me from day one, I should do unaccompanied. We were close to preview time and I still had not got it right. When I suggested this alternative – a capella, no orchestra – the musical director hit the roof; after all, she had written the music, so who was I not to fall in line with what she wanted? Her reaction knocked my confidence somewhat. The next day at rehearsals, I engaged the help of the director and a few members of the cast and sang it for them in the way that I thought I should do it. They said the rendition was great and fitted in nicely.

I still had problems with the other songs, especially with the orchestra, my having to come in at the right time, breathing at the right place, holding the note – the list goes on and on. But deep down I felt that if I could crack that one love song and do it my way, the others would somehow become easier. In other words, it was becoming a psychological battle. So, I suggested to the director that he have a word with the musical director that night, as a run of the play was arranged for the next day.

For this rehearsal, with all the cast present in the auditorium, it was decided that we would do the songs first as she had to leave early. And I would show her how I wanted to do the love song.

She took control of the session: 'OK, let's hear what you have then.'

I did a bit of the scene followed by the song, which was not fantastic, due to nervousness, but her comments cut through me like a sharp razor.

'Well, if that's the way you are going to do it, then I might as well not bother to have written it, so you'd better drop the song.'

With that, she stormed out, just as the director walked in, and for the first and only time in my long career, I disappeared into a dressing room, locked the door and cried. The tears just poured out. It was as if the many years of struggle and fighting against the odds had come to this. I could not help but think that had it been any of the leading white actors in the company, she would have been unlikely to disrespect them in the presence of other actors. I do not think so.

A couple of actors and the director tried to talk to me through the closed door, but I needed time to compose myself and temporarily work the anger out of my system before I returned to rehearsals, determined to rise above it all.

The previews began and, as far as I was concerned, they were an absolute disaster, especially the love song with the orchestra, which I was doing exactly as the director had wanted. But even a calypso which ought to have been effortless for me went haywire. A saviour came in the person of the author, Derek, who flew in, although we still had a number of previews to be completed. I had no alternative but to pull him aside and explain my problem. He watched the rehearsals that day and immediately agreed with me to do it my way. The only disappointment was that he cut the calypso.

The first night I did the main song without the band, it went like a dream and I never looked back for the rest of the run. Depending on how the mood hit me on any given night, or the mood of the audience, I was able to experiment. I might render it slowly, or quickly, just changing the pace, but always with that genuine, loving feeling that it was meant to transmit. It was amazing how my confidence in that number positively affected my performance of the other songs. I was able to detect if the pianist, or the drummer, or the bass player missed a beat; I was able to tell who was off key and who was slow in coming in. Invariably, because there were often different musicians on some nights, as I had all the confidence in the world, I was able to hold it together. I was in control. I did not know how it sounded to others, but it was well executed as far as I was concerned. Nevertheless, it was one of the most painful experiences that I had undergone in the theatre.

Outside the theatre, in society as a whole, some seriously scary stuff was happening, and it became impossible for almost anyone not to be aware that racism was still very much a fact of life and how poorly black people in particular were often treated by the authorities. This came to a head with the murder of Stephen Lawrence in 1993, killed in an unprovoked attack while simply wanting to catch a bus to go home. Darren was now in his early twenties, living in London with his girlfriend. How safe was he? Lorna and I worried. How safe were any of us if the police didn't do their job well enough to protect anyone in the Black community from racist attacks?

'Institutional racism' was the term used about the police, after an investigation into how they had dealt with Stephen Lawrence's murder; most West Indians didn't need telling this – it was often part of their everyday reality. The police, for many, were simply not to be trusted.

A few years later, in 1995, the role of the police featured in my life in a very different way. I was asked to go to Central London for an audition for *The Thin Blue Line*, a new comedy series written by Ben Elton. Ben began as a stand-up comedian, then moved into writing with some hugely successful shows under his belt, especially the *Blackadder* series which he co-wrote with Richard Curtis, and which starred Rowan Atkinson. He was now planning a new vehicle for Atkinson, and a Ben Elton series was pretty much guaranteed a primetime slot. As a left-wing comedian known for social satire, I felt he would pull no punches in the show, and a part in a series of his would be good on any actor's resume.

As was expected, there was the usual cohort of actors attending the audition. The audition was slightly different because the majority of it was about my work, and we joked about life in general. Just when I thought that would be all, Ben asked me if I would not mind reading a few lines from a scene. I was a little tempted to refuse, but instinct told me to go along with it, in spite of feeling that at that stage of my career, most of the British directors and producers must have seen and known about my work.

A few days later, I was asked to return for a further audition. On that occasion, Rowan Atkinson was present. Once again, I was asked to read and again, I left with no indication from either of them whether or not I would be chosen for the role.

'We'll be in touch.' The standard sentence!

A few days later, I was sent a scene from the script and was asked to look through it. Obviously, I needed to learn it. Then, for the third time, I attended another audition. By this time, I was feeling a bit fed up. Why were they taking so long, and why did I have to be repeatedly doing the same thing?

Once again, I left the audition room none the wiser. I called my agent that evening and said that if they called, I did not want to go back. She listened to all that I had to say and then quietly said, 'You'll have to go back again tomorrow – they called just a few minutes ago.' She also added that it was a choice between a white actor and me for that particular role; not turning up would just be handing it over to him. So now there were two factors that would persuade me to take the final plunge. Firstly, Ben Elton and Rowan Atkinson were involved, and no actor would be foolish enough to turn down an opportunity to work with two of Britain's top comedy writers and actors. Secondly, I now realised that the part had not specifically been written for a black actor. That really spurred me on!

I felt extremely tense and apprehensive on the following day, especially now knowing that the competition was just between another actor and me. Would it be a case of so near and yet so far? However, the greater part of the session was spent just talking shop. After a very uncomfortable and restless night, to my relief, the call came from my agent that I was the one they had chosen to play the role.

Even better, the part had not been written for a black actor but since I had the role, the writers got to work and added more background, so I became Constable Frank Gladstone, a Trinidad-born constable.

You might think that working on the show would have been a constant comedy sketch, however, both Ben and Rowan were serious writers and consummate professionals. Watching Rowan go from behind the scenes to "performer" was an amazing transformation. I learned a great deal during my time on the show.

The series was a monumental success, so when the second series was commissioned, it did not come as a surprise to any of the cast. *The Thin Blue Line* only recorded two series, but it became a British classic. I appeared in all the episodes.

Darren and Sheona – each now pretty grown up – both loved it! They hadn't been very old before they'd realised that Dad was doing something that was very public: something that millions of people were watching. Although I had to laugh when my daughter Sheona – when very young – once claimed that she could not understand how Dad was on television, so she went behind the box to see if she could see me properly and wanted to know how I could be standing in two places at the same time: in front of her and in the box!

I was a well known face and this brough its own difficulties at times. However, I accepted it in good humour, with the exception of the time a gentleman asked me to shake his hand whilst we were at a urinal! Unlike Paul Newman, this incident did not stop me from giving autographs but it did highlight just how people can forget that you are a human being too. I always try to be gracious, the only time I might not give an autograph is if I'm eating, but I endeavour to find the person afterwards and have a chat with them.

I am of the view that you cannot have a successful career in TV and theatre and not give back to your audience.

On a sad note, just before the start of the second series of *The Thin Blue Line*, I travelled to Trinidad to see my mother who was gravely ill and in the hospital. It was very painful to see her, a woman who was so vibrant and always active, lying in the hospital bed, helpless and having to be washed and cleaned by the nurses. Her condition brought much sadness to my heart.

When I flew out to Trinidad, I was hoping against hope that it was not going to be the last time I would see her alive, but unfortunately, it was. She was so very sick, barely even recognising me. I came out of the hospital ward realising that in all likelihood I would never see her again. Two weeks later, I was in the middle of rehearsals when I had a call from Trinidad telling me that she had passed away. My sisters had been with her since I left but I had gone back to the UK and continued working. Rowan Atkinson and the writers on *The Thin Blue Line* asked me if I needed the time to go straight back for the funeral, so I decided not to go as I had only just seen her and already shed my tears at that time. My sisters were there; if they hadn't been, I would definitely have gone to Trinidad for that final farewell.

It was a painful time. Very final. The closing of a chapter in my life.

Some years later, my father in Trinidad also died. I regret that because of my relationship with Ralph, or lack of it, I seldom visited him on my early trips back to Trinidad, even at the height of *Love Thy Neighbour*, the hit comedy TV series which catapulted me to fame and was transmitted in Trinidad with huge success. I heard that my father saw and loved the series, but it was only really at the suggestion of my son, Darren, who was about fourteen at the time, that I started paying my father regular visits. Slowly, over the years, we warmed to each other and at the time of his death, in 2002 aged ninety-four, I was calling him Dad and Pops. But I was still not totally sure he really was my father.

I was unable to fly down to Trinidad for his funeral but a call from his adopted daughter, who lived with and looked after him for several years, was to cast a shadow over our father-son relationship. Amongst the wailing relatives and long-time friends was a man the spitting image of Ralph, who claimed to be his son, although he didn't want anything my father possessed. As I mentioned before, I never questioned my mother about her decision to marry my father. She never referred to him as my dad, she would call him Ralph to me and over the years this led me to have my doubts that we were truly related. After all, I looked more like my mother and not like my father, so this revelation felt like a double blow. Was he not my son's grandfather? I wished I had known, but it was too late now, and too late to forge a brotherly relationship with a stranger. What was past was past.

Another chapter closing at this time was the relationship between me and Lorna. Although we would always both be there for our children – both nearly fully adult by now – we sadly decided to divorce. Lorna had been an amazing mother to both Darren and Sheona, now makes an amazing grandmother, and we have remained great friends and have never lost respect for each other. But sometimes, a marriage simply has run its course.

For the time being, Lorna remained in Reading, but I moved back to London, to East Ham, only a short tube ride away from all the theatres.

But London was just a base for now, and since the success of *Love Thy Neighbour*, back in the early 1970s, I had regularly travelled abroad – not just to and from Trinidad, but further afield, to Nigeria, Ghana, Kenya, Zimbabwe, South Africa, America and Australia.

PART FOUR

Around The World . . .
To A Big Red Book

BIRTHDAY GREETINGS

Greetings to you, my dear friend,
On this long-awaited day,
'Tis my affectionate desire to extend
Best wishes on this happy day.
I know your heart is filled with joy,
For I can see it in your face,
But to good I hope it will employ
For the gate to happiness is at your grace.

by Malcolm Walker, aged 15

CHAPTER 13

The World Is My Stage

'The good thing about being an actor, and the gift of being an actor, is that you are beautifully forced to see the world with different eyes' Javier Bardem, Oscar-winning Spanish actor and producer

To this day, without a doubt, *Love Thy Neighbour* was one of the most significant roles I have undertaken, simply because it propelled me to a higher level, so that in layman's terms, one might say that I became famous. I walked the streets and people recognised me. I cannot knock that, but it also had its downside. For instance, my car mechanic in London was a Trinidadian; he'd regularly serviced my old Rover 90, for what I knew was a reasonable price. After he had seen me performing on television, however, he decided to charge me exorbitant prices. Asking him why, his answer was simply: 'Now that you are famous, you can afford to pay more.'

Since then, I have not used his services. Indeed, because of the television hype, people feel that all actors earn substantial amounts of money. Unfortunately, even during my *Love Thy*

Neighbour series, I was never in that bracket. And anyway, an actor's job is always precarious. Should the series end, there was no guarantee of further work. No job security. On top of that, the pay structure in the industry did not do any favours for black actors.

But the 'fame' that being on a top TV series gave me certainly brought some terrific new experiences too. One such was having to walk the famous red carpet in London for the Annual TV Awards, televised live from Leicester Square, London. That year, 1972, together with Kate, Nina, and Jack, I won an award for the Joint TV Personality of the Year. Dressed in my black tuxedo and matching bow tie, I arrived with my then wife, Lorna, in a chauffeur-driven car and was stopped and interviewed by the press on the red carpet. I would be lying if I said that I did not enjoy every minute of it! But the elation only lasted for a few days; soon I was back down to earth again, working away as a black actor in this society.

As a result of my popularity, EMI Music Publishing Industry approached me to cut a fun record singing 'It Was Love' and 'Reggae Woman'. I thought that at the time a much better idea would have been to take some of the old English songs like 'Pack Up all my Care and Woes' and perform them with a sort of reggae-type beat. That might have been a lot funnier and gone down better with the audience, especially as I knew I was no singer. They enlisted the help of Eddie Grant, whom I knew, to produce the record – I remember him saying that he was appalled that I would not make a penny out of it. The few days in the recording studio were a bit nerve-racking, and we tried all sorts of interpretations and beats, ending up with a kind of cross between calypso and reggae. To my horror, at some stage, they said there was every possibility that they would have me appear on Top of the Pops, singing the record. Well, that never happened!

Promotional work can be very important around a long-running series, a chance for fans to meet the stars of the series and for interviews for press and other media. And as *Love Thy Neighbour* had been so successful worldwide, this brought really exciting opportunities for me to travel a bit. It also meant that I had met a lot of influential people, and many of those had connections in other countries, people with whom I could stay if I wanted to visit.

Obviously, I'd been back to Trinidad a few times since leaving, and my mother had been over to see me too, enjoying very much her time with the family – I will never forget seeing her dancing around the room with my son Darren on her shoulders – but travelling elsewhere felt very exciting, different places, very different experiences, and a score of lessons learned from each. Most excitingly, I decided to visit Africa. While growing up in Trinidad, we were fed unflattering stories about life in Africa. As schoolchildren, we knew more about English history than of our own: Milton, Shakespeare, the Tudors, the Industrial Revolution, and Queen Victoria. Nothing about V.S. Naipaul, Canboulay, or the University of Timbuktu. We delighted in the antics of Tarzan, Lord of the Jungle on the silver screen, watching him lord it over 'the natives', everything around us showed a glorification of the Mother Country and the depiction of Africa as uncivilised and ignorant. It was no wonder that when I arrived here in England and met African students and read African literature – books like Chinua Achebe's Things Fall Apart – my eyes were quickly opened to the true and real Africa. In the 1960s, I admired those remarkable activists like Roy Sawh and Tariq Ali who made strong, well-informed public statements about the struggles of black people. Roy Sawh, a Guyanese, had an incredible mastery of the English language, and quickly silenced any heckler who would dare contradict him at Hyde Park's Speakers' Corner. I enjoyed it most when there were many hecklers, it was pure theatre. A Sunday for me in the summer would be to get on a number 8 bus from Islington, get off at Hyde Park, walk to the Serpentine, hire a boat and row around the lake for about an hour, then join the crowd at Speaker's Corner. From there I'd take the long walk along Piccadilly from Green Park tube station to the Wellington roundabout, admiring the work of a large number of artists displaying their work on the railings at the side of the pavement.

I choose not to be a platform speaker, preferring instead to demonstrate my competence and expertise in my profession as an actor; any statement I wanted to make had to be in the context of my work, not on a public platform. And I wanted to help create harmony, respect, unity, love for one another and fair play in all societies, especially in my native homeland and in England. I also would not have had the confidence to face hecklers; the quality of my work could speak for me, but I still feared my lack of education might show if I tried to stand up away from my work.

By the early 1970s, however, I was aware of a growing movement to acknowledge our African ancestry: from Marcus

Garvey's 'Back to Africa' movement, to the rise of Black Power among cultural and political activists both here in the UK and the Caribbean. Soon certain symbols became associated with the consciousness of being from Africa – natural hair, dashikis, African names. For some, a physical return to Africa was the most important demonstration of this commitment. And so when I was offered the opportunity to visit that vast continent, it was something I leaped at.

In 1970, I flew from Heathrow Airport, London, with Nigerian Airways and was welcomed on board by the pilot, whose accent ushered in a strong sense of euphoria. I had a feeling of elation because on my previous travels on airlines, I had heard only a very cultured English or English Trinidadian voice; to suddenly hear a cultured English-speaking voice but with a strong Nigerian accent was both a novelty and pleasantly surprising. 'Wow, how refreshing!' I thought to myself as I was being served by Nigerian stewardesses.

We eventually touched down in Accra, Ghana, sometime after midnight, due to a late departure from Heathrow. On disembarking, like the Pope, I kissed the ground instinctively. The airport was in absolute chaos. Swirling crowds in a colourful array of clothes, strident voices, and excessive heat. We would soon reboard and continue to Nigeria, so we felt a sense of trepidation. Might we have to stay overnight at this airport? The confusion created was unbelievable.

After what appeared to be a few hours, it was decided that all passengers would be accommodated at a hotel in Accra and the mode of transportation was to be the mammy wagon — a small, light truck used locally to transport people and goods to the market. This was necessary since there was no airport transportation readily available. This meant that we had to share the space with the market vendors and their big baskets. Although I was the only West Indian within the group, I had become friendly with three Nigerian passengers who had been on my flight.

When it was time to board the mammy wagons, which already had several locals on board, there was bedlam once again. I found myself organising passengers, getting mothers and children on first, at times having to hand the children through the window. In spite of not being able to speak any of the local language, every passenger without exception followed my instructions.

When I finally got on board the last vehicle, together with the three friends I had made, we discovered that the clueless driver had absolutely no idea where he was going. Passengers took the initiative to direct him: 'Turn right.' 'No! Turn left.'

The first vehicles were nowhere in sight. At one point, our driver attempted a three-point turn on a dirt road, upon which the people at the back of the vehicle started shouting with anxiety. We were near a ditch, and even though the night was pitch-black, because they were accustomed to the terrain, I suppose they knew the imminent danger to which we were all exposed.

Throughout all of this, I was dying of laughter. I found the whole incident so refreshing and amusing. After many twists and turns, we finally arrived at the hotel about three-thirty in the morning. The other passengers had long since arrived and gone to bed. A few of us decided not to turn in, but stayed up, playing cards, drinking coffee, telling jokes, and talking.

We had no idea what time the plane to Nigeria was meant to depart. It seemed as though we were in that hotel for hours, from where we continually telephoned Nigerian Airways, only to get negative responses from the staff. I did not think that they themselves were even aware of the complete disorder and confusion that existed.

Eventually, a call came through that the flight was preparing to leave, but no time was given, and we were simply instructed to be ready in half an hour. Two mammy wagons and one car arrived – it was obvious that we were going to be packed in like sardines. Once again, I took it upon myself to organise the passengers, and to get the families and older people off first.

All's well that ends well, and around midday we finally boarded the flight for Lagos.

My stay in Lagos had been arranged by a Nigerian actress, who lived in the impressive St John's Wood area in London, a property she owned, just a couple of blocks away from Lord's Cricket Ground. She insisted that I stayed with her parents and brother, and I was told that the father was a chief, and the family supposedly very wealthy indeed.

I was met at the airport by her brother, a very dapper young man. We drove in his sports car directly to his home: an enormous house on two floors with a Bentley and a Rolls-Royce parked under the house. I had not anticipated such a display of wealth but was grateful as it made my first visit to Africa immediately memorable, not least because it highlighted my ignorance of the continent.

A young man over six feet tall, as if by magic, just appeared from nowhere and hurriedly took my suitcases out of the car and disappeared upstairs. He did not even appear to acknowledge me when I greeted him, so I began to think that I might actually be in the wrong place – they'd collected me by mistake! I was then taken upstairs to what appeared to be a kitchen, but which was also used as a dining room and a sitting room and which seemed unkempt. There I was introduced, first to the father, an elderly guy with a big stomach who was sitting at a table reading the newspaper. His wife, slightly younger, was sitting in the corner of the room. She just smiled and said, 'Hello!' and then remained silent. My first impression was that she did not want me there, and if that was the case, then where would I stay for the next eight days? I was on a very small budget and still had to complete the other leg of my journey: ten days in Ghana.

My introduction continued as the son then took me along a corridor, negotiating old furniture and pieces of odds and ends, to a spacious room with a half made-up double bed in the middle and a single put-u-up or settee bed leaning against the wall. The room was clean and tidy with minimum furniture and my suitcases were placed on the floor next to the put-u-up. This, apparently, was the son's room, and I was going to be sharing it with him. He told me that he was out most of the time, so I would enjoy a degree of privacy and added, without my asking the question, that his mother, although she appeared cold, was hospitable but spoke very little when his dad was around.

I quickly and quietly scolded myself for this very stereotypical thought. 'Stop it, Rudy. That's your English attitudes talking,' I told myself in sotto voice.

However, the room was clean and there was no need to venture to other parts of the building. In fact, I would be out all day and I would only be there to sleep. I was prepared to mix the rough with the smooth, but there was something not quite right about the chief, who was supposed to be very wealthy; I just could not understand the neglected appearance of the place.

The son suggested that we go out for a meal and by then I was really hungry, so I welcomed the diversion. He took me to a popular restaurant in downtown Lagos, where I sampled a real Nigerian dish: okra soup, jollof rice, a stew. By the time we had finished eating, I was dog tired, so he took me back to the house.

As the car pulled up, the tall guy appeared from nowhere and opened the door for the son and then just vanished, when he realised that he was not needed as the son was going on to a club, and only dropping me off. Once again, he did not respond when I greeted him. I then assumed that he did not speak English, so I decided that the first word I had to learn in Yoruba was 'Hello'.

The house was very poorly lit, so finding the toilet and bathroom required some degree of a detective's work. I was up early, feeling rejuvenated as I had slept through the night without a hitch and the other bed did not appear to have been slept in at all. I could see no movement in the kitchen area or around the house and I was not going to explore. I found a tiny galvanised enclosure in the yard that turned out to be a shower. I returned to my room, got dressed and decided to find somewhere to have breakfast. Firstly, I had to find somewhere to change some of my traveller's cheques. I found a bank and took out enough of the local currency to last me for the duration of my stay there. Eventually, I found a little café, not far from the bank, where I enjoyed a hearty breakfast.

I discovered by then that most people spoke English as a second language, so I wondered why the tall young man at the house did not respond when I spoke to him. After breakfast, I decided to go for a walk, just to explore the area, and found myself in a market area. To my surprise, I encountered the servant and at the same moment, he spotted me. 'Hello!' we both said simultaneously. He even shook my hand and introduced himself. He spoke standard English, and then said something that left me speechless. He explained that he was just the servant and could not be seen talking to any of the chief's friends!

I told him a bit about myself, what I did for a living and how I came to be staying there, as well as some of the things I wanted to see whilst there. In particular, I wanted to buy some of the local carvings, because I knew about the artistic skills of the local craftspeople, mostly men. Hence, the servant became my guide and took me to where he knew I could purchase the best carvings.

The trek was about to begin. He took me through the marketplace, made accessible by so many narrow roads that I began to lose my bearings, yet knowing that somehow I had to trust his instinct and let him lead. Fortunately, we found a sculptor who agreed to carve a couple of masks that he promised would be ready for early the next morning. A price was negotiated by my guide, who had already informed me that when the carver asked for a down payment, I should refuse him. I needed to change some more money to pay for the carvings, but when I suggested going to the bank, he said that he could have gotten me a much better rate of exchange elsewhere. He then took me through areas that I would not have seen otherwise, some seedy and frightening, and because he was extremely tall, he made one stride to my three, so I was playing catch-up all the time.

I also felt that because of his servant mentality, he did not want to walk beside me, and that made me feel uncomfortable and vulnerable, because it was not my lifestyle, and because I was in a strange land with customs that were alien to me. Although they were all people of my colour, I felt my safety was at risk. We were on a narrow road with a number of small, dilapidated shops and cafes, when he stopped suddenly, looked around, then knocked on a door, while he continued to take furtive glances until someone said something on the other side in a language other than English.

The door was then opened by a woman, who took a quick look outside before taking us up a flight of stairs to a little office where a little guy, probably in his 40s, was sitting behind a desk. He asked how many travellers' cheques I wanted to change. His rate was exceptionally high, and I declined to change them all, just signing over a few. It was clearly an illegal operation. I came out of that building sweating, and with my guide advising me to tuck my money safely away.

We ended up in a restaurant for a meal. By then, much to my relief, our communication had become less of a servant and master relationship. We returned to the house that afternoon, but as was expected, he left me as soon as we got to one road away from the house and reminded me that I had to continue on my own.

Late that afternoon, the son returned and offered to take me to a local shabeen. It turned out to be a place where a number of young men and women hung out, drank, talked, smoked a lot, danced a bit, and more than likely ended up in bed. My host seemed to be very popular. After ten minutes of sipping my first orange juice, I wanted to leave but thought it was best to remain there for about an hour, although I was rather tired after the day's adventure. My host readily agreed to drop me back at the house, quite rightly so, as I was proving to be rather boring company.

On the following morning, I was up early, had my shower and came into contact with the chief. We exchanged civil greetings and I asked for the use of his telephone so that I could call my Ambassador at the hotel. The Ambassador agreed to pick me up that lunchtime for us to have a meal. I had just enough time to collect the carvings, return to the house, have another shower, change and be ready for pick-up time.

As pre-arranged, I met my guide a block away, went to a café for breakfast, then collected the carvings, which were beautifully done with only the final polishing to be completed. We returned to the house, adopting the same routine as the day before. I showered, changed and was looking out for the Ambassador's car, obviously to go out and meet him the moment he arrived. About fifteen minutes before the appointed time, a car pulled up outside the house, and to my surprise, out stepped Jocelyn, a fellow Trinidadian ex-wife of a Nigerian chief and senior politician, whom I had met twice in London; she was also a friend of the Ambassador. Was it a coincidence that she had arrived just a few minutes before the Ambassador?

She paused, looked around, a bit uncertain that she was at the correct house, and as if by magic, the servant appeared. They spoke briefly and her expression changed when it dawned on her that she was at the right house. I dashed back inside to dab on a little more aftershave, and the new cologne I had bought in the duty-free shop, and by the time the servant tapped on my door, I was sufficiently spruced up.

I expressed delight in seeing her and she the same. She said that the Ambassador had an urgent request to call on the President. He had tried several times that morning to contact me, eventually asking Jocelyn to make contact, and if possible, to take me to lunch. The Ambassador also regretted that he was unable to have me stay with him, having just arrived in Nigeria and staying himself at a hotel until the Ambassador's residence was ready.

As I was about to escort her out of the room, she told me to pack my suitcase and bring it with me. It was an order, not a request.

I paid my respects and thanks to my host for his hospitality, promising to carry his salutations to his daughter in London, and explaining that I was being collected by the diplomatic representative of my country of birth.

We drove to Jocelyn's apartment, just on the outskirts of Lagos centre, where I spent the rest of my stay in Nigeria.

Just over a week later, I was back in Accra, Ghana, where I stayed with the Busby family. There could not have been a greater contrast to my welcome in Lagos. The house itself was similar in size and age but that was where the similarity stopped. It was warm and welcoming. I had known the late Eileen Busby in London, for some time, and when I mentioned my desire to visit Ghana, she had immediately suggested I stay with her parents who lived in Accra.

Her father, Mr Busby, was a retired medical doctor, born in Trinidad, who trained as a doctor in London but felt that his skills would have been of better service to the people of Africa, so he set up his practice there and saw patients from his own home. He talked at length about those early days, when his only means of transport was his legs. It was not unusual to be woken up in the middle of the night and walk for a mile or more through the bushes, to attend to a sick person. He was also a very close friend of George Padmore, Pan Africanist and fellow Trinidadian, who had emigrated to Ghana, and Kwame Nkrumah who led the Gold Coast to independence from Britain in 1957. Mrs Busby, one of the most beautiful and warm women I have ever met, was Ghanaian by birth.

Since this first trip, I have travelled to many parts of Africa – Zambia, Zimbabwe, Kenya, Nigeria and Ghana – but I felt myself physically and spiritually locked into Ghana, the people, their warmth, their history and their sense of humour. I experienced the pain of seeing the dungeons on the shores of Accra, from where it is possible that my ancestors had been chained and shipped out to the Caribbean. I experienced the absolute joy of dancing the popular West African dance, the High Life, with villagers whom I had never met and who kept talking to me in Gha, the local language, because they were convinced that I was Ghanaian. I was even offered a piece of land by a chief, because I was a friend of Dr Busby.

Eileen, who had surprisingly flown into Accra the day after I arrived, decided to take me, together with her sister, Margaret and their mother, on a day trip to Takoradi and Sekondi. The journey was quite a long drive from Accra. We were going into Takoradi, when I had the most extraordinary experience. I started describing things around the corner as though I knew the whole area. It all felt and looked so familiar, as if I had been there before – just such a wonderful, spiritual feeling. We were visiting their grandmother, a strong and active old lady, who was in her 90s. The house itself, like many other houses in the area, was a mud hut, but very clean and welcoming. The toilet facility was a cesspit in the yard, and the water was fetched from a standpipe just a block away. We had travelled with our own picnic lunch, so after eating, we paid a visit to a cousin, who lived not far away and who was a presenter on Ghana Television.

Her home was modern and filled with modern-day luxuries, befitting such a high-profile person. By the time we had talked and had drinks, it was far too late to make the long journey back to Accra, so they decided to stay the night and leave early the next morning. I had the choice of staying over with their cousin or with their grandmother – I chose to go back to the hut.

That night, I slept close to Mother Earth and it was the most beautiful, peaceful and comfortable shut-eye that I had ever experienced. Early in the morning, I went out to a standpipe and stood there in my birthday suit to have a shower, using a calabash – a utensil made from the hard shell of the calabash fruit – to pour the water over my head, just as I did as a child growing up in Trinidad. Then I threw the wrap that the grandma had lent me over my body and took a walk along the coast.

From this trip onwards, Ghana has become one of my spiritual homes.

My love/hate relationship with Nigeria continued, when in 1983 I returned to shoot a film entitled The Death of a Black President, a movie written, produced and directed by a Nigerian friend, who in the 1970s lived and worked here in England, as an actor. The casting of most of the principal parts was done in London, with one exception. An actor, who was a part of our circle of friends in the 1960s but was then living in Los Angeles, flew in to join us. There was much unease amongst many of the actors as to the legitimacy of the project, which seemed uncertain to materialise. One week, it looked as if it was cancelled, with the director having flown back to Lagos, then the next it was on, and that continued for several weeks, until finally a contract of sorts was signed. As a result of the uncertainty, my then agent insisted that most of my fees be deposited here in London and my return ticket be issued before I departed.

I had visited Nigeria before, so I was well aware of the do's and don'ts and the precautions that I had to take to safeguard myself. However, I certainly was not prepared for the repercussions that occurred when one of the actresses in the company whipped out her camera in the airport and took a photo of us. Within seconds, we were surrounded by the military police – as in many countries, it was forbidden to take photos in the airport. Fortunately, she was able to keep the camera, but only after a stern warning not to take any further photos.

We were to be transported in minivans, but I was invited to travel in the car owned by the director and his wife, whom I knew from London. I insisted on sitting in the back as it appeared to have more leg space there and also a place to put my hand luggage that contained my personal documents. A local newspaper in English was on the back seat of the car and on opening it, there staring at me was a headline: BRITISH GOVERNMENT CANNOT GUARANTEE THE SAFETY OF ITS NATIONALS. As I read further on, I realised that it was referring to our group of actors and technicians, who were out there to shoot the movie!

The movie was about a military coup that had taken place just a few years before and a number of prominent people including the ex-leader's family disapproved of its filming. I knew then that there was no turning back as if I had said then and there that I wanted to return to England and had refused to do the film, my life might have been in danger. It did not help to ease my discomfort when after only about ten minutes of driving there was a military roadblock.

The car was searched at gunpoint and then waved on. There were two more such roadblocks with the director giving one of the officers what appeared to be a monetary bribe, and to top it all, further on, I saw the body of a dead man at the side of the road.

We arrived in the village of Badagri, on the outskirts of Lagos and drove into an enclosed compound, developed on about three acres of land, with a number of huts scattered around. We were told that it was going to be our base for the next four weeks; but for some others, it was only to be for two weeks. A surprised look registered on all of our faces, because we were all used to staying in a hotel when on location, not in huts. Somehow, though, I liked what I saw and welcomed the opportunity to be amongst the local people.

A few expressed their displeasure, but the main objector was the actress who had almost ended up behind bars for taking the photo at the airport. With this in mind – and the newspaper headline fresh in my memory – I immediately worked out that the reason behind having us located out there and not at a downtown hotel was to avoid attracting attention.

The first day of filming set the pattern for the rest of the schedule. Some of us were told to be ready for a 7.30 pick-up the following morning but the minibus did not arrive until nine. An hour after we got to the location, the director turned up and announced that there was a change of location, so back in the vehicles we went, and eventually shot completely different scenes from the ones that were scheduled.

On the third day of my stay, I was able to get hold of a telephone and I called my Trinidadian friend in Lagos. This came as a total surprise to her, and it was yet a bigger surprise when I told her about the movie that I was shooting, because she had heard about it and was fully aware that there could have been some danger attached. She even offered me the security of staying at her place and having a car pick me up each day and take me to the location, but I declined the offer.

In spite of the cloak and dagger existence of the filming schedule, I was enjoying the challenge of working in a different environment, and in addition, the village and villagers outside the compound became a haven of spiritual fulfilment. Whenever I got a break, I would wander through the village and just talk to the old people, most of whom spoke English, or just sit by the side of the road. The people were poor compared to Lagos, but there was a pride in the way they conducted themselves, and the effort they expended in keeping the village clean. As a result, I did not refuse when I was asked to share some food with a local family.

Our filming in Lagos was not a case of all work and no play. For example, we were invited to a typical Nigerian wedding that was an all-day affair. We were all discussing what would be the most suitable wear, whether men should wear suits, but in fact, none of us, men or ladies, had African-styled clothes. Eventually, one of our actresses turned up in a hat and elbow-length white gloves, befitting Ascot! We also went to a house party, where we were having a really enjoyable time until about midnight when I announced that it was time for me to be taken back to Badagri. Only then was I told that we all had to stay there until it was daylight. It was then explained that although there was no curfew in place, it was unsafe to drive when it was dark. After this, I readily declined any other invites that I got.

Since the film was completed a few days ahead of schedule, I was free to go out and explore the markets, or visit homes of Nigerians I knew. The day before I flew back to London, Jocyline – my Trinidadian friend living in Lagos – took me out to lunch and arranged for me to visit the home of a diplomat friend of hers, someone she felt I should meet. I was to spend some time with him whilst she went on to fulfil a previous engagement before collecting me later in the afternoon.

The security surrounding that house was quite disconcerting, for not only was there the installed alarm system but also two ferocious-looking Dobermans. We had been talking for about an hour when the telephone rang and although the diplomat spoke in Yoruba, I sensed something was very wrong. After he hung up, he said that he had to attend to urgent business. He hastened to add that while it was possible for him to take me along, he was not sure what time he would be back, so he suggested that I stay at his home until my friend turned up in approximately two hours' time or when his daughter came back from school. He left snacks for me to nibble on and, as he left, indicated two doors then gave me a stern warning not to open them: the Dobermans were in there and I would be dead meat if I did!

For two and a half hours, I sat in one place sweating, not daring to move, listening to every movement coming from the rooms and going over in mind every conceivable scenario. Were the doors actually locked? What if the dogs found a way of opening a door from the inside. What means of escape were open to me? What if the daughter turned up using a different entrance and opened the door not expecting me there? If I opened the door to go outside, would it trigger an alarm? Nearly two hours later, my friend arrived and blew the car horn. The dogs barked and I moved from that seat so quickly that those Dobermans would have needed wings to catch me. I heard more ferocious barking, but I was already opening the car door and did not even look back. I spent the night at my friend's home and arranged to have my suitcases brought to the airport the next day.

Seven of us were flying back to London – four technicians and three actors. We all checked in our suitcases, but I also saw that the actor, who was based in Los Angeles, was being spoken to by an airport official and then taken to a back office. I wasn't worried because the body language of both parties had not been aggressive. However, a long time elapsed, and none of the other members of the airport staff seemed to know what was going on. Finally, I was approached by the same gentleman who had taken my colleague away and he asked me quite nicely if I were a friend of the actor. I answered in the affirmative and gave him a brief history of our working relationship in London.

'That's fine, then I'll allow him to join you all, and he must thank you.'

When I asked him why that was so, he simply said that I should let the actor himself tell me. My colleague emerged a few minutes later, sweating profusely, and continued to do so until we got on board. When I asked him what that was all about, it turned out that he was carrying illegal drugs and as is the norm 'I could have been locked up and the keys thrown away'.

It was then my turn to sweat because I had left my suitcase with him the day before to take to the airport with the rest of the luggage. What if he had opened my suitcase and put his drugs in there, even though I had it locked?

I only relaxed when I got through customs in London.

The film was released in the UK as part of a Commonwealth Institute event; I saw it on its release and was quite pleased with the story and how it came across but it was never expected to be a blockbuster movie. It was also shown in several venues throughout Africa.

Ghana may well have become a spiritual home; but my heart will always belong to Trinidad, a Trini to de Bone. After nearly ten years away, I made two trips back home within the space of a few months. There was great excitement and expectancy on the part of the members of my immediate family and those who were awaiting our arrival at home. I was married to Lorna at that time, a fellow Trinidadian, whose father I knew disapproved of our marriage: at that time, actors did not have a high reputation amongst the older West Indians, acting not being regarded as a 'proper job'. We had a handsome eighteen-month-old son, Darren. It was around winter, so we were well-clothed for our departure from Heathrow. On our arrival at Piarco International Airport in Trinidad, the heat came at us like a fiery furnace. We were in total discomfort, sweating profusely as we queued to go through immigration. After the usual greetings of various uncles, aunts, cousins and in-laws, we headed for my mother's place; a house I had not visited before as she had moved since I left the island.

As we were driving along the Eastern Main Road, the first thing that registered was the sight of a security guard, carrying a gun, not just a baton. I also noticed houses surrounded by iron bars or burglar-proof gates and doors.

'What is happening here?' I wondered. 'This is not the Trinidad I left ten years ago. People are caged in!'

The journey lasted about half an hour and for the first time I saw armed policemen in the country of my birth. The house where my mother lived was not yet burglar-proofed, but later that was to change, though not with iron bars but with wooden latticework. We joked about our relatives and friends having to live behind bars, as if they were living in a jail, like domestic prisoners.

I was immediately engulfed in the humour of Trinidadians, which as previously mentioned was quite unique and spontaneous. I remembered going for a walk on the first night with my sisters and cousins when a cyclist rode past, pretty close to us, so I shouted, 'Aye way yuh light?'

As quick as a flash, he replied, 'In meh pants.'

On this first night, there was a full moon illuminating the darkness, and there was something magical about being in Trinidad on a moonlit night. H. D. Carberry, a West Indian poet, captured it nicely in his poem, 'I Shall Remember'. I suggested that we all took a walk over to one of my favourite roaming spots, The Coconut. It was an ideal place to stroll through with a girlfriend, under the light of the moon, or to use a clearing there at the weekends for a wind-ball cricket match. For young children, it was also just right for playing hide and seek games. Regrettably, I was to receive a rude awakening when my cousins told me that the trees and vegetation in the area had been bulldozed and there was now a large housing estate there. Sadly, I was told that what little of the magical playground of my youth that remained was not safe to roam around at night anymore.

There had been many other changes in the ten years that I had been away. Some of the older folks had died, most notably my Aunt Ada, my sister's father, two adopted uncles, and an older cousin – all people whom I had loved as a child. I was, however, consoled by the evidence that at least the priceless and spontaneous Trini humour was still intact.

As an example of this: My then wife, Lorna, gave a taxi driver the wrong fare for a trip and by way of apology she said, 'Oh dear.' Immediately the taxi driver responded, 'Madam, is not deer in season you know, is manicou.' His witty response came with a pun on the word 'dear'; since a deer is an animal and so too is the manicou, a marsupial opossum.

On another day, while walking through Woodford Square in downtown Port-of-Spain, I could not help but notice a woman, who was clearly in her late stage of pregnancy, wearing the shortest mini skirt imaginable. A guy, who obviously knew her, shouted from across the park, 'But eh, Agnes, yuh pregnant?' Then taking a slight pause for effect, added, 'An ah could see de baby head.' That of course, was his humorous way of telling her that the dress was far too short!

My two weeks' stay in Trinidad was short but rewarding. My son Darren was able to meet relatives on his mother's side as well as mine, able to see the village in which I had been born and to experience the rich culture and, even at his early age, enjoy some of the humour. However, I realised the relationship among neighbours was not as close as before, that 'the village' was no longer 'raising the child'. Whether it was modernity, progress or technology, life as I knew it had changed irrevocably. I do still feel nostalgic for my past, its communal values, and it frightened me then to see the issues we faced in Britain being replicated in the Land of the Steel Band.

The next time I returned to Trinidad was in 1972 as a result of the success of *Love Thy Neighbour* – a very different sort of trip. It began with a special flight from Heathrow, London, to the Piarco International Airport in Trinidad: the inaugural flight of British West Indian Airways (BWIA). *Love Thy Neighbour* was an extremely popular show in the Caribbean, especially in Trinidad, so it was inevitable that Nina and I, as Trinidadians, together with Kate Williams (Jack Smethurst was unable to come due to other commitments), would be invited to join the members of a very high-powered group of dignitaries from Trinidad and Barbados.

As soon as we stepped off the aircraft, we were greeted by the scintillating, refreshing, breath-taking music of a steel orchestra playing the *Love Thy Neighbour* theme tune, which was followed by the latest calypsos for the season. We were given a red-carpet reception at the airport and after press interviews, driven to the Hilton Hotel in Port-of-Spain to start two weeks of receptions and sightseeing in Trinidad, then Tobago, and lastly Barbados, before flying back to London.

On my return to London, the manager of BWIA invited me to become their public relations (PR) representative in the United Kingdom. There was to be no salary attached, just the opportunity to fly to Trinidad at least twice a year when a space became available. The project would also give me the opportunity to promote my homeland, Trinidad and Tobago, of which I am very proud. I did not hesitate to accept the offer, even though I knew that it was going to be a challenge to get the time off due to filming schedules, and also I knew nothing of the aviation industry. I was given an airport pass – 007 – which was the envy of many airline staff members since 007 is of course James Bond's number. This pass allowed me to go on board and meet the aircraft passengers and crew when the planes landed at Heathrow Airport. If there were any problems being encountered by passengers, I could act as a mediator.

I threw a lot of energy into improving the image of my country and the airline, for a number of years. The activities included organising promotional tours throughout the length and breadth of England, and even as far afield as Sweden. Many of those I worked with on this advised me against giving my services free of charge, but I did not listen. Neither did I pay much attention when the then head of the Barbados Tourist Board let me know how much she was paying a Public Relations Company in London for work that didn't generate as much coverage as I got for BWIA; I only got occasional free trips. Her advice was also reinforced by a relative of mine, who held a senior position in the airline. He even went a stage further and suggested to me that I should try to secure a written contract. Their warnings were well-founded because a few years later, the management of BWIA – or *Bwee* as it was fondly called or *"Best Women In The Air"*–even *"But Will It Arrive"* engaged an English PR company at an exorbitant cost to do the same job.

It didn't really bother me, because the airline had grown and they had moved out of their small office in Maddox Street to Regent Street in London. I also had to prioritise, and my career had to come first, so there were times that I would be unable to go on a promotional tour to any out-of-London venues. What was disappointing to me, however, was the lack of courtesy displayed by the manager, because the PR firm was taken on before they'd even told me they were going to do so. I got not even a letter or a phone call, and the first I heard of it was from a staff member, who called to say that a flight to launch a new aircraft was coming into London in a few days with a number of VIPs from Trinidad, together with the Trinidad media. I wondered why my name hadn't been included on the list to greet them, as I was usually an automatic choice, especially based on the fact that I'd laid a solid foundation in promoting the airline.

On arrival, the Trinidad press actually asked for me and were told by the Bwee Manager that I was working and unable to be present. That was totally untrue. I had never been asked! Nevertheless, I did attend a reception that was held on the following day at their offices in Regent Street for the travelling VIPs and travel agents. I was asked by several journalists from Trinidad why I hadn't been at the airport the day before. Quite understandably, it was the last day I worked for Bwee under that management.

Some years later, that manager left due to ill health and the new manager immediately called me back to help promote the airline and, most importantly, Trinidad and Tobago. Until the airline closed in 2006, I then enjoyed a happy relationship with every manager since then.

I felt sad and disappointed when the airline had to close. Progress is important, but sometimes the cost to society is very high. It is my belief that the family shop at the corner, the coffee shop and the post office, all act as the nerve centre for the community. It is where friends are made; it is where families bind together. The small- to medium-sized BWIA airline could have been considered as a family company. Some of us did not mind working long hours into the night to get things done. Like a village shop that has now been overtaken by the huge supermarkets, so too the huge airline companies that hold a monopoly and lack sensitivity to human needs have swallowed up the smaller operating airlines.

Nonetheless, I was pleased to have been a non-paid staff member of my National Airline, BWIA, in the 1970s and 80s. I felt that it was one way of being of service to my beautiful twin-island state of Trinidad and Tobago. I am also proud and satisfied with the achievements we had made during those wonderful years and that I have had the opportunity to make a substantial contribution to it. Furthermore, I was able through my association with the airline to visit several countries, experience different cultures and appreciate time away from my work.

I did enjoy travelling, so when I was invited, together with Jack Smethurst and Nina Baden-Semper in the early 1970s, to do a tour of a country I felt was the other side of the world, Australia, with a specially adapted stage play of Love Thy Neighbour, I jumped at the offer.

My trip there was memorable for a number of reasons. At the time, the policy of the Australian Government made it impossible for any non-white to immigrate to their country. I found that disturbing, especially as at the same time the British newspapers were full of advertisements begging British nationals to apply for UK citizenship. I had read reports about the treatment of Australia's original inhabitants, the Aborigines, so I wasn't at all sure what to expect. I was somewhat surprised, therefore, when on arrival I received the red-carpet treatment. Obviously, my stay was only temporary, and as a celebrity I offered no threat to the host nation in terms of increasing the black population.

My first stay was in Melbourne and lasted a few weeks. The hotel in Melbourne was the one that had been used by the touring West Indies cricket team not long before, so the members of staff were accustomed to dealing with West Indians. I was therefore well looked after. But it was cold! Some days were just as cold or even colder than in Scotland, something I had never envisaged.

The TV series was extremely popular in Australia, so there was no shortage of invitations to attend a number of functions, give talks and have press interviews. However, what really left a lasting impression on my mind was a visit I took to a couple of homes of some of the Aborigines. Their stories of harassment, unfair treatment, third-class citizen-status, all the ills that beset our society across the globe today; they were living it.

I was extremely fortunate to work with a very talented British actress, Amanda Muggleton, who had emigrated to Australia and was cast as my girlfriend for the stage tour. We also put together a show directed by her boyfriend, using excerpts from plays, poems, and songs, and staged it for only one evening at a small theatre space in Melbourne. The reception from the invited guests was fantastic.

Meanwhile, the Australian press was looking and trying to dig up sensational stories about the cast members. They were obviously a little bored with me because I insisted on talking only about my work and not of my private life; all they knew of that was that I was married, had two young children and my family were flying over to join me imminently. But two of the female members of the cast had been contacted separately, with the reporters trying to find out if I had slept with any of them and if so what I was like in bed! There was nothing to tell, but the actresses could have easily made up some story and gotten quite a bit of cash on the side . . .

The ordinary Australians, especially the women, were very hospitable, particularly when I made a very simple gesture that was part of my upbringing, like opening a car door or just treating them with the respect they deserved. It appeared to be something to which they were not accustomed. But the apprehension I had felt before I left England about any racism in Australia was demonstrated by one unfortunate incident. It took place while I was in a department store, standing in the queue, waiting to pay for my items. There were people behind me and about three ahead, but the guy immediately before me, about six feet tall and heavily built, turned around and saw me. In a very strong South African accent and loud enough so that most customers in that part of the store heard, he exploded:

'Jesus Christ, I left South Africa to get away from you black bastards, why don't you just get lost!'

The store went quiet. He obviously was challenging me to respond with violence, but I drew myself up to my fullest height possible, all 5ft 10ins of me, looked him straight in the eye and manufactured a smile. 'You have a problem, I haven't.'

He disgustingly chucked the goods he had in his hand on the counter and stormed out.

'Have a nice day!' I added with a smile, and as perfect an English accent as I could muster.

The people around went very quiet, the tension unbelievable. Then a false and belated, supportive kind of smile crossed some of their faces, probably because they had recognised first my voice, and then my face from *Love Thy Neighbour*. At heart, sadly, many of them probably agreed with the racist. That incident and the sad stories of the native Aboriginal peoples really set me thinking, and were indeed the main contributors to my bitter-sweet experience in that country.

I had to find ways of channelling my energy, so I embarked on a keep-fit – or more like get fit – routine that entailed going for a run (I hated running!) very early every morning. I also worked out with a karate instructor every other day, played quite a lot of tennis and made sure I had an hour's kip every afternoon before the show. By the time I left Melbourne, about six weeks after arriving, I was in the fittest shape I had ever been.

The tour then moved on to my favourite city, Sydney, the most cosmopolitan in Australia, where I stayed with a friendly couple, an English guy with an Australian wife. After Sydney, we continued the tour on to Adelaide, and I was also able to visit places like Brisbane in Queensland and Ballarat in Victoria for the occasional night or two during the tour.

It has always been important for me, especially when working in the theatre, to surround myself with actors who are prepared to work hard, who are extremely professional, but who also have a very good sense of humour. At times, I have been known to reduce my fellow actors to tears of laughter on stage whilst not allowing it to get completely out of hand. Throughout this tour, I developed a tremendous rapport with two Australian actresses working with us, who invited me several times to their homes to dine with their family members. We were continually trying to corpse – or make each other laugh – on stage, and invariably they came off the worst.

But they were plotting their revenge . . . On the final night in Adelaide, I sensed that they were planning something spectacular for me, and at half time, I discovered what they had in mind. I had to wear a pair of long pyjamas on stage, and in one scene I had to embrace one of the girls on the floor of the stage for no more than about a minute. I discovered that they had cut the cord, which held the trousers up, so I knew instantly that she was going to pull down my trousers on stage!

How could I turn the tables and not alert her that I knew? Well, I was able to get hold of a small folding umbrella and just before I walked on stage, I repaired the pyjama cord and stuffed the umbrella into the front of my underpants, with the pyjama top covering it. It served as a perfect camouflage. Out of the corner of my eyes, I could see the actress's other partner in crime, standing in the wings, a position she never occupied before, because it was still some time before she came on. She was clearly waiting for the moment when my pyjama bottoms would be pulled down. I am extremely good at holding myself back from corpsing or bursting out into laughter on stage, but it took extreme will power to hold on and act through the scene as normal, knowing what was to come – and I was aware that the actress too was finding it difficult to hold in her laughter. The whole scene up until this moment of physical contact was about ten minutes long and it was noticeable that she tried to avoid making any eye contact with me throughout that period, which was very unusual. Then came the moment when we got to the floor and had to embrace. She immediately tried to pull at my pants, and of course, they did not budge. At the same time, I pressed myself against her hard, and she went into an almost uncontrollable laughter when she realised I had turned the tables on her.

I held on tight, and I kept whispering in her ear so the audience could not hear: 'Can you feel that? Can you feel that?'

To top it, I forced her upstage hand onto the umbrella. The audience did not know what was happening but was finding the whole thing hilarious and they were rolling about in laughter. We rolled apart eventually and the actress then had to make an exit up a flight of stairs in the middle of the stage, delivering a few lines as she went, so I positioned myself with my back to the audience and indicated what I had in my pants, just as she was about to deliver her lines.

That was over twenty years ago, and I am still waiting for her lines to be delivered! The actor waiting in the wings to come on was furious, but the scene went on with the audience none the wiser and loving every moment of it.

The boot was on the other foot, however, when I was involved in doing another play at the Lyric Theatre in Hammersmith, England. The actress with whom I was working throughout the rehearsals and well into the performances, hardly smiled. She looked and felt very uptight. I was quite prepared to go through the entire production without any further attempts at getting a smile out of her, but on impulse, one night on stage I began stroking her hand during a speech, but after a few seconds she pulled her hand away without as much as a flicker. Immediately after the play ended and before the curtain call, I got what I deserved.

'I'm a serious actress! I will not be a party to any foolishness on stage, don't do it again!'

I apologised and that was the end of that. But I preferred to work with professionals who also did have a sense of humour!

Poverty, it seems is always amongst us. I had witnessed the poverty of the Aboriginal people in Australia, and more than twenty years later I saw something very similar in the Caribbean when I went to the Dominican Republic in the north-central Caribbean to film *Bitter Harvest* for the BBC with the much-talented actress Sue Johnson. I was immediately struck by the extent of poverty that existed, especially among the Haitians, who had fled Haiti.

But on a much more positive note, I was struck by the beauty and the rich mixture of the people. It was captivating, but also frustrating, simply because there I was, wanting to talk to people who spoke only Spanish but behaved just like

Trinidadians: the way they moved, their simple way of life, their dance – the salsa, that I loved, and which we call the merengue in Trinidad. There was an enviable ease too with the way mixed relationships seemed to work. It was not uncommon to walk down the streets and see a white wife and a black husband. Nobody was paying the slightest attention, as it was just the norm. In fact, there was a lot more integration regarding colour and race in the Dominican Republic than I had experienced anywhere else.

How wonderful it would be if this integration could be more common throughout the world, making it a better place to live for all people, of all colours, of all religions and of all races.

CHAPTER 14

Is This My Life?

'We will all, at some point, encounter hurdles to gaining access and entry, moving up and conquering self-doubt; but on the other side is the capacity to own opportunity and tell our own story' Stacey Abrams, US politician

---

The stages in one's life are marked by anniversaries and milestones – significant turning points, or moments in life by 'big' birthdays. Many people celebrate these milestones in different ways, and over the years, I have chosen to ignore most of them! My thirteenth, my first teen year – just another day, as was my eighteenth and twenty-first, and that was so until I reached my fiftieth birthday.

I returned home from rehearsals to be greeted by a room full of friends singing 'Happy Birthday'. The party had been organised by my wife Lorna, my son Darren, and daughter Sheona, and was filled with friends, many from my local tennis club. The following decade brought lots of work, not only in the theatre but also appearing in The Bill, one of the lead roles in a Thames TV film called The Pirate Prince, a part in a comedy from Universal Films, a part in Lovejoy – a medley of different roles, which was both challenging and fun.

I have always had very strong internal guidelines as to the parts that I choose to take, ninety-nine percent of the work that I have done over the years have been roles that display a tremendous amount of dignity in the character. I always feel that there should be a reason why he's a bad guy not just bad for bad's sake, so that I generally look for roles that show an alternative to a character, that there is a good side or a kindness in its simplest form. I don't take roles where the person is portrayed in a derogatory way. I have never taken roles for the sake of money, there has to be a greater value to me.

I have been fortunate to not regret turning down any jobs offered to me, although I don't live a life of regrets, I am who and where I am today because of the decisions I made good, bad or indifferent, and that has always been my driving force.

However, I'd have loved to have been Doctor Who. I did episodes in the show and it occurred to me then that if that was offered to me, I would have jumped at it because I can imagine the fun I could have brought to the character.

There were also personal changes. Most notably, Lorna and I were divorced, not without its pains and tears. Darren by then had moved out and was living with his girlfriend and it was decided that Sheona would stay with Lorna. I moved back to London, to East Ham, and later got married again in 1998, to fellow Trinidadian Dounne Alexander. A year later, my 60th birthday was approaching on Tuesday 28 September 1999 – the sort of milestone many people definitely recognise and celebrate and, of course, the last birthday I would have before the millennium. I had, however, planned nothing except for attending a regular get-together with The Bunburys, the celebrity cricket club of which I am a member. This year, we'd be at Lord's cricket ground, hopefully followed by a game, so we had been told to come in cricket whites.

The morning started in a relatively low-key fashion with a quiet breakfast, then a shower. It was a gloriously sunny day, perfect end-of-season cricketing weather. I had discussed with both Darren and Sheona the possibility of going out for a meal that day, but nothing firm had been agreed. However, when I tried calling my daughter during the morning and got no reply, it crossed my mind that my son and daughter and the others might have planned an evening meal at home: a good home-cooked meal with all the trimmings, probably eaten picnic-style on the sitting-room floor. Very appealing. That would have been a perfect end to the day.

It was about 11 o'clock when I negotiated the busy St John's Wood roundabout, drove past the imposing Victorian pavilion and turned into the Lord's car park. I left my cricket bag in the car and was escorted to the lift and up to the Tavern meeting room, just as I had done on previous occasions, feeling innocently relaxed. The first thing that struck me as the lift doors parted was the sudden burst of noise as party poppers flew. From there on, everything happened so quickly as if in a whirlwind. A series of snapshots, floating balloons and there was the actor, Fraser Hines, holding out a square green cake with flickering candles – a replica of a cricket field. Of course, those rascals from The Bunburys, led by captain David English, had planned this 60th birthday party for me. I was thrilled to bits that they had gone to so much trouble for me.

I turned to see who else was present. The blur of a grey suit, blue shirt, dark tie, shock of silver hair, that unmistakable voice, and those immortal words: 'Tonight, Rudolph Walker, *This is Your Life!'* And Michael Aspel handed me the Big Red Book.

In a rush of excitement and adrenaline, I recognised perhaps for the first time, how far I had come.

What was by now a well-oiled machine kicked in, and within a few minutes, I found myself in a chauffeur-driven limousine on my way to Thames Television Studios in Teddington. I was met by the floor manager and taken to my dressing room, all very familiar, because it was one of the dressing rooms I had occupied on a regular basis, over twenty years before when filming *Love Thy Neighbour.* I was then left alone. Alone, because that was how they, the secret-planners, had organised it. Perfect torture. A rack held my clothes for the show, no doubt supplied by my 'devious' family. I smiled to myself, wondering how they had managed to keep all of this, which must have taken months of preparation, a secret. I know that those who appear on *This Is Your Life* always say that they were unaware of any plans, but I truly did not have an inkling.

There was a variety of sandwiches, but I was far too nervous to eat; and with it, a huge basket of fresh fruits, which I love, so the odd grape found itself into my mouth followed by lots of chilled fizzy water that was also at my disposal. The bottle of champagne sitting in the ice bucket was never opened.

I sat alone for what seemed like hours, seeing only a runner and the producer. That was the time when I really started thinking and was able to ask myself so many questions. 'Who have they invited? Who is there? Who is coming?'

I was kept away from everybody. It was an uncomfortable kind of tension, not because I feared any awkward circumstance would emerge, but I started thinking who or what the researchers might have dug up. Would they have tracked down Charles Marowitz or Dr Jonathan Miller? What would they say now, twenty-plus years later on? What would any of them have to say about me? Would I have to help them out of a hole if they had nothing to say? Would the programme makers be able to fill half an hour? This could all turn out to be an embarrassing shambles. Are any of my elderly relatives living in Trinidad going to be there? Perhaps Uncle Roy, and Aunt Milly, his wife, one of my favourite aunts, who was now living in Brooklyn?

Since I had been with my then wife for only a comparatively short period, she would not have had my complete history and would have had to do a lot of research. How much had my son and daughter been able to tell her? How far back had they gone? I started thinking about all the people I would have invited if I were organising the event, like Carmen Monroe, my favourite actress and mentor, now living in Florida. My sister in the States, of course – but I had visited them only a few weeks before. In retrospect, I remembered my nieces had been questioning me quite a bit about my family tree. Who might be a surprise guest? Perhaps my cousins living in Trinidad? Or my father, Ralph? Now that would have brought tears to everybody's eyes – including mine – and triggered a number of embarrassing questions.

They had already done Jack Smethurst and Nina Baden-Semper, my co-stars in Love Thy Neighbour, though both Kate Williams and I had said at the time that we wanted no part of it. My reason at the time was quite personal and straightforward: the TV show had been the first big series I'd done that got me public recognition. What life had I to fill the show at that time?

My imaginings were eventually interrupted by a knock at the dressing-room door and an immediate rush of adrenaline. The moment had arrived. A researcher, looking a little like a cyber-creature from *Doctor Who* with her headphones, microphone and battery pack, gave me a smile that was meant to cheer. My mouth was dry, and my hands were wet as she led me into the vast studio. The lighting was bright, and it was difficult, or almost impossible, to see past them. A gentle push and I was on set.

I was taken aback by the burst of applause as I entered. I looked around, hardly able to take in the pointing and laughing from all the actors who were there and the 'We got you, Rudy!' smirks from The Bunburys cricket team as well as my family, who were all seated in the audience. I was immensely moved as they all stood and clapped. It was the first time I had been given a standing ovation. I cannot recall exactly how I got to the chair provided, but I sank into it gratefully as my knees were turning to jelly. This was more of an ordeal than I had imagined.

Before I had time to think, Michael Aspel opened the famous red book, and it all began.

'Gathered round tonight, as you see, Rudolph, are family and friends including a Bunbury or two, and a talented line-up from your day job in television and theatre and the cricketing world.'

Many of my friends, family and colleagues had turned up to pay tribute to my long career in film, television and the theatre. My long association with players of the successful West Indies cricket team of the 1960s and 70s also had a representative. There were clips that I had not seen for years, bringing distant memories to life: *Fable, Othello, Black Silk, The Thin Blue Line, Divorce His and Divorce Hers,* a made-for-TV film of the early 1970s with Richard Burton and Liz Taylor.

'Perhaps one of the surprises would be a message from Elizabeth Taylor,' I mused.

The show was moving along nicely without any hitches, far too smoothly. But I cringed and wanted to disappear into the woodwork as Michael Aspel continued: 'Well, with your TV career coming along, you decided to try your hand as a pop star.'

I knew then what was to come: the record I had made twenty years ago – '*Reggae Woman*' and '*It was Love*'.

Twenty years later, it sounded even worse!

I was a bit embarrassed, but deeply touched by the tributes paid to me by colleagues and friends: Jack Smethurst, Mona Hammond, Kate Williams, Nina Baden-Semper, Floella Benjamin, Kika Markham, Doña Croll, Sir Trevor McDonald, as well as those whose mere presence in the audience spoke volumes of their appreciation of me.

This special day was also shared with so many others: my fellow sports devotees – the great Clive Lloyd, Frazer Hines and David English from The Bunburys; and those who loved music as much as I did. Even Eddy Grant flew in from Barbados. Most importantly though was my family: my sisters, Aliena, who had flown in from the United States, and Veronica; and my children Darren and Sheona. My initial fears were eased at who came to support me and although, sadly, neither Carmen Munroe nor Earl Cameron could be there and Lorna, too, was absent since I was there with my new wife, this was understandable and I could see the effort that had gone in to make the show special.

The great sadness I experienced, though, was that the one person who would have appreciated this tribute more than anyone else could not be there – and that person was my mother. I so wished that she was present to share this momentous occasion with me. I certainly missed her on that night of celebration, that night of reflecting on all that I had achieved. I had reached the age of sixty, and on that night I was being presented with a rich tableau, an affirmation of how far I had travelled.

Yes, this was Rudolph Walker's life.

Little did I know that even more dramatic, painful and controversial chapters were yet to be written.

Top: With Virginia Wade & Cliff Richard, Birmingham Arena, Cliffs Celebrity Tennis & Show; Middle Right: In The Book Liberator; Middle left: In Black Silk with Kika Markham 1985; Bottom left: A trip to Zimbabwe with students and actress Joan Ann Maynard & Marsha Miller 1995; Bottom Right: With John Goodman on the set of King Ralph 1991

Top right: Emma Award 2002; Top left: In Thin Blue Line 1995; Middle Left; The Crouches 2003; Middle Right: Race in media awards presenting with footballer Garth Crooks 2000; Bottom left: With my late Cousin Gloria 2002; Bottom Middle : Carol Haye first Winner of Inter Schools Drama Award

Top : Princess Ann presenting me with my OBE 2006;
Top Right: On The stairs of Buckingham Palace 2006;
Bottom: Receiving my CBE in 2021

Top: WithPrince Edward and the Duke of Edinburgh Awards 2005;
Middle left: With my teacher Miss Alcantara at her home in Trinidad 2015; Middle Right: 9. With my friend in 2020;
Bottom left: With Tameka Empson on my 70th Birthday; Bottom Right: Sir Viv Richards with my grandchildren Loveday & Latimer

Top: The Cast of EastEnders 2011;
Middle: The cast of EastEnders 2015; Bottom left: National Television Award;
Bottom Right: Pride of Britain Awards Gee walker with Danny Dyer and Diane Parish 2021

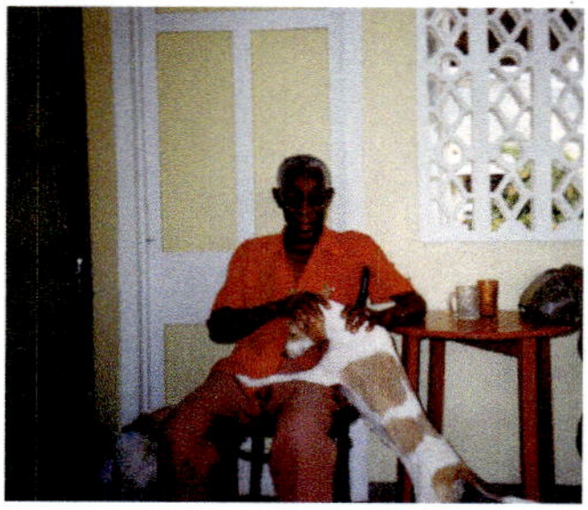

Top: Yeah Man! Patrick on set with Nicholas Bailey & Gary Beadle;
Middle: With Roger Griffiths, Wil Johnson, Mohammed George, RW, the late Malcolm Frederick, Jimmy Akingbola, Danny John-Jules
Bottom left: With Cynthia Lennon; Bottom Right: My father Ralph Walker

Top: Winning Outstanding Contribution at the British Soap Awards 2018; Middle left: Celebrating my 80th birthday on set; Middle Right: With my on-set family;
Bottom left: Make-up jinks with Diane Parish; Bottom Right: With Harry Kane & Diane Parish

Top Left: Relaxing on set of EastEnders; Top Right: Best Actor Award presented by the late Horace Ove, Director; Middle left: With Baroness Patricia Scotland, Baroness Valerie Amos, Lord Simon Woolley & Juliet Alexander 2024;
Middle Right With Diane Parish
Bottom: With Darren, Sheona, Loveday, Latimer & Josh at the WOMAD Festival 2024;

PART FIVE

Life on a Famous Square

SUNSET

I gazed at the far horizon
Out in the distant blue
And there I saw the beautiful setting sun
So magnificent that no mortal knew.
I saw the lights of the village
Turn on one by one
And the mysterious night took over
From another day that is gone.
Once more I peered at the far horizon
Now lost in the distant grey
It seems to be very tranquil
Out yonder far away.

by Malcolm Walker, aged 13

CHAPTER 15

'Yeah, Man!'

'Take a stand for what's right. Raise a ruckus and make a change. You may not always be popular, but you'll be part of something larger and bigger and greater than yourself. Besides, making history is extremely cool' Samuel L. Jackson, American actor and producer

---

It was coming up to my sixty-second birthday in September 2001 when I had a call from my agent Michelle Burke saying that Mr John Yorke, Executive Producer of *EastEnders*, would like to see me. No conversations took place with my agent prior to that with the possibility of joining the cast but I was soon told that there were certain well-known actors they have listed and who are approached when an opening occurs.

It appeared as though I was one of the fortunate ones. *EastEnders* was – and is - hugely popular, regularly attracting 35 to 40 per cent of the total TV audience and, in 2001 when I joined, it had clashed with ITV's rival soap *Coronation Street* in the schedules for the first time, with *EastEnders* drawing 8.4 million viewers to *Corrie's* 7.3 million. That's a lot of viewers!

Appearing on screen at the time were Corinne Skinner-Carter, a fellow Trinidadian, playing Mrs Audrey Trueman, who ran a bed and breakfast place; she had two sons, Gary Beadle as Paul, and Nicholas Bailey as Anthony. What part did the producer maybe have in mind for me?

My meeting with John and the casting director Julia Cramsie was a very relaxed and enjoyable one in which they hinted that they would like me to be part of the Trueman family but minus Corinne, whom I was told was shortly being written out. Although the scripts and storyline were still being developed, I found out that I would play her ex-husband, returning for her funeral and reuniting with my sons after many years apart.

I felt a real dilemma once offered the role – a dilemma that many actors would love to have. There were several burning questions I had to ask myself. Did I want to give up the freedom I had been enjoying for so many years, the freedom to switch from TV to film, to radio, to stage? A freedom, although punctuated with many disappointments, frustrations and anger, that had given me tremendous satisfaction in the quality and variety of work I had produced over the years and a decent standard of living?

I also had to ask myself, *'What contribution could I make to an already established series?'* It took some time before I finally decided to take the plunge, and during that period the people who were very close to me - my son Darren, my daughter Sheona, and my agent - were instrumental in helping me make the final decision, reminding me of the impact a few members of the *EastEnders* cast had had when visiting their school, Highdown, in Caversham, Reading.

The then Executive Producer, John Yorke, also played a very important part in my decision-making. His vision, his sincerity, and his assurance that I wasn't going to be just token black character gave me hope. John's recognition of the absence of black stars on the cover of magazines, and his determination that he would do everything within his power to change that also influenced my decision. He felt that the Trueman family would have just as much impact as the other families in the Square.

In our discussions, John and I talked about the type of character I'd like to play - a true, true Trinidadian of the old school, who had travelled the world, got into all sorts of trouble, and whatever knocks and setbacks, and heartaches he had suffered, he comes out smiling - a lovable rogue. I felt that the character would be a great way to bring a bit of comedy into the show. A true Trinidadian! Using jokes and humour to get himself out of sticky situations.

And so, I said yes!

I received a call from the costume supervisor to meet her on King's Road, Chelsea to look around for outfits that would suit the character. It was a challenging but enjoyable experience. Finding clothes that had a touch of the old fashions, but still trying to keep up with outfits of the day. Wearing a hat, and keeping his paper money in it, was an old Trinidadian habit I wanted to include. A waistcoat and pocket watch would be a touch he acquired when first in the UK, plus pointed boots and a leather belt. To top it all, I suggested Patrick should have a gold tooth - a trademark of some of the older Trinidadian men.

At the time, there were stalls in Shepherd's Bush market where you could buy clip-on gold teeth, so I tried one out and it was agreed that this would be part of Patrick's wardrobe. The make-up department then sent me to a specialist who modelled me a bespoke fitting that was like a very thin veneer over my front teeth, including the signature gold tooth. It was easy to fit, never budged an inch, and lasted absolutely ages. I had two, just in case of emergencies – and still use them all the time. Sometimes I leave my dressing room after filming, get home and realise I'm still wearing it!

It was a nerve-wracking experience as I walked onto that set for the first time. Even with all the TV work I had done over the years, I still suffered from butterflies in my stomach on that first day, even though I had nothing to say in my opening shot. Over twenty years in the series and I still get butterflies when I walk on set, especially if it's a big scene.

That first day, I was warmly greeted by Carolyn Weinstein, the *EastEnders* Company Manager, then introduced to Angela at the *EastEnders* reception desk. Then I had the excitement of meeting a few of the international and *EastEnders* legends who were relaxing in the artists' green room waiting to go on set: Barbara Windsor, who played Peggy Mitchell, landlady of the Queen Vic pub (Who could forget her *'Get out of my pub!'* line?); June Brown, who was launderette legend Dot Cotton; not to forget Pam St Clement – Pat Butcher, with her trademark big earrings! They were all very welcoming, remembering their own first days on the set.

Scenes are sometimes filmed out of story order; you might start the day filming scene 6 of Episode 17 in the Vic, and later that day or the next or even the following week, return to film an earlier scene of that same episode. It can feel confusing. But I was fortunate that my first scene to be filmed for *EastEnders* was my arrival as Patrick Trueman. And the writers couldn't have written a better entrance for me - the scene is still being talked about today, over twenty years after it was first transmitted. A chauffeur-driven limousine pulls up in the Square, the camera pans as the passenger door opens, then a pair of brown pointed cowboy boots appear. The camera slowly moves upwards, showing a slick dark suit with a waistcoat, a gold pocket watch, and then up to my smiling face under the trilby appearing on screen. It could have been a scene out of one those great Western movies starring Clint Eastwood. Plenty of opportunity for me to present a real character straight off!

As with every job in the past, I have thrown a hundred and fifty per cent effort into the show and enjoyed what little contribution I have made to the continued success of *EastEnders*. Storylines included an early marriage (to Yolande, played by Angela Wynter, with whom I am still in touch although she left the show in 2008), and made a welcome return to the show in 2023, an affair with Pat Butcher (Pam St Clement) when Patrick rented the car lot, the loss of a son to drugs, a row with Phil Mitchell over his son Ben (Steve McFadden has played Phil, a stalwart of the series, for many years), more affairs - I think *EastEnders* does see Patrick as a bit of a ladies' man! - and, recently, the chance to play a more confused Patrick after he suffers a series of mini-strokes. But he does manage to fit in another marriage! This time to Sheree Baptiste, played by Suzette Llewellyn. Throughout it all, I've kept up Patrick's favourite saying, *'Yeah, man!'*

I have been allowed over the years to make little changes within the script, mainly to do with the rhythm of the dialogue. There was however one moment that I was over-ruled and glad I was. It was a scene when I got into bed with Pat Butcher and left my hat at the foot of the bed. I questioned as to why Patrick would do that, as in reality he would hang it in the hallway together with his coat. I must admit however that when I saw the scene played out on screen it was absolutely hilarious!

Working with Pam St Clement was a joy - her timing, the twinkle in her eye when we were doing our flirting scenes, and her support from day one was invaluable, and I was extremely saddened when such an iconic character was written out of the series.

Some of the storylines really have tackled social issues of the day too; one episode in 2007 focused on racism with the Truemans responding to racist insults; and in 2009 there was a TV first for *EastEnders* with an episode featuring an all-black cast. As Patrick, I was reminiscing about my first days in London in the 1950s – well, since I'd first come over to the UK in 1960, it was easy to draw on my own experiences to portray this effectively, and hopefully get viewers talking about what happened back then, in particular at the real-life Notting Hill race riots which featured in the episode. And to discuss, as the characters did, whether racism still existed in the same way. The BBC described it as *'an opportunity to explore in some depth the background and experiences of Patrick Trueman, one of*

EastEnders' longest-standing and most popular characters', but were surprised when there was criticism about it not being advertised in advance. In their view, they often focused on one particular character for a whole episode and this was no different.

But if you were a member of the Black community, it was a big deal. I remembered the 1960s, when children, if while looking at television, saw a black face on the screen, would shout to their mother in the kitchen: *'Mom! Look, a black man on the telly!'* However, by the time Mom got to the room, the actor would have been gone and might never appear again. As was the case with my *'carrying a dead body'* across the back of the scene in my first-ever TV appearance!

Now, children of all races and skin colours growing up in the UK could see an episode of a major TV soap where everyone in the episode was black. A small step forward.

Working in *EastEnders* for over twenty years, there had to be moments I cherished or regarded as challenging. Filming in the winter at a seaside resort with the late June Brown and having to escape from her bedroom through a window on the ground floor in only my underpants and having to do several takes was challenging! Less so was having to dance with her and acknowledging that she was a very good dancer and full of fun.

I will never forget receiving my CBE from the then Prince Charles and inviting him to pay us a visit at the *EastEnders* studio . . . he did come, and remarked on the day, much to my surprise, that I had to take the blame for him being there. There were also the unscripted exchanges - a once-in-a-lifetime experience. There was one moment off camera during the visit that captured the relaxed way in which Prince Charles engaged with others. Just as we were all getting into position for a group photo Letitia Dean said she was feeling cold, and the then Prince Charles removed his overcoat and placed it over her shoulders.

In 2015, I filmed my 1,000th episode as Patrick! I hadn't even realised, so it was a total shock when the crew and cast gathered on set – in the laundromat – to mark the occasion. *'A thousand episodes? Are you sure?'* I queried, adding, *'I look forward to coming here. I look forward to working. I still have that child-like feeling I had when I was fifteen or sixteen, walking onto a set for the first time.'* I would never have believed, when first signing up for the series, that I would still be part of the *EastEnders* family now, more than twenty years later.

It's all been huge fun! But also, hard work. It still remains a very challenging job, and I am fortunate to enjoy the loyalty and friendship of cast, crew and staff.

Whatever happened in my personal life, I went to the extreme not to let it affect my work. And during these years on *EastEnders*, I did face some very low and dark times in my life. One such period was a few years ago when I separated from my then wife, Dounne, and was forced to move out of a flat I had been living in in East London. It necessitated me spending nearly all my life savings on legal fees and I suddenly found myself, in my seventies, starting from scratch again with nowhere to live and very little money in my bank account. I had to put all my furniture in storage, and for nearly two years I sometimes lived out of a suitcase, going from pillar to post as my mother would say. I would sometimes book into a hotel near the studio or a hotel in Reading. When I had a late shoot and an early call time, I always accepted any offer the studio made to accommodate me in a local hotel.

I recall staying in a Reading hotel for three nights that drove me to utter despair. The hotel looked homely from the outside, very old-fashioned in appearance. I was arriving back in Reading late from filming, so I was unable to check it out before, and it fell well within my budget. On arrival I was just about able to squeeze into the one parking space that was left, the indication that the hotel was full. I rang the bell and waited long enough to look around, and a feeling hit me immediately: *this is not me*. Guests were coming and going, quite a mixture too - from suited, to guys who could easily be from a building site, the majority of the guests being men. The receptionist finally arrived, confirmed my booking, and took me to my room. It was a tiny room on the ground floor, overlooking part of the car park, with my car just outside my window. A wash basin, small bed, and a TV in the corner, with a communal shower and toilet in the corridor. I sat on the bed and cried. Questions of: who am I? Why am I in this position? *'You make your bed; you lie in it,'* was an old saying from my dear mother. I had slept in surroundings a lot more challenging and have survived, but by the time I got to bed, I felt emotionally exhausted.

My daughter Sheona came to my rescue and was able to find an apartment to rent for a limited period; this was followed by help from Lorna, who was able to persuade a friend to rent me an empty flat she owned for a couple of months before it was sold.

In one property I rented, the bedroom was in the basement, and I arrived from filming one evening to find it covered in about six inches of water! Using a saucepan, I was able to dip out the water. That night I slept upstairs on the couch. I had a few days and nights like that before the problem was solved. But it was hardly the life of a high-flying TV star! Throughout that period no one knew the full extent of how demoralised I felt, nor what I was going through - not even my children, who I was very close to, knew how I really felt. Some days on my way to the studio, I would pull up at the side of the road, have a good cry, pull myself together, then arrive at the studio and immediately the environment would act as a tonic, and I was ready to go. On the TV I was celebrated as an actor, but my personal life away from work was pretty awful at the time.

There was only one actor who really picked up on it, saw beyond the mask I put on – Diane Parrish, who played my on-screen adopted daughter; she would suddenly pull me aside when there was a break, and ask me if I was OK. Somehow, she had got to know me well enough over the years. Even then, careful and guarded, I would admit to only part of the unhappiness.

It was a difficult time in my life, and I had to a certain degree, isolated myself. I opened up to my sister, living in the UK, other than that, I had certain friends that I would spend several hours chatting with over a meal and their support meant everything it was a time of great pain and loneliness.

Over the years, I have generally avoided making public speeches – as I have said before, I don't want to be some kind of spokesperson for black actors, or for West Indians in general, but can often be perceived as such. Just give me a script and a character to play and that will be fine. But then something turned up that I absolutely felt I had to do . . . though my initial reaction was one of horror.

I had just collected my car from the mechanic and was on my way home when I received a call on my mobile from the show's Executive Producer, Louise Berridge. *EastEnders* was up for an award at the 2003 National TV Awards – transmitted live from the Royal Albert Hall on ITV and hosted by my good friend, fellow Trinidadian, Trevor McDonald. Louise informed me that, if we won, I was delegated to accept it on behalf of the show. I could not believe what I was hearing, so to avoid crashing into another vehicle, I quickly pulled up at the side of the road and asked her to repeat what she had just said. Then I made all the excuses possible to opt out, but she would have none of it. How I got home from there I don't know, but I sweated for the rest of the journey.

I did not think that Louise, or anyone who was not black, would realise the enormity of the impact that gesture had on me. To most people perhaps, it would simply be a matter of going to the podium, saying thanks to all who contributed, smiling appropriately and going back to one's seat. But for the key actor to collect the award to be black… well, if we won, this was going to be a bit of history - and more so Black British history.

For once, I did not tell my then wife or children what might be about to unfold. I decided to suffer silently. I got home and tried desperately to write something for the awards but just could not find the words and ended up going to bed without having written a word. It was a restless night, so I awoke about four the next morning and as if by divine intervention, the words just came – a short speech, as it had to be, time being a factor.

On the day of the function, seated in the Albert Hall with my wife lodged between Louise and me, it was not until Louise leaned over and asked if I had my speech ready, just in case we won, that my wife became aware of what I was about to do.

Until that time, I had tried to present a very calm outlook but as if a tap was suddenly turned on, I just started to sweat.

Would we win? Or would *Coronation Street*, or *Emmerdale*, or *Hollyoaks*? I was filled with trepidation.

'And the winner of the Most Popular Serial Drama is . . . EastEnders!'

The hall erupted. It was a very popular decision, and as I stepped forward, I was conscious of the millions of people watching throughout the United Kingdom; and here I was standing, a proud black man, accepting an award on behalf of the Company. The continuous applause when I was about to speak threw me off just for a few seconds. I was not sure if we should soak it up until it started to die down, or ride it, but it allowed me the time to pull myself together. Trevor's hug and compliment afterwards were a moment I treasure.

The following year, for the second time in a row, we won the award, and I was again asked to accept it on behalf of the Company. It did not hold the same magic as the previous year, but was just as nerve-racking.

Initially, I was not a fervent believer in having separate black awards for theatre, television, films and radio but I did appreciate that it was a way to get the recognition those of us working in these industries deserved. No one was truly recognising the contributions that peoples from the Caribbean and Africa were making to Britain, while other communities had several well-publicised and transmitted award ceremonies and the British music industry, of course, have the MOBO awards for performers of music of black origin (with the majority, but not all, of the musicians being people of colour). Then there are the British Academy Film and TV Awards (BAFTA) and Oscars, which for many years were predominantly of one colour. When one looks at the transmission of those award ceremonies, one is hard pushed to see a (non-white) black Afro-American/English face in the audience, let alone one being nominated. With that in mind, I saw nothing wrong with having a high-profile black Oscar ceremony that recognises excellence, innovation and quality: a platform that is an outlet for creative diversity. But of course, if that were to be suggested, the cry of separatism and racism would go out.

Only a handful – twenty or so – Oscars had gone to black actors or actresses since they first began the Academy Awards in 1929 – Sidney Poitier, Denzel Washington, Mahershala Ali, Halle Berry. Where were the British names? Happily, many voices have pointed this out and the Oscars are now far more inclusive.

Not being seen as a black actor was also noticeable and openly displayed in other situations. In March 2005, the BBC published the *EastEnders* 20th Anniversary book. I am referring to the same *EastEnders* that I represented at the Award ceremonies. The first time that I heard about the book's publication was via a phone call from a colleague, a BBC radio producer, who suggested that I get hold of a copy and read it. I could detect anger in her voice, but she would not say why so I came to the conclusion that something had been written about me that was derogatory or uncomplimentary. I must say at this point, that the book had not been written by anyone at *EastEnders* so I was unsure as to what to expect.

I acquired a copy the next day at Reception and began flicking through the pages to spot the references to me. I noticed Gary Beadle (who played one of my series sons) had a small photo on the front cover, followed by three other black actors, who had been unheard of before joining the series. I turned to the back cover and there was a small picture of Nick Bailey, my other screen son. Then I thought I must have missed something, so I had a second look, much slower this time. My picture was nowhere to be found!

Surely I'd missed it, I thought. So, I looked up the index, first for my name, and then for Patrick Trueman's. There was not even one mention of either name. It was at that point one of the actors, Shane Richie, walked by and teased me about checking out how big a spread I had in the book, and I revealed that I was not even in it. He thought I was joking and after a little banter between us, another actor, Adam Woodyatt, arrived on the scene and joined in. He seized the book and looked through it himself. Both their reactions were ones of total and mutual disgust and they even went as far as to say that the book should be withdrawn and reprinted.

A call to my agent followed, and after expressing her total disbelief, she wrote to *EastEnders*. *EastEnders* expressed their disbelief that such a thing had happened and explained that all the editorial work done on the book was in the hands of an independent editor and not *EastEnders*. The editor, in his defence, stated that at the time when the final decision was made to go to print in 2004, they had to choose the actors with the strongest current storylines. Well, that argument fell flat on its face on all counts. Firstly, was he saying that for the three and a half years I had spent in the series, that I had not been given the sort of storylines that were worthwhile? Secondly, was he also saying that the Ferrara family, who came after the Truemans, enjoyed far better and stronger storylines? Finally, was he also saying that the Millers and their dog, who had not yet appeared on screen but had only recorded several episodes, also had stronger storylines? By the end of 2004, I had appeared in more than 300 episodes over three years and in 2004 had eight 'doof-doofs'! The doof-doofs, of course, relate to the final notes of each episode when a character is highlighted as part of a big storyline.

The absence in the book of one of the first black family in the Square – despite their small photos, there were only scant references inside to Gary Beadle or Nick Bailey either - caused many eyebrows to be raised and questions asked. It certainly didn't go unnoticed by the Black press, or many within the Black commseunity, so there were questions from them about it. I refused to give any interviews. John Yorke had only just returned to the BBC and unfortunately wasn't around at the time when those decisions were made and implemented, but it was inevitable, however, that I had to have a meeting with him to express my total disgust at the way they conducted their printing/publicity/PR business. John totally understood my position and certainly never tried to stop me talking to the press. But we have an old saying: *'Never bite the hand that feeds you.'*

I took that saying on board then, and now, in 2024 as I reflect on over twenty-three wonderful years I've been in *EastEnders*. I am proud to have been part of its journey, to witness the diversity, and not being afraid to explore issues that affect us all in our daily lives. It consistently sets a very high standard, and includes characters from diverse ethnic backgrounds, especially in the last three years, having the brilliant actor Colin Salmon as The Queen Vic landlord, that thought wouldn't have been entertained a few years ago, and including the most recent storyline in which I was involved, and at this time in writing it is still ongoing.

It was at the beginning of 2024 I was invited to a meeting with our Executive Producer Chris Clenshaw, and regardless of how long you've been in the show, or how confident you feel in the work you are doing, there is always that part of you that says *"this is it, thank you for your contribution, but we have to let you go"*, and you start planning your departure speech. My approach to his office was as I've done, that is to joke, have fun with the staff, make sure they are in a good mood. When Chris came out and ushered me into his office, his first words were, there is nothing to worry about I just want to get your feelings about an idea we want to work on that'll involve Angela Wynter and myself. My tension dropped and the sweaty palms stopped instantly.

We are planning to write an entire episode for just two people Angela and me, (a two-hander it's called), how do I feel about it. If I was standing you could have knocked me over with a feather, it was the last thing I expected to hear.

I must have hesitated because Chris chipped in with *"there is no pressure, if you don't want to, I quite understand or needed time to think about it, there is no rush"*. But I had made up my mind within a second, it was too great an opportunity to turn down. I was unable to obtain the storyline then because nothing concrete was written. My only request was that we get a copy of the script as early as possible, ahead of what is the norm a week or two before we start filming. It was only after I walked out of Chris office the enormity of it sunk in, a two-hander only happens rarely.

The entire episode was recorded over two days. Two challenging days. The topic – someone in authority who uses their position to be abusive.

After the transmission the public reaction was fantastic, and at time of writing both Miss Wynter and I have been nominated for the National TV Awards. What a long way from the emotions I had sixteen years ago.

It was in May 2008, I sat in my car, which was parked on the banks of the river Thames near Greenwich. It was indeed a beautiful spring afternoon. The tide was very high, so the water was beating a steady rhythm as it splashed against the river wall. This was accompanied by the occasional journey of a boat, which depending on its size, increased the rhythm more forcefully, and added to that, there was the occasional sight of a bird. It was extremely quiet; the perfect setting for me to relax mind, body and soul.

Less than a week before, I had been walking ten feet tall and on cloud nine, having just returned from two enjoyable and revitalising weeks in Tobago, where I attended the Tobago Jazz festival, followed by a weekend in Atlanta for Maya Angelou's 80th birthday celebrations, an invitation that when it came filled me with great excitement. Just to meet and be in the same room with such a great and inspirational black woman!

However, all good things do come to an end, and as another saying goes, *nothing lasts for ever*. For me, both sayings have been proven to be true. Quite unexpectedly, that serene, peaceful refreshing atmosphere was changed as I received the news that my co-star in *EastEnders*, Angela Wynter, was about to be axed from the series, at the end of her contract. The news upset me very much and immediately changed my joyful mood to anger. It wasn't just about losing her from the series either. There was a deeper part of me that was very saddened by Miss Wynter's pending departure. Within the context of the series and working with her on a day-to-day basis, she had become a true friend and soulmate. The break-up of such a relationship could not be taken lightly, especially as I held the view that our on-screen relationship had not been fully explored.

As would be expected, the thought of my future with the Company did occur simultaneously, even though I had been given the assurance that I was an important and integral part of the *EastEnders* series family. Miss Wynter, in her very philosophical and sisterly way, said that I must stay and insisted that I must not even think of leaving. This was the same advice I had been given previously by a very senior and highly respected actor and mentor throughout my early career, Earl Cameron, when I had contemplated leaving because of the lack of challenging storylines.

And yes, there was a part of me that was extremely happy to continue in the show, especially knowing of impending storylines that were likely to pose a challenge to my acting skills. And in any serial drama, changes of characters within family situations can bring more exciting storylines. Sometimes the producer decides that it is time for a change – as with Angela – and at other times, the actors themselves decide that they want to branch out and do other work. This is more likely with younger performers who don't already have a body of other work behind them, and fear being typecast.

Myself, I already managed to fit in other work around my *EastEnders* obligations. Steve McCrum, a well-established and respected comedy producer, sent me a script which he felt had the potential of a possible comedy series for the BBC. After reading it, I had some reservations, none of any major significance, but I felt it was worth doing.

I had no regrets whatsoever doing the first series of *The Crouches*, a sitcom about a three-generation black family living in SE London. A bonus was that while I played Grandpa Crouch, my screen wife was my old friend Mona Hammond. From day one and throughout the making of the series, the writer, producer, and his staff showed me a tremendous amount of respect. When things went wrong, as they did from time to time, I always had a personal call from the producer either to apologise or to thank me for something simple I might have done or said that eased the tension. It was a respect that was given and not one I sought, and I would like to think that the same would have been accorded to any senior leading white actor.

Before the series was transmitted, the first and most scathing attack on it was by a section of the Black press bemoaning the fact that it was written by a white man. And, by implication, a criticism of me for accepting a role in it.

I cannot escape the fact that where I am today is because ninety per cent of the parts I had played from Shakespeare and *Love Thy Neighbour* to *EastEnders* have been written by white writers. Yes, I have felt and still feel that our involvement falls far short of what is required and necessary to make ours a more balanced and harmonious society, but were my critics saying that I should never have accepted those parts? Never take a job if a white person was in charge in any way? And as such risk throwing myself on the scrapheap where the statistics, forever increasing, show many black men with no hope and relying on the state or drugs to keep them going?

In discussions that I had with the producer, prior to and during the making of the first series of *The Crouches*, it was his intention to bring on board black writers for the second and third series because it had the ingredients to become a blockbuster, thereby releasing more opportunities for black comedy writers.

The BBC reacted to the criticism by offering the next series to a brilliant black producer/director, Miss Paulette Randall, who engaged several black writers. I was informed of the sweeping changes by Steve McCrum. However, life for *The Crouches* ended with barely a whimper. Unlike the success enjoyed by the comedy series *Goodness Gracious Me*, dealing with life in the Asian community, even poking fun at themselves. That series starred two excellent actors with whom I'd had the privilege in the past of working with, Meera Syal and Nina Wadia, and I found it extremely funny and informative. But why did that series and its format succeed while *The Crouches* didn't? A better time in the schedules? Less press criticism while it was getting established? I really don't know.

CHAPTER 16

Endings, Beginnings . . . And Returns

'As a kid, this is what I wanted my life to be. Not in my wildest dreams did I ever dare to dream that it would be this' Smokey Robinson, American R&B soul singer, songwriter and record producer

There were other endings too. When long-standing characters were written out of *EastEnders*, it could feel like losing a family member. And sometimes over the twenty plus years I've been in *EastEnders* I have actually lost a friend or seen them struck by illness. Seeing John Bardon – who played grumpy grandad Jim Branning - on set in a wheelchair after he had his stroke and then his passing; also the loss of Barbara Windsor to Alzheimer's – I remembered how she had welcomed me with open arms when I arrived; and June Brown who had qualities as an actor that were very special. If the actor had left the series, then it was likely I would be invited to the funeral, unless they had specifically requested a small family event. But when they were part of the series at the time, the producers would film a funeral for the character. Hence there was a funeral scene for June Brown's Dot Cotton, and filming her funeral as the character Dot was a very emotional event. I did not attend June's funeral (close family only), but it felt on the day as if I was saying my final goodbye not to Dot but to June. But alongside the sadnesses, there were also joys, for instance, the absolute pleasure I get when I visit a school and am able to communicate with the students. Or when I visit a hospice and speak – as Rudolph Walker, but also to many as the character Patrick - to the patients and their carers.

I often hear "Patrick" or "yeah man" shouted out to me if I'm seen out and about.

Another joy comes with my growing family. I had become a grandfather: my son Darren now has three children – two sons and a daughter – Josh, Loveday and Latimer. We don't get together as often as we'd like, but we do make time for a weekly Zoom call with the whole, immediate family, so that we can catch up on what everyone is up to.

And when I had the opportunity, I would try and get off to warmer climes – the British winter is not my favourite time of year. My ideal scenario would be to pack my bags around the end of November, when it is not too cold, jet off to Trinidad and Tobago and return to England at the end of March, although then it could be still bitterly cold. However, it is comforting to know that warmer weather is just around the corner. I imagine this is the dream of most of my generation, reinforcing our right of return and maintaining the dream of retirement 'back home'. Hence a large percentage of people do pack up lock, stock and barrel and emigrate to Spain, South Africa, Australia or the Caribbean when they retire. But I was still working. So, any breaks away I got had to be fitted in around the *EastEnders* schedule, and any other commitments I had made. But yes, I did get away on a few occasions, one remaining in my mind since it was at Carnival time, and I had negotiated a break of a few months. . . .

It was 8:00 a.m. on a cold, grey Saturday in early February and I was at the BBC's studio in Elstree, filming a short scene in the Minute Mart with Angela Wynter. One take. The scene was over. The all-clear came from the director. The temperature was freezing. Removing my winter coat and jacket, I sprinted from the exterior set and headed up a flight of stairs to my dressing room. No make-up to be removed as I only used an anti-shine cream on set. I felt sure I set the record for quickest costume change ever. On my way out to the car, which was there waiting, engine running, and with suitcases already in it, the receptionist appreciated that every second counted, so I was forgiven for not leaning over the desk and giving her a hug. However, I was still able to get a kiss on the cheek from Miss Wynter on her way from the set to her dressing room as I was about to get into the car.

I was heading for Heathrow Airport to catch a flight to Trinidad, in time for the annual Carnival celebration, described as the Eighth Wonder of the World: The Greatest Show on Earth. A visit to Trinidad, especially at Carnival time, was my personal answer to resolve any problems or stress I am feeling. It probably cost about the same as seeing a counsellor but guaranteed a time of lasting and wonderful memories, cushioning all the challenges I was sure to encounter on my return to cold, damp London. For me, Carnival time is always a three-week period each year when I relax, unwind totally and laugh almost continuously. The drive from the studio to Heathrow on the M25, then M4, at this time of the morning was surprisingly quiet and, just as well, because I only had a little over an hour to get there on time for check-in. I was not US President Barack Obama, and my so-called celebrity status cut no ice with the airline; no one was going to hold the aircraft for me! However, recognition by fellow travellers, wanting selfies or signed autographs, were a result of my growing fame. I say 'fame' only because there were not many black men invited into the nation's homes on a nightly basis. So I was stopped frequently. I willingly responded with smiles and signed several autographs after coming out of the car and waiting at the check-in desk. Luckily, the desk clerk had upgraded me to first class, so there was still time left to get to the duty-free shop and sign a few more autographs.

One such encounter was a slightly painful one. A West Indian guy, possibly in his late fifties, with a strong Barbadian accent was accompanied by a much younger, taller and very attractive lady, whom I thought was his daughter. He must have read my thoughts or have been at the receiving end of jokes from his friends because he chipped in quickly and introduced her as his lady friend. He greeted me with exaggerated friendliness, called me Rudy, and gave me a strong handshake, which, had he continued a few seconds longer, would have caused serious damage to my fingers. I hadn't yet recovered from the excruciating pain that shot through my hand when he gave me a forceful thump on the chest. It was all done to impress upon his lady friend that we were good buddies from way back.

In the theatre, we have something called the rule of three. If, for instance, there are a series of jokes, the comedian/actor starts with the minor one, followed by the next funny, and the final joke is meant to be the funniest, the one that brings the house down. The rule could have been applied in my situation quite easily: a handshake, followed by a punch. What next? I braced myself, but thankfully nothing happened. A few discreetly placed questions revealed that we had met nearly thirty years ago at a celebrity cricket match in which I played at Edgbaston with the legendary cricketers Rohan Kanhai, Clive Lloyd, Alvin Kallicharran, Desmond Haynes, Gordon Greenidge, Michael Holding, Derek Murray and many others from the great West Indies cricket teams. I realised from what he said that the man had sat at a table next to me and had been a guest of one of the Warwickshire players. I am extremely good at faces, but I honestly could not remember this guy. Nonetheless, I continued to participate in the charade because to do otherwise would have blown away his standing with his young lady. I caught something in her eyes though that said, 'I know he is a show-off, so thank you for not making him feel small.'

I hurriedly made my way to the first-class lounge, trying to recover from my bruised condition. If I were to encounter another well-intentioned brother, I'd plead that my hands were full to avoid a handshake and I would only have to do a Muhammad Ali shuffle to dodge another thump. I had been invited to the first-class lounge before, but I never knew there existed a separate section where one was invited by the duty manager, away from the majority of the other first-class passengers. I could only assume that was where the mega-stars or the very rich hung out before boarding their flight. As I was neither, I was humbled by the privilege. Sitting in the lounge was John Hurt, the brilliant actor and keen cricketer, with whom I had played in a number of celebrity cricket matches throughout the country, for the Vic Lewis' Celebrity Eleven. The late Vic Lewis was a legendary big jazz band leader and also a member of the MCC. The teams over the years had included: Robert Powell, famous for playing Jesus Christ in the film *Jesus of Nazareth* and as a Staff Nurse in BBC series *Holby City*; and John Alderton, who starred in the television comedy series *Please Sir!* We chatted for a while, remembering classic matches and other cricketers like Wes Hall, Charlie Griffith, Rohan Kanhai, Sir Everton Weeks and Sir Garfield Sobers who played alongside us. We also spoke of the footballer Malcolm McDonald, known in his heyday as Super Mac.

The flight was slightly delayed, so I had the time to make my final call to the people who were very important to me - my son, Darren, and my daughter, Sheona. At the airport, a buggy was sent to take me to the plane. I was approaching my 70s, still physically active on and off the cricket field and the tennis court, and I thought only wheelchair-users or passengers with special needs were transported in those things. I was fairly fit, and I was not overburdened with only three pieces of hand luggage that consisted of a briefcase, some duty-free items and my much-travelled tennis racquets. Furthermore, I did not think the encounter with the enthusiastic brother had left any visible sign to warrant a buggy, but I graciously accepted the offer. Even though we were whizzing through, people still recognised me, but at least I did not have to stop and sign autographs, otherwise I would have missed the flight. I caught myself smiling like a Cheshire cat and waving like royalty. I quickly exchanged my ordinary spectacles for a pair of dark shades and a knitted cap with the peak pulled down as low as possible over my forehead. That seemed to have done the trick. I got to the final check-in desk before boarding the flight without any further encounters. I must point out though that I am not the only actor who received that kind of royal treatment by fans and, contrary to what one might be tempted to think, we do appreciate all the accolades. However, at times, the attention can be overwhelming and even disconcerting.

An example of another of my experiences that day will hopefully explain the dilemma that we can encounter on any given day. Word had gotten around that I was on the flight, so there was a buzz in the air, and people slowed their pace to say hello to me and smile, ignoring the requests to board. As soon as I stepped into the holding lounge, I was greeted by a fellow Trinidadian of East Indian descent, who strategically placed himself next to the check-in clerk, greeted me with one of the broadest smiles imaginable, and with the immortal words, 'Rudolph Walker, yeah man!', clicking his fingers the way I do as Patrick Trueman in *EastEnders*. 'Man, is good to see yuh again after all dese years.' He spoke loud enough so that every Tom, Dick or Ali within a mile radius could hear. Next to him were his wife and three children, to whom he introduced me. His wife extended her hand, saying, 'My husband speaks a lot about you and your schooldays together, since you appeared on TV.' Now this gentleman was at least ten years younger, so that was my first clue that he had the wrong person. The second clue was that anyone with whom I grew up or went to school with knew me as Malcolm. They would never call me Rudolph or Rudy. However, the look of excitement and expectation on the children's faces when I turned to them was so exhilarating that once again to save embarrassment, I quickly asked them their names and ages, shook their hands and signed three autograph cards that I had tucked in my pocket. Then as if by magic, the flight manager intervened and told the family that they had to board the flight immediately. The father still had time to say, 'Man, ah glad we on de same flight, we go ole talk, yeah, man!' Clicking his fingers, he turned to the flight manager. 'Ah know dah star-boy fah years, we went to de same school, we used to lime together.'

The flight manager looked at me, then at him, and became a little firmer in insisting that they proceed to the aircraft immediately. Finally, I was on board. I do have a very strange habit of falling asleep within a few seconds of settling into my seat before the aircraft takes off. It is as if the months of packing, unpacking and repacking, the excitement, the tension, all finally take their toll the minute I settle into my seat. On this trip, it was about fifteen minutes into the flight when I felt a gentle prodding from the air hostess, who was offering me a beverage and a mixture of nuts: cashew and chana (fried chickpeas), a delicacy from my native home. That was my cue to embrace, hook, line and sinker, my Trini heritage, mannerisms and language. My dialect became very

Trinidadian, so everything was 'dat' instead of 'that' and the 'g' got lost in pronunciation, so I would say, 'Yuh jokin', or 'Yuh comin', or 'Yuh goin.' I usually take a leisurely walk in the cabin, talk to families and sign autographs for the children, which activity, at times, could take up to an hour. The journey down the aisle this time was going to be a little different from all the others because I knew that I would meet again the two men who claimed to know me well but with whom I was pretty sure that I had no previous interaction. When I got to the guy from Barbados, he was fast asleep and surprisingly his companion did not attempt to wake him, so we had a quiet chat.

It was her first visit to the Caribbean and to Barbados, because she was born in England and had been together with the gentleman for only a few months. As soon as I sensed that her friend was beginning to stir, I quietly moved on and stopped to talk to another long-standing friend from Trinidad. We were just catching up on family news when I felt another thump on my back and turned to see my fellow Trinidadian minus his family. He was in full flow yet again, 'Rudolph, yuh son-of-a-gun, so good to see yuh again, man,' and he continued, addressing the entire plane. 'Ah went to school wid dis star-boy, yuh know, in San Fernando, an ah go tell all yuh someting, dis man, yuh see him quiet, quiet so now, but he was a tough fella, yuh know, you didn't want to mess wid him in school.' As a man, if another man starts to shower you with praises like that, or as we say in Trinidad 'big-you-up', you might assume an air of importance, puff out your chest and look around to see if any of the beautiful female passengers had started to look at you in a sort of come-on flirtatious way. However, this compliment did not sit too well on my shoulders and it began to have the opposite effect on me. I did not want to embarrass him, even though I knew he had mistaken me for someone else. Firstly, I lived and went to school in Barataria, in the north of the island and not in San Fernando, which is far south. Secondly, I was ten or more years older than he was and I am referred to as Malcolm by everyone with whom I went to school. Furthermore, I was my mother's only boy child, so when my new best friend claimed that I had an older brother, who was as hard as nails, and all but described my entire family as borderline criminals, even my legendary patience was sorely tried, and some choice Trinidadian phrases were about to escape my lips.

Enjoying the unfolding spectacle and my obvious discomfort was my family friend, who knew me well and knew that this was a case of mistaken identity. He also knew me well enough to know that I was not going to embarrass the guy, but he enjoyed watching me sweat and waited to see how I would manoeuvre myself out of the tricky situation. Fortunately for both of us, the air hostess appeared and asked me to take my seat. Not to be outdone, my newly acquired friend quickly suggested that he could slip into a spare seat up front, so we could continue our talk about the old days. Again, the hostess came to the rescue, politely informing him that there were no available seats next to Mr Walker. Relieved, I returned to my seat and spent the remainder of the flight leafing through the local papers, catching up on Trini news and gossip, checking out live shows and events.

The flight to Trinidad is a long one - almost nine hours - but luckily, I do like flying and once I am on the plane, I relax and allow myself to get into the holiday mood. I seldom watch the movie as most of the time, I have a book to read, and I do enjoy solving puzzles. The plane touched down at Piarco Airport at 5.30 p.m. I fully expected my newly acquired friend to be present when I was collecting my suitcases, but his absence was very noticeable. What I found out later was that my family friend, after he had enjoyed my discomfort, had pulled the guy aside and quietly put him right; he also told a number of passengers nearby of the mistaken identity.

I have made countless trips to the Caribbean, especially to Trinidad and Tobago, the place of my birth, and each time, I pause to reflect on my childhood, from where I have come, where I am today and what part I have played and continue to play in various lives, for better or for worse. The first sound you hear as you disembark is that of a steel band playing calypso music on the airport's forecourt. This day, I resisted the temptation of chipping along to the rhythm, only because with mobile phone cameras around there was every chance that within seconds the images of me dancing on arrival at Trinidad's Piarco Airport would have travelled thousands of miles, and I could hear my son and daughter saying, 'Dad, what are you doing? You are the only person dancing, very embarrassing.' It was a week away from this pre-Lenten Festival of Carnival, so the welcoming music was just to get visitors in the mood. Tony, his sons Michael and Emmanuel, the son and grandsons of an old school friend, George Joseph, were waiting to hand over my faithful old Volvo estate car that I had shipped down to the island from the UK. It is a half hour drive to my house in Barataria, approximately one hundred yards around the corner from where I was born and where I spent the first twenty years of my life, and it is just four miles outside the capital city of Port-of-Spain.

As I opened my front door and walked in, I was reminded once more of how far I had come, how far I had travelled, in more ways than one, and that now it was good to be home again. This house was the place that had equipped me with an inner strength to cope mentally with the pressures I experienced daily, living in the UK. There was even a welcome gift. My house guest, Dr Jenny Rouse, a very close family friend, had left me some fresh local fruits on the table. The temperature, even though it was about 8 p.m., was hot - especially for someone who only ten hours earlier had been wearing a heavy winter coat. A quick shower and I changed into a pair of shorts and a merino (a sleeveless vest), and then it was time for me to sit on the back porch and enjoy those sun-kissed mangoes, bananas and pawpaw that were juicy and delicious and a far cry from their frozen, vacuum-packed cousins found in some UK supermarkets.

The heat crept under the merino and brought with it the sounds of my neighbourhood. The belly-laughs of the couple next door were mixed with the canned laughter of the latest offering on television of *Westwood Park*, a popular local television soap. Along with all of that came the melody of the crapaud serenade (distinctive croaks from our local frogs as they leap around the garden) and the ever-present mosquito drone that was swiftly followed by my accompanying slap to crush them.

Then there were the smells! The wind changed its direction and blew away the last remnants of burning grass and I pleasantly inhaled one of my favourite smells. I could sit in the open gallery at the back of the house and be transported straight back to my youth and the sights and smells of neighbours clearing their yards and burning the leaves and grass. Then the sights! The mesmerising aerial dance of the insects-seeking bats; the inky, black backdrop of night, fireflies and stars almost within touch and the full moon that would have every dog, pregnant woman and poet tossing and turning until dawn when the cock crows. The full moon seemed to have had the same effect on me. The roller coaster of emotions over the last twenty-four hours began to take its toll, so I retired to bed for a well needed sleep.

At 4.00 a.m. the next morning, just after the heavens had washed the sleep from the island and just before the sun awoke to dry its face, I was up and off to San Juan's Saturday market. As a child, I got to the market by treading along the grass verge in my washeycong or plimsolls, jumping over open drains onto the roads or hitching a ride on the back of a donkey cart, with a warning from my mother not to gallivant, otherwise I would get a licking.

Now I was walking on roads that had been paved with drains that had been concreted. Significantly, what had not changed and was so refreshing was for me to get a good morning greeting, accompanied with a smile, from every stall holder in the market, be it man or woman, Indian or African

Trinidadian. I soaked up the atmosphere, and looked for the stall vendors, who never seemed to age, or the sons and daughters of the ones who, since my last visit, had departed to enjoy life in the other world. I was greeted by the sounds of the market women, who all seemed to have had lessons in voice projection, long before I did, and whose strong voices bellowed from one end of the market to the other. A masterclass in performance techniques, which would have left many of our Royal Academy of Dramatic Art (RADA) trained actors standing in awe. With each stall presided over by an eagle-eyed, sharp-tongued well-upholstered market woman, the excitement grew.

As a boy, I had no time to linger and enjoy the atmosphere or touch the produce, as the mission was to get the goods and get home as quickly as possible. Now, I was even allowed the opportunity to have a free taste of a governor-plum or balata or some other local fruit that was in seasonal abundance. I needed to get fresh fish, which had just been caught that night, and fresh vegetables. It is amazing to think that all those vegetables we cooked regularly as part of our daily diet were now being hailed as super foods with health-giving properties. Pommecythere (ambarella), also referred to as Golden Apple or June Plum, contains iron; sweet potato has potassium, and soursop (*Annona Muricata*) is said to be a natural form of chemotherapy. Yam can control hormonal balance and weight; dasheen and eddoes give energy and must be used in moderation. In addition, there were the green vegetables like spinach, which we call bhaji, dasheen leaves, called callaloo bush, okra also called ladies' fingers, and watercress - or cressles, as we call it. We had been eating a healthy diet, without knowing it.

Here in Trinidad, the kitchen was my territory, and on this particular day, I was planning to prepare one of my specialities, fish broth - a recipe I learned from my mother, albeit the hard way. It was only 5.30 and in the UK most people would still be in bed, but I had completed my market shopping and was now heading for Woodbrook, a residential area just outside Port-of-Spain and the home of my late cousin Miss Pat Bishop. The 'Miss' an important prefix that demonstrated the respect we had for her. Patricia Alison Bishop TC, to give her full name, was a musical genius recognised as such with a national accolade, The Trinity Cross (TC), and the recognition of her peers with the title of The Archbishop of Pan. Pat propped herself up in bed, still in her nightdress. She prefers it when I fly into Trinidad if I visit her first thing in the morning when it is quiet, no visitors and phone calls to disturb us. I generally perch myself at the end of the bed if a chair is not readily available. She would ask her housekeeper to bring me a glass of coconut water. It was just gone 6.30 a.m. and I was making my way to the Colonial Life Tennis Club, which is situated at one side of the Queen's Park Savannah, in Port-of-Spain about a ten-minute drive from Pat. The savannah is reputed to be the world's largest roundabout and is ringed by poui trees (*Tabebuia Rosea*), with the rolling hills of the Northern Range in the distance. I arrived and was greeted by one of the players, Shirley Kelsick, a senior club member. She questioned jokingly, 'But A! A! Rudy, you come again?' To which I retorted, 'I haven't stopped coming since I left here three months ago.' All ten players burst into laughter. That was followed by some picong, a continuous and spontaneous verbal teasing, satirical or comic banter. This is an important feature of our communication, verbal gymnastics that can easily become insulting. Not crossing the line is a skill that many have.

I love the description that playwright Horace Carter, son of a Trini mother, made of this practice – 'a verbal battle of insults hurled in rhymed verse'. This picong continued throughout the games across all three courts. Therein lies the tonic – games, picong and camaraderie – that I so desperately crave for during those cold winter months in England. The standard of tennis is quite high as some of the players have represented Trinidad in their youth. The players are of all creed and colour, covering the whole spectrum of the society: cabinet ministers, housewives, doctors, mechanics, shopkeepers, bankers, calypsonians, Africans, Indians, Whites and Syrians. Players such as Glenda Morean-Phillip who became High Commissioner for Trinidad and Tobago in the UK. Shirley Kelsick was one of Trinidad's leading tennis players, Dr Keith Rowley who is now the Prime Minister of Trinidad and Tobago, the late Bobby Thomas a highly respected broadcaster and a Director of TTT, Neil Giuseppi, who remained a very close friend and many, many others.

My standard of tennis is just above average compared to most of the players, but I do so enjoy these encounters. It is a time when the phrase, that is common to us, 'all-ah-we-is-one', can be aptly applied. As a child, I walked past those same courts, peeping through the wire fence, but then I could just have had a glimpse at the players, people of light colour in their white shorts and tops. Furthermore, I knew the likes of me were not allowed anywhere near the compound, simply because I was black and poor. In any case, tennis in those days did not hold any interest for me; cricket did and was certainly within my reach. However, I am always aware of the social boundaries that I have crossed over the years and on many occasions I find myself retracing my steps in life as I look back upon my early life experiences that are all so vivid in my mind.

As are more recent experiences. And despite wanting real stability in my life, unfortunately this has not proven to be the case although I am still very friendly with my first wife Lorna, and we are both proud of the two children we created together. Sadly my marriage to Dounne had failed and I married Evangeline Vincent-Davis in 2016, only to see this marriage unsuccessful too. It is a sadness to me that my marriages failed as I have always aimed for a long-term relationship with the women in my life. Looking back, I can see that I have attempted to find an ideal wife, based on the women I knew growing up and the values that I attributed to them, including the strength and independence of my mother. Lorna came very close to this. Being in the public eye is hard on relationships, having to share your partner with fans and cameras can be difficult to deal with and not everyone, especially if it's not a world they're familiar with copes well. I felt sorrow to hear that Evangeline died from a brain haemorrhage whilst she was in Trinidad in 2024. But if my personal life has had its ups and downs, my professional life has continued over the decades.

Now, 2024, an established actor still working both on the stage when roles are offered and in *EastEnders* – even being awarded the 'Outstanding Achievement Award' at the British Soap Awards 2018 for having played Patrick for seventeen years, I know I have crossed many boundaries. I had also been honoured by being awarded an OBE in the 2006 Birthday Honours for services to drama and charity and a CBE in the 2020 New Year's Honours. The letter for this came through in 2019 but I only got the award later the following year as the country came out of the Covid lockdown. I collected it at St Jame's Palace from Prince Charles (soon, of course, to be King Charles) and as we were talking, he referred to *Coronation Street* instead of *EastEnders*. I corrected him – me, a once-poor boy from Trinidad correcting a future king! – and invited him to visit the set after he talked about how both he and his mother had visited the set of the northern serial drama. Apparently, this invitation was noted and both he and his wife Camilla, then the Duchess of Cornwall, turned up in Elstree. We then filmed an unscripted scene in the market, including Camilla being offered a tot of rum by Patrick! All alcoholic drinks on the set are usually just watered-down cola or cold tea or just lemonade or water, but on this occasion, in honour of the royal visit, real alcohol was on offer, so the rum offered to Camilla was actually rum!

What a long way I had come. I count myself so blessed.

PART SIX

Final Reflections

I WAS BORN A HERO

I was born a hero brave and free
With strength to fight my foes
My lion heart that man did fear
And my ever-bloodstained sword.
I fought many a battle on land and sea
And gained victory over all
I stormed the decks; I walked the planks,
But thank God I still lived on.
My life was filled of adventures
Adventures great and small
Adventures that other men were afraid to face
For they were not brave and strong.
… I'll always dream of those adventurous days
At nights when I go to sleep
How I was victorious over all my foes
And a hero on land and sea.

by Malcolm Walker, aged 14

CHAPTER 17

'Where Do You Go from Here?'

'*My humanity is bound up in yours, for we can only be human together*' Desmond Tutu, South African theologian and human rights activist

---

This book has taken several years of gestation before its birth and during that time, and certainly over the last few years, we have lived through some major events that impacted on the social, political and cultural landscapes in the UK. As I began writing, we were expecting to come out of a national lockdown and to herald a new normal. In every facet of our lives since then, there have been changes and challenges – and some, like increased working from home in many professions and the familiarity of mask-wearing, feel to be permanent.

Throughout the lockdowns, the theatres were dark and quiet – closed doors, cancelled shows, careers stalled. But the profession rose to the challenge, with monologues instead of TV dramas on our screens, small productions streamed out into people's homes, acting classes by Zoom, outdoor performances when feasible with audiences in 'rings' or 'bubbles' on the grass

– and bigger shows like *EastEnders* working through the problems by installing screens between performers and focusing more on individual performances. I think we did pretty well, in fact! Then, as the lights went up again and social distancing became a distant memory, we needed to step up again to re-engage and work towards ensuring that equality and creative diversity remained on the agenda.

Between 1948 and 1964, it is estimated that over 300,000 people from the British Caribbean migrated to the UK; coming here in nine ships, the most celebrated being the HMT *Empire Windrush*, its passengers including four calypsonians from Trinidad – Lord Kitchener (Aldwyn Roberts), Lord Beginner, Lord Woodbine and Mona Baptiste. Who could forget Lord Kitchener's instant calypso 'London is the Place to Be' which he made up immediately on arrival in the UK!

Many others came here by aircraft, mainly British Overseas Airways Corporation (BOAC). Perhaps that's why my fellow Trinidadian, Ansel Wong, one of the founders of Black History Month, refers to himself as being of the BOAC Generation rather than the Windrush Generation!

As each generation grew, we became integral to every facet of British society. And yet our presence in the social, cultural and political landscapes of the UK remained at best patchy, unrepresentative and tokenistic. There is a multiplicity of reasons for this absence and too much of our time is spent trying to storm the barricades or smash the glass ceilings.

In my world, theatre and TV, black actors should not have any barriers to being cast for any role. Talented actors of any colour should be able to perform in every aspect of theatre, from farce to comedy, to drama, to Shakespeare.

Yes, there have been changes. But too often they are episodic, knee-jerk reactions to external events – the racist murder of Stephen Lawrence by a gang of white thugs in 1993 led to an investigation into institutionalised racism within the Metropolitan Police (and as I write, another similar investigation is now underway, over 20 years later) while the activism of Black Lives Matter showed a ground roots cross-cultural revulsion to racism. We can come together to campaign on issues, but the impetus is never maintained beyond the rally or the demonstration. There is often no continuity, or momentum, to maintain real progress.

Television media is one of the social agents that can foster/provoke change in society. It is a very powerful means of communication and it reaches many more people in a shorter space of time than can be done in the theatre. As a result, it should be showing more positive images of the Black community. As I have said previously, there should be a higher percentage of black producers, directors, writers and camera persons, but their inclusion must be based only on their excellent accomplishments and not on a quota system.

I tell all the young people I meet that whatever profession they want to pursue, if they enjoy it and their gut feeling is that it is what they want to do, they should go for it. There is no crystal ball to foretell their future, no guru to accurately predict their progress. It does no one any good to sit back and say, 'I wonder if I should? I wonder what it would be like?'

In the acting profession, my advice is to accept the competitiveness, be ready for the intensity of proving your suitability for roles, prepare for nuanced practices and prejudices. But, overall, don't give up. You must have the will to succeed, the inner strength to overcome all obstacles, believe in yourself, in your potential and be prepared to learn all the time.

For me, every person I met, each challenge I faced and every rejection I was given provided me with lessons to learn. Yes, I would lick my wounds. Cry. Swear. Threaten retribution when I achieved success. But that bitterness never lasted long. And if I had to walk away, I always walked away with dignity.

I bring to the theatre what I think is me and I always try to bring truthfulness to what I do. I do not know what style that is, whether it is something I picked up from looking at older actors or developed on my own. And I had a personal vision of where I wanted to be - in five years, in ten years, by the time I die. Aspirational goals and achievements, re-shaped and re-set every time I achieved one or was knocked off course.

I knew what I wanted so I stuck it out and was determined to succeed. I knew my capabilities, even though at times I was reminded by individuals, friends, relatives or fans that I could have been more ambitious, aimed higher. Other reminders were less supportive, and I needed to learn how to be thick-skinned as the criticisms could be harsh and unfair. Sometimes I watch videos of my work, but I tend to wait until sometime after their transmission to watch them, for like many actors I am my worst critic - there is very little that I have ever watched for the first time and thought that it was well done! I pick out all the holes and think that it should have been better.

It is different in the theatre, because at some performances I could be conscious that something had not quite hit the mark, something was not quite right, but there was always another opportunity to rectify it at the following performance.

I have never really felt overpowered by an audience. Like Vivian Richards - that skilled, aggressive, West Indian batsman. The Master Blaster always strode out to the playing arena with total confidence, even though there were times when he managed a mere ten, a four or a duck, yet at other times his fifty or a hundred or two hundred were spectacular, and he would take every bowler to task.

In like manner, when I walk on stage, especially to a packed theatre, there is always a wonderful feeling, a high, as I sense the rapt attention of the audience, the fixedness of their eager eyes, the degrees of expectation and the peering look on their faces. Although I always believe that when I walk on stage, I exude confidence, that does not stop me from being very nervous. This happens at every performance, not just on press night, but within a minute of walking on and facing the audience and the lights, I become transformed.

I remember when I was on stage doing *The Fatherland* at the Tricycle Theatre, I played the role of two characters; one was a that of a West Indian and the other an African. At the end, pleasing remarks were made by members of the audience, but I found it very difficult to believe that it took them a long time to realise that it was the same person who had come back on stage as an African. That was very rewarding.

Just before the press night, I felt more nervous than usual and an experienced young black actor, having detected my nervousness, took me aside, saying: 'God has given you a wonderful gift. You have done all your homework, as long as you focus and think positively, walk out on that stage with confidence, it will happen. You have no reason to fear, walk ten feet tall.'

Since then, whenever I feel somewhat nervous before I go on stage, I always remember the words of that actor.

Confidence and self-belief are crucial to an actor; it is important to believe, when given a role, that you are capable of playing it well. Why would the director have chosen you otherwise? Just as I am my own worst critic when watching replays of my performances on screen, I have been my own saboteur too when taking on a new part. Especially at the beginning of my career.

One part I played sticks in my mind in particular. In February 1967, the formidable director, Dr Jonathan Miller, was casting for *Benito Cereno* by Robert Lowell at the Mermaid Theatre, a play he had successfully directed in the States. I was one of the many black actors he had auditioned for the part, but because of my little experience I did not think I had the slightest chance of being chosen.

When I did get the part, I was excited but filled with nerves. It was the first time I had met and worked with Norman Beaton and Nina Baden-Semper, and I felt very insecure when conversations went beyond the boundaries of the play, making me very aware of my own academic shortcomings in comparison. I often felt that more educated people could be rather intimidating, making it all too obvious – body language, condescending behaviour etc - that they considered me on a different level from them. All I could do in return was throw my energy into being the best I could be, watching and listening to every bit of direction from Jonathan.

One day, my self-confidence was further boosted when Jonathan pulled me aside. 'Now, Rudolph,' he said, 'you have a fantastic voice, but I want you to forget it!'

At that moment, I knew exactly what he meant - not that I must ignore that gift God gave me, but that I should maximise it only when it could be effective, impacting and meaningful. I had seen actors with good voices falling into the same trap of using the voice rather than their soul - that inner part of their being. In essence, I'd been saying, 'Listen to my beautiful voice!'

Jonathan was involved in many other projects, always in demand and often away for brief spells. A week before the play closed, he flew back to see it. None of us was aware that he was in the audience that night, and a very close friend of mine accidentally overheard him, in the foyer after the show, telling a group of his friends that the greatest pleasure for him was coming back and seeing how Rudolph Walker's performance had grown in stature. Wow!

I did not rest on my laurels; although I had fantastic reviews, there were always greater depths to any character I played. Sometimes, finding those depths can itself be a salutary lesson. One of the scenes in the play took place on board a ship, requiring Babu - my character - to serve a meal to two actors, then stand behind them whilst they ate the meal. On one night, the scene appeared to be taking unusually longer than normal, because as I stood there behind them, I was feeling sick but could not move because I had dialogue coming up. I could feel the perspiration pouring off me. There was a break of just a dozen lines, and I dashed to the back of the stage with my back to the audience and vomited and was back again for my next line. I was sure the audience thought it was part of the play, though my fellow actors knew precisely what happened.

Perhaps, if Jonathan were in the audience that night, he might have thought that I was a real genius to add that touch to the play!

Gerald Harper, who I had worked with on TV, was always extremely supportive, and he came to see the show and took me out for a meal afterwards. He then said something that rang alarm bells in my ears that evening and beyond.

'Rudolph, what I saw you do tonight was fantastic, but you are black, where do you go from here?'

There was no need to question what he meant because it was so clear.

Later, more experienced, I still ran into problems when trying to be part of a development team for a new project. I was attending an end-of-shoot party at the Elstree film studios for the cast and crew of *Man About the House*, a popular sitcom that was made into a film, and both myself and Jack Smethurst, at the studios to make the film version of *Love Thy Neighbour*, made guest appearances in the sitcom. During a break in our shooting, one of the guests attending the party was Jimmy Leggett, a well-known and highly respected casting agent, who told me that I ought to have my own TV series.

'Come on, Jimmy, you must be joking! Me? Have my own series?'

'Why not? You are well respected in the business, you have what it takes to carry a TV series successfully, and I am certain that if I go to any TV company with an idea, they will snap you up, and welcome you on board. Tell you what, Rudolph, I'll go away and write you a format for a series and give it to you. It will be my present to you. You can own it and do what you like with it.'

I smiled in appreciation and thanked him sincerely, but I thought that was the end of the conversation.

About a month later, through the post came a three-page format for a television series about a young black copper, who had aspirations of becoming a lawyer. My agent, excited about the prospect, arranged an interview with the appointed head of drama at London Weekend TV.

Jimmy's assessment appeared to be correct, because there was no problem getting a meeting, in spite of the fact that we did not send him a copy of the format in advance. The meeting went fairly well. He quickly read it, was not gushing with enthusiasm, but said he liked the idea and dropped a little bombshell at the end, by saying that he was moving on shortly and he would leave the final decision to whoever would succeed him.

I went back to my agent and gave him the news.

'Let's not leave it lying there, try somewhere else.'

My agent then called the head of drama at the Associated Television (ATV), who was based at the same location where I am now filming *EastEnders*. Once again Jimmy was correct, and the door was immediately opened. Yet again, they loved the idea. This time they were much more positive, suggesting that we should have several meetings to follow through and that we did. I even got a message from the head of drama himself, saying how delighted he was to have me on board.

A black actor in those days was never accorded that sort of respect and being part of a development team was unheard of. Nothing, however, was written down or recorded. And in spite of my excitement, I was realistic enough to know it could all go horribly wrong.

A number of weeks went by and no call came, so I asked my agent to find out what was happening. My agent was told that the series was going ahead – but the executive producer was clear that this was 'not Rudolph Walker's idea they were using, nor Jimmy Liggert's'. No, apparently it was an old idea they had in the locker for some time, but obviously when it came to casting, I would be considered. It was the last I heard from them. The producer of the short-lived series was the same executive producer who I first took the idea to at London Weekend TV.

Jimmy, too, had not been informed, nor his format recognised. But the very idea that he thought so highly of me makes that incident a fond memory and I thank you, Jimmy, for your belief in me and the most gracious interest that you have shown in my career.

There were others who were vocal in their support of me and questioned why more opportunities were not created for black actors to gain a much higher status. That letter from

Michael Hastings who wrote *For The West*, was an example of such sentiments.

This wasn't the first time something similar had happened to me; I'd collaborated once before with an actor to develop a new format with myself in the key role, he'd sent it out to varied producers, only to discover something almost identical being produced about a year later with a white actor as the principal character.

This was the last time I tried to be part of a development team for a new TV series – twice bitten! It was too disheartening, and I preferred to focus on the acting roles I was being offered, so I could give 100% to my work there.

CHAPTER 18

Meeting The Greatest

'I've learned that people will forget what you said, people will forget what you did, but people will never forget how you made them feel' Maya Angelou, American **memoirist**, poet and civil rights activist

I have always paid tribute to the many actors who have opened the door to allow me an easier path into the business; to allow me to take up the baton and move forward. They have all built the platform for many others, including myself, to reach where we are today.

One of those stages, only dreamed of by earlier generations, was my two appearances on the National TV Awards show, historic because they were 'firsts' and so deserved archiving as evidence of how far we had come by that stage. They were historical, and tapes so produced should be kept in libraries, not only in England but also distributed and preserved in the archives of all African Caribbean countries. In turn, they should be made available to our grandchildren and the generations to come. More importantly, events like those should be written about as part of our history. It is important too that when the baton is passed on, the generation to come acknowledges that success did not come overnight; seeds were planted and nurtured with blood, sweat, tears, hard work and very many sacrifices. My children, Darren and Sheona, my grandchildren Josh, Loveday and Latimer, their children and future generations, need to see in print the contributions that their parents and grandparents made and the challenges they experienced and had to overcome to pass on the benefits that they are enjoying today.

My educational pathway had been rooted in a colonial relationship that Trinidad had with Britain. Not only from what I learned in school but from what my experiences of day-to-day living taught me about myself, my family and my country.

I could not play for the Queen's Park Cricket Club unless I was of a certain colour. There were clubs I could not join - for example, the Maples Club in Port-of-Spain, whose members were predominantly white. There were also places I could not go. But there were winds of change blowing as the drive for independence from Britain gathered momentum in my native Trinidad and throughout the Caribbean.

This was the period that historians called Doctor Politics as all the proponents for political change were PhD graduates of Britain. Ironic, yes. But an English classical education drove the move for political, cultural and social change.

Dr Eric Williams was one such agent of change. I left Trinidad before all the dramatic changes took place only to arrive in the UK to realise that the situation was much worse here.

In the early 1960s, when I arrived in London, it was not at all surprising to see pictures of Elvis Presley and John F. Kennedy side by side with the image of the Sacred Heart of Jesus on the walls in a West Indian house. And it was not just the framed pictures on the walls but also the furniture and decorative elements – from the glass fish to the polished wooden radiogram. With each passing year, the photos changed as a reflection of each period of settlement. And Elvis was replaced with Bob Marley.

We were, as young Caribbean immigrants, looking for heroes, icons and leaders with whom we could identify and also emulate. For me, the emergence of Muhammad Ali filled that void. Ali emerged as a figure of immense power. His rise through the ranks of Olympic champion to world boxing champion was phenomenal. He became a topic of heated debates in African Caribbean barber shops and social gatherings. Like the millions of other people around the world, we were treated to a larger-than-life character, a superb showman, and arguably the greatest ever boxer.

He was a hero to me, and I had the amazing opportunity of meeting him on 2nd December 1974 when he was invited to address the pupils of Tulse Hill Comprehensive School.

Ali was staying in the London Hilton Hotel on his way to Chicago coming back from retaining his world heavyweight title belt against Big George Foreman in one of the most famous boxing matches ever, 'The Rumble in the Jungle' in Zaire, now known as Congo, Africa.

Paul Stephenson, a friend who was one of Tulse Hill's school governors, met Ali in a hotel foyer and asked him to come as a guest to Tulse Hill school. Ali's response was, 'I'm a very busy man, how much are you going to pay me?' When Paul said he didn't have so much as a dime, Ali said, 'Man, you have got more nerve than Joe Frazier,' then he smiled and agreed to visit the school.

I was contacted by Paul and invited to the school to be a member of the welcoming committee. I cancelled every appointment I had that day as I was never going to miss this opportunity, but I was more excited that these students at this school were going to get the chance to meet one of the greatest sports icons in the world at the time, and I wanted to see their faces. The headmaster had also decided to keep it a secret as he wanted to surprise them.

Ali arrived and was hidden away in the headmaster's office, as all the teachers gathered all the pupils from every classroom into the assembly hall. The children didn't know what was happening. Over a thousand young people with teachers crammed into this hall, waiting and wondering why they had all been gathered together. A few of us were on the stage and Ali was in the wings on the stage out of the sight of the students as Paul came on the stage and announced, 'We have a young man who's made a great impact in Africa and is on his way to Chicago now but has decided to come and see you.'

Ali emerged from the wings, and as recognition set in, the place erupted! The noise was deafening. It wasn't only the students making the noise, it was the teachers too!

Finally, everyone calmed down and Ali was able to speak.

The showman was in action. The presence that he had was phenomenal. He spoke about getting an education and having respect for your teachers. Everyone, including myself, was inspired. Then he picked out one tall young man and started sparring with him. Inspiring and entertaining, that was Ali. He left the school with one of his rhymes: 'I like your school, Mr Stephenson, I admire your style, but your pay is so cheap I won't be back for a while.'

Everybody laughed. It was typical Ali style.

After the assembly we went back to the headmaster's office and I was so surprised and taken back when Ali invited poet Clarence Thompson and myself to the Hilton hotel, where he was staying, to have lunch with him that very day. No one says no to Ali, and I wasn't going to start that trend.

When we arrived, Ali was in his room, and when he came down there were large groups of photographers. Ali said, 'Take your pictures and then disappear, this is a private lunch and I want privacy.'

When the photographers left, the showman left too, and what we had was this bright intelligent man who inspired us for two hours. This time spent I will never forget. What I ate for lunch that day, I can't even remember, because the best food I received was the knowledge that came from the multi-talented Ali. This period in his company was far beyond my expectation. There in our presence was this public figure, this larger-than-life character, who suddenly switched and became the seeker of knowledge, the adviser, and the prophet. He was interested in what was happening with black people in the United Kingdom. He was interested in world affairs and in what was taking place in the West Indies. All the while, those interchanges were conducted very quietly and without any histrionics as was seen in his public persona.

Many things were discussed, but I would like to honour him by keeping most of what was said private and in my heart.

I asked Ali if I could bring my son Darren who was just over three years old at the time and was already doing the Ali shuffle to the hotel to meet him, and Ali immediately agreed. It was arranged for the following morning. I was once again excited and so was Darren, to meet someone he only saw on TV. After waiting in the foyer for a while Ali came down with his large contingent of people, came over and lifted Darren. And Darren, very much unlike my son's usual behaviour, just started to cry, so I quickly had to rescue him. I don't know if it was Ali's height, or suddenly coming face to face with a hero that set him off.

Over the years I saw in Ali a man who was becoming more influential than any other political leader on this planet. I saw a man who could bring people of all colours together, a spiritual leader; a man, as he grew older and departed the boxing arena, who could continue to challenge the status quo. A man capable of getting to the core of world poverty and affecting changes.

I felt a sense of pride in the way Ali sacrificed and positioned himself to positively influence the world. It was refreshing to hear Muhammad Ali say in one of his interviews, 'Boxing is only a means of getting the platform to facilitate the work I came to this earth to fulfil.' That statement only confirmed the beliefs that I held.

'The Greatest' gave me one of my greatest memories and inspired me and a whole school in South London, England. I would love to know what those young people got out of that visit and some of the testimonies of what they have achieved since they met him. What a day!

However, he made a statement at that lunch that was to be embedded in my memory over the years when he told us that the only time America would give the Presidency to a black man was when the ship was sinking.

In November 2008, more than thirty years later, Barack Obama was elected as the President of the USA.

I often compare the impact of Ali's presence and public profile on the global stage with our community leaders in the UK or political leaders in the Caribbean. In the Caribbean, we have had some notable individuals who championed the drive to political independence from Britain, but after that the well ran dry.

My one glimpse of hope was the West Indies cricket team of the 1960s and 70s: a classic example of what strong and well-respected leaders could achieve. Starting with the late Sir Frank Worrell and later Clive Lloyd, they were able to pull together a team of cricketers who were world beaters and achievers. They were talented individuals from different islands, with different cultures, different ideologies, different likes and dislikes and even different accents but they were able to bond with one another and make a difference in the game.

In the UK, we are still looking for strong leadership among the Caribbean community. Two individuals who I can single out with pride are the late Bernie Grant MP and the late Rudy

Narayan, the barrister. Bernie's untimely death robbed us of the only black political aspirant who had the potential for national leadership. It was not unusual to visit his surgery in Tottenham to see people of all races, colour, creed and religion waiting to see him. And Rudy Narayan fleetingly occupied the national stage as a campaigning barrister, championing black victims of the judicial system. Fearless, articulate and debonair.

Many reasons have been suggested of why we have not been able to have an individual from our community to unite us and lead the struggle for equal rights. Where is our Nelson Mandela? Our Dr Martin Luther King? Many have tried to make inroads, but no one has yet taken on this mantle. Island nationalism? Poverty? Slave mentality? Ethnic and colour rivalries? I am not sure if any of these are the reasons.

It is said amongst the African Caribbean community in England that we don't have a history, but we do. It's just that not many of us put pen to paper, and time and time again when books are written, documentaries and films are made about England we are pushed in the background into insignificance. For many years, there was no physical or cyberspace to house the history of our presence in Britain. But we now have the fledgling Black Cultural Archives, the Home of Black British History. Based in Brixton in SE London, the collection draws together artefacts and other evidence of the histories of African and Caribbean people in the UK, to inspire others to learn about and appreciate the richness of this history. In the words of Kwame Kwei-Armah, actor, writer and broadcaster, it is a 'goldmine of information about Black cultural identity in Britain'. My hope is that this venue will become a place that will archive our history, encourage the teaching of it in schools and universities and be accessible for families to learn of their parents' heritage and history. And the archives go way back, back to before the Windrush years.

It is only within the last few years, for instance, because of public pressure, that it became widely known to the public that West Indians played a very important part as pilots and soldiers in the Second World War. It wasn't all white heroes! Regrettably, it is only within the last year I became aware that the Jamaican nurse, Mary Seacole, played an equally important role - and some have said, a far greater role - in the Crimean War than did Florence Nightingale. An article by Helen J. Seaton in the Victorian Web, on political history, explains that 'the sands of history seemed to have buried Mary Seacole's deeds until, in the 1970s, when it was rediscovered and has now become a symbol to black nurses'.

All this partly fuelled my decision not to seek roles in the USA – something I had been encouraged to do at varied times. But I wanted to stay in the UK, not just because of my family responsibilities but a kind of pioneering campaigning spirit that fired a burning desire, as a black actor, to walk the walk in England.

I watched a lot of what was taking place on television, in films and in the theatre and realised that there was not a single Caribbean actor in England who could be described as a household name. The only person, who came near to achieving that status was Errol John, and even so, it happened only for a limited time. After fifty-three years in England and fifty years in the industry, I have yet to see the British make a national or international star of one of their home-grown Caribbean trained actors. The actors who have gained international acclaim had to cross the waters to the United States of America to achieve respectability. The practice in England seems to be that one is honoured today and dropped tomorrow. It seems simply to be a token gesture. Idris Elba, John Boyega, Bonnie Mbuli and Adrian Lester, to mention just a few, had to cross the waters to gain recognition and respect. However it's encouraging to see a number of young actors are producing their own films and working in collaboration with other mainstream production companies.

CHAPTER 19
Giving Back

'I would like to be known as a person who is concerned about freedom and equality and justice and prosperity for all people'
Rosa Parks, activist in the American civil rights movement

Setbacks and disappointments have made me a stronger person, both mentally and spiritually, and prepared me for what lay ahead. Over the years, I have had many low points when my self-confidence has taken a beating from the pressure, the anger, the frustration, the demands from people around me and the need to keep up appearances. I have, during those periods, taken refuge in prayers, in my spirituality and in my belief in myself. I do it on the cricket field, on the tennis court and whenever I travel. I keep true to myself, to my beliefs. And to my family. To my children, my grandchildren, a handful of very close friends, and the work I do with The Rudolph Walker Foundation, the Haven's Hospice, Errol McKellen Prostate Cancer Foundation, and Sickle Cell Society - they are my bedrock, they keep my feet on the ground. Help me to keep it real.

And one way I have striven to *'give back'*, to help a future generation face their own challenges, is in working with young people.

During the high public profile of *Love Thy Neighbour*, I was invited and accepted invitations to visit a few schools throughout the country, especially the ones with a high percentage of black pupils. Two schools in particular held great interest and appeal to me, more so than the others. They were the Dick Sheppard School and Tulse Hill Comprehensive School, both in London.

In both cases, I was deeply concerned about the alleged harassment some students faced from the police on their way home, after leaving school in the evenings, or congregating outside the library in the centre of the borough. There seemed a real lack of worthwhile and stimulating activities in which they could be engaged after school. As a result of those concerns, the Rudolph Walker Drama Award was born. I had the full support of one of the Governors of Tulse Hill School - Mr Paul Stevenson, a highly respected civil rights activist - and Mrs Margaret Broadley, Head of Dick Sheppard School, who both encouraged drama in their respective schools.

The format was quite simple. The students, who could come from any year group, organised themselves in groups of no more than six, selected a director and a stage manager from the group, and among them wrote a scene lasting no more than fifteen minutes. They could choose their own storylines – and many focused on topical issues like stop and search, exploring it on stage to stimulate discussion. Depending on the number of entrants, the school would then select the best three to represent it at a special gala evening alongside a similar number from the other school. I was able to obtain some high-profile celebrities to come on board to judge and award trophies for best actor, actress, director, stage manager and play, thus giving the children a great incentive to achieve high standards in whatever they undertook.

The main requirement, however, was that the pieces should have been written and rehearsed outside of school hours and with no help from the teachers. The students took rehearsals in turn, working at each other's homes where possible, thus ensuring some quality time being spent after school, if just for one evening each week.

The heart-warming response and enthusiasm from the pupils and parents was astounding. And although the programme was set up to allow expression and build confidence in pupils that they could be part of something successful, in some cases the talent shone through and pupils went on to bigger and better things, building careers within the drama world. One example of this was Paulette Randall, one of the first students, who has gone on to be one of the most sought-after directors in the UK. I was fortunate to have her directing me in a number of episodes in *EastEnders*.

The closure of both the Tulse Hill and Dick Sheppard schools meant the end of the Drama Awards. But my concern for the welfare and well-being of youngsters continued with visits to a number of schools from London to Birmingham and Bristol, talking about my life experiences and trying to inspire as best I could.

In 2003 I had a call from Mervin Cato who at the time was working for Edmonton County School. He requested if I could come and speak to a whole year group of 300 students at his school. I arrived early and he asked if I could also visit the home of his parents who were great admirers of my work on TV.

That first talk at Edmonton County was amazing as I was able to interact with the students and it wasn't just me talking at them. It became the first of many visits to schools in the Enfield area. Mervin Cato invited me to speak to individuals, classes of thirty children, whole year groups and even whole school assemblies of 700 students plus. It was a nerve-racking experience to start with, as I never prepared a speech and just hoped and prayed that I'd be up to the challenge and not left with egg on my face.

The power of TV and the popularity of *EastEnders* meant that I was always greeted with rapturous applause and excitement throughout the school.

Mervin also invited me to a Pupil Referral Unit (PRU) which was a centre for students that have been permanently excluded from school and most of them had problems with the law and in gangs or had gang affiliations. I was warned before I arrived of the high security within the corridors, and how fights could break out. The group of youngsters I was meeting were apparently a very tough bunch.

The door opened and I was greeted by almost total silence for the first time. They knew who I was, but they didn't care. I could just imagine the thoughts of some of them: *'What you are doing here, old man? We don't have anything in common.'* And, *'You probably have a big car with a driver waiting to take you to some big party.'* They were a mixed bunch of youngsters. A few of the lads had their feet up on chairs and made no attempt to remove them when I entered.

I indicated to Mervin to leave the room: he was reluctant, but I felt confident about speaking to them alone. There was a table with a chair placed behind, presumably for me to sit there. I removed the chair, set it amongst them, and turned it around so I could rest my arm on the back it. Then I set about talking about my life, and wherever I was able to add a little humour I did, also sharing the painful times with them. One by one I got them to talk a little about themselves; not all did, but enough were drawn in to have a healthy discussion.

The session only ended when Mervin knocked on the door and announced that I had a school to visit. They were all by then sitting up in their seats, very respectful; one who wore a hood and had his face covered when I arrived had removed it by then - not by me telling him to do so either.

Mervin's remark when I got out into the corridor was: *'How did you do that? I've never seen that group so quiet.'* His observation was immediately followed by one the youngsters coming out of the room to shake my hand and say thank you, sir. It turned out that same youngster told Mervin the next day that my conversation with them had been so inspirational that he was determined to change his life around.

I felt then that I had to return to the Drama Awards and ensure that I did my small bit to help provide a positive experience for youngsters to engage in with their free time. And this initiative has now become an established programme, Rudolph Walker's Inter-School Drama Awards (ISDA), that works with several schools to provide young people with a sense of purpose and opportunities to engage in theatre arts. Youngsters aged 11-18 can submit a video presentation showing why their school should be picked, and then six schools are chosen. Each is matched with a celebrity actor to help them develop a ten-minute play about any topic they choose. Over the years that the competition has been held, this has involved the support of people over the years like Carmen Monroe, Little and Large, Cleo Laine, and many others. I am so grateful to them for helping me with the project. The rehearsed plays are then performed at an annual Finals.

At the time of writing, I have just seen the performances for the 2023 Award – which was won by FreshSteps Independent School. It was a remarkable performance from a group of youngsters with special needs that brought tears to our eyes. I particularly appreciated a comment by one of the parents that she had seen a side of her son that she didn't know existed and thanked the Foundation for the work we are doing.

Along with the new Archives and the UK Black History Month, first celebrated in the UK in October 1987, initiatives such as mine hopefully help young people of the future each work towards the futures they can create for themselves, free of discrimination. The sankofa image that is the symbol of the UK's Black History Month creates a perfect message: *'Sankofa'* is a combination of three words in the Twi language of Ghana that, combined, mean *'going back to fetch'*. It is an illustration of the importance of turning to our past and heritage in order to chart our progress and the journey to our goals.

As a young actor, I felt the urge to make a difference and, in my mind, I kept thinking, *'Rudy, you have a job to do in this country, you have to break down some barriers.'*

Today, that feeling is still very much alive in me.

I'll end this section with Archimedes. A quote over 1500 years old, but still valid:

'Give me a lever long enough and a fulcrum on which to place it, and I shall move the world.'

Or at least, a little bit of it . . .

CHAPTER 20

Final Thoughts

Over the years I have achieved many of the dreams I set for myself as a small boy. I am often asked *"what next?"*. At 85 you might think that I am ready to put aside the clapper board and retire from the limelight, however, you'd be mistaken. I believe that age is no barrier and as long as I can continue to remember my lines, give a good performance and that people want to see me or hire me, I will keep going.

There are so many great actors who felt that they needed to step aside because they feared they were no longer relevant once they reached a certain age. I do not feel today that this is the case and just recently reading the story of 94-year-old American actress, June Squibb, appearing in her first starring role in the film *Thelma*, shows that time need not dictate why any of us should give up doing what we love doing prematurely. So, I intend to continue on for as long as it is humanly possible. And I still have several things on my 'to do' list – mostly focused on continuing to find more positive ways to inspire young people.

I would love to produce and am already developing an idea for a television series. So, if you are reading this and think that you could help me get this show into production, please don't hesitate to get in touch.

I also want to expand the Foundation's work nationally and internationally, especially our REACH programme for students who have been excluded from school or are at risk of being excluded. This programme gives them a range of creative experiences, using the power of the performing arts to support young people going through difficult times. My hope is to see children in Africa, the Caribbean and further afield having the same opportunities as I am able to provide for young people here in the UK.

I am still living life to the fullest. Just this year I attended the WOMAD Festival (as I have almost every year since it was founded in 1980 by Peter Gabriel) and had the dubious experience of sleeping on a waterbed in a tent. Now I have slept in a great many different types of bed over my years, but this was something I am not keen to try again. Firstly, it was cold and attempting to get into a sleeping bag whilst rolling around on a less than fully inflated waterbed in no mean feat! Not to mention the difficulty in exciting it at a fast rate with a full bladder, I look back now laughing but at the time I wondered at my sanity in agreeing to it.

I still love all festivals, Notting Hill of course being one of my favourites. I do feel that this festival would benefit mightily from a stand at Hyde Park Corner, this would allow bystanders to watch the procession and see the final judging take place. This is how it's organised in Trinidad and it takes away a lot of the fear people have from crowds. I have suggested this to the powers that be, but as yet they're not sold on the idea. I am thrilled by the sites and inclusivity, the festival has grown so much over the decades and attracts people from all over the world. I recall attending with Lorna and the children and being swallowed up by the crowd and struggling to get through. Suddenly a group of young men recognised me and immediately cleared a path shouting "Clear out of the way for Mr Walker and his family, move, let them pass," and as we were going through the ones who recognise me patted me on the shoulder. I attend the carnival every year and enjoy the warmth of the people of ages and background. This sums up the nature of the people and how they take care of those around them. If you have never been, I urge you to go and experience pure joy and extravaganza.

I live in a fabulous little cul-de-sac just outside of Reading and I have the support of fantastic neighbours. When I first moved in my daughter spoke to Christine next door, explaining that there could potentially be an issue with Paparazzi and autograph hunters, we were given a clear indication to her character (she was a feisty lady) when she said "They'll have to come though me first." Sadly Christine passed away but her husband, Richard, who's in his nineties often sites on his front porch and we chat about our days. This is a great comfort to me and is very reminiscent of how we spend out evenings in Trinidad.

So, where will the future take me? All I know for certain is that the passions that have driven me all my life are still very much alive inside me, and I will continue to walk my life with purpose, and with dignity.

Appendix

Awards

Belmont CYO 1959
Best Actor - The Robe
Variety Club of Great Britain 1972
Joint ITV Personality of the Year
Timeout – 01 for London Awards 1988
Reader/Viewer Performance Awards in King of England
Black Celebrities Awards 1991
Lifetime Achievement
The Voice – Annual Community Awards 1999
Contribution to the Arts
Black Entertainment Comedy Awards 1999
Lifetime Achievement
The Executive & Professional Network – Men & Women of Merit 2002
Lifetime Award
Trinidad & Tobago Association 2002
Services rendered to the nationals of Trinidad and Tobago & the community
EMMA Awards 2002
Best TV Actor
Windrush Foundation Awards 2003
Outstanding Contribution to the Arts

The Trinidad & Tobago National Foundation Honours 2003
A Celebrated Actor for Outstanding Services to the Community
Screen Nation Film & Television Award 2003
Inspiration Award
Reading Refocus Community Awards 2004
Contribution Awards
Best TV Personality
GG2 Awards 2005
(GG2 – A Division of the Asian Media & Marketing Group)
Leadership & Diversity Award
BAS 2006 (British Association of Steel Bands)
Contribution to the Promotion of steel band, music, art & culture in the UK
High Commissioner for Republic of Trinidad and Tobago – 2006
Outstanding Achievement
Scarf Award put date (sickle cell anaemia charitable group)
Recognition of Long Standing & Continuing Support
Norman Beaton Fellowship date?
Achievement Award
Silver Star 2008 Award
Outstanding Charitable Work
Golden Calabash Award 2008
Outstanding Achievement
The British Soap Awards 2018
The British Soap Award for Outstanding Achievement

Acknowledgements

I wish to thank the following people for their help with my writing this book:
Rhonda Alcantara
Juliet Alexander
Yusuff Ali
Bessie Bonair
Mervin Cato
Sue Cook
Sarah Moore-Eckert
Jonathan Etuk
Gabby
Colleen Hue
Evangeline Vincent-Davis
Verna Wilkins
Ansel Wong CBE
Anton Phillips
Michelle Burke (of Gavin Barker Associates)
Rick & Beverley Mayston
Taryn Johnston & The Chronos Publishing Team